Discourse and Reproduction

Essays in Honor of Basil Bernstein

Edited by

Paul Atkinson

Brian Davies

Sara Delamont

University of Wales, Cardiff

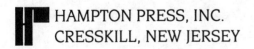

HAMPTON PRESS, INC.
CRESSKILL, NEW JERSEY

Printed in the United States of America

Library of Congress Cataloging-in-Publication Data

Discourse and reproduction : essays in honor of Basil Bernstein /
    edited by Paul Atkinson, Brian Davies, Sara Delamont.
            p.   cm.
        Includes bibliographical references and indexes.
        ISBN 1-881303-04-7 (cloth). -- ISBN 1-881303-05-5 (paper)
        1. Sociolinguistics. 2. Educational sociology. 3. Language and
    education. I. Berstein, Basil B. II. Atkinson, Paul, 1947-
    III. Davies, Brian, 1938-   IV. Delamont, Sara, 1947-
    P85.B46D57   1994
    306.4'4--dc20   94-23554
                                                                    CIP

Hampton Press, Inc.
23 Broadway
Cresskill, NJ 07626

Contents

Acknowledgments

We are grateful to Pauline Donovan, who did the administrative work on this volume, and to Anna Weaver, who worked on the chapters as an editorial assistant. We are also grateful to Amanda Coffey for her editorial help.

An earlier version of Geoffrey Walford's chapter appeared in the *British Educational Research Journal*, 12(2), 183-195, and we are grateful to Carfax Publishing Company for permission to print the revised paper.

The British Academy provided a small personal grant in 1983 to support Paul Atkinson's bibliographic work on Bernstein, in preparation for his 1985 monograph. This volume too reflects the Academy's support.

Introduction

THE BACKGROUND

Nineteen ninety saw the retirement of Basil Bernstein from the Karl Mannheim Chair at the Institute of Education, University of London, and the publication of Volume Four of *Class, Codes and Control* (*The Structuring of Pedagogic Discourse*). It is, therefore, a particularly apt time for the publication of this collection of essays which are in the nature of a Festschrift for Basil Bernstein. It should be emphasized at the outset that these are essays *for* Bernstein. His life and thoughts have been the catalyst for the work we have brought together here. It is not, however, primarily a book *about* Bernstein. In preparing this volume we asked our contributors to concentrate on producing ideas and reflections of their own that had particular origins in or points of contact with Bernstein's work. We did not solicit chapters with the primary purpose of providing general introductions to Bernstein's ideas. The authors' personal and intellectual relationships with Bernstein differ widely. Some are former students and colleagues; others have enjoyed less intimate personal acquaintance and have been influenced by his published work. All have found the man and his ideas to be catalytic in some way. This volume is in no sense valedictory: Basil Bernstein may have retired, but he has continued to be prolific. The publication of *Class, Codes and Control* 4 and the existence of the as yet unpublished *Class, Codes and Control* 5 reflect the continuing fecundity of his ideas. The flow of work from students and collaborators —in this book and elsewhere— also testifies to his continuing intellectual influence.

This book was not intended to be an exegesis of Bernstein's work, nor a comprehensive review of it. The collection edited by Sadovnik (1995) deals with the controversies surrounding many aspects of Bernstein's thought, and all three editors of this book have contributed our own assessments to that particular volume (Atkinson, 1995; Davies, 1995; Delamont, 1995). Our authors were not, therefore, asked to produce a collective, shared response to his work. They were free to choose how far, if at all, they wished to discuss Bernstein's own writings and to respond to his intellectual influence how they felt most appropriate. Some of the chapters are more closely grounded in Bernstein's theories (e.g., Edwards, Walford); others take some of his ideas as points of departure (e.g., Apple, Young). Some reflect the author's biographical engagement with Bernstein (e.g., Goodson, Davies); others less so. The contributors inevitably, and quite properly, differ in their enthusiasm for Bernstein's work and their interpretation of it. No editorial "party line" has been imposed on them. Moreover, Bernstein has not seen these chapters prior to publication. They therefore in no way reflect an "approved" version of Bernstein's thought and its implications. He has inspired work so diverse, and elicited responses so varied, that it would be absurd even to attempt to find or impose uniformity. That was certainly not our intention in any event.

There is, we hope, little need to justify the idea of celebrating Bernstein's intellectual contribution. His is widely acknowledged to have been one of the most original and creative contributions to post-war British sociology. His reputation is international. His ideas have inspired a great deal of empirical research and theoretical speculation throughout the world. When Atkinson undertook a citation analysis of Bernstein's influence for his monograph (Atkinson, 1985), he turned up references to Bersntein's published work in huge numbers, not only throughout the English-speaking academic community, but from every continent and across a bewildering variety of disciplines and institutions.

It is, however, important to emphasize that this collection of essays will not stand or fall solely on interest in Bernstein. As we have indicated, the purpose of the book is not to collect memories and celebrations of Bernstein. Our authors are all substantial scholars with international reputations; all the chapters that have been collected together here are original contributions in their own right. The authors explore their own intellectual preoccupations and analyses. It is a fitting tribute to Bernstein that we should not be engaged in the sterile rehearsal of old debates and positions.

Given the global impact of Bernstein's work it is appropriate that the contents of this volume are international in scope. In addition to authors from the United Kingdom, there are British authors working in Germany (Chisholm) and Canada (Goodson), and contributors from the United States (Apple, Cazden and Hymes), and Australia (Young). We were unable to include contributions from Scandinavian, Japanese, Hispanic, Lusophone, or Francophone academic worlds, but we could appropriately have done so. Our volume reflects, perhaps, the breadth of Bernstein's intellectual contribution; it lays no claim to a comprehensive coverage of it.

SOME COMMON THEMES AND MISSING ISSUES

Several common themes run through the chapters in this volume. First, several of the authors (mostly notably, Young, and Dickinson and Erben) compare Bernstein's work to that of Continental European theorists. Bernstein has never been a comfortable part of the English, British, or Anglo-Saxon empirical tradition of sociology. Although his substantive preoccupations are firmly rooted in the recurrent issues of British education and society, his ideas have never been bounded by the Fabian tradition of political arithmetic (as were those of many of his contemporaries). Although he has never chased after fashionable theories, he has drawn on a wide range of inspirations in classic and contemporary social theory. When Young writes of Habermas, or when Dickinson and Erben draw attention to the links between Bernstein and Ricoeur, therefore, they exemplify the theoretical scope of Bernstein's oeuvre. They illustrate the recurrent affinities between Bernstein's scholarship and strands of social thought from continental Europe. His avowed debt to Durkheim is self-evident; less overt but of equal importance are the inspirations Bernstein derived from Marx and Mead. His affinities with modern French thought—most notably with the theoretical and substantive themes of Pierre Bourdieu and Michel Foucault—are also explicitly acknowledged in Bernstein's more recent work (as are his reservations and differences from them). In addition, Silverman draws attention to important comparisons with the sociology of Harvey Sacks, whereas Young's chapter invokes Habermas in a discussion of pedagogic discourse.

It is, indeed, remarkable that a sociologist who has prefigured and reflected fundamental themes and issues in contemporary social thought should not be regarded more widely as a central figure in the academy. The reasons are not hard to find, however,. For despite the evident importance of his chosen themes, and the affinities with other scholars who enjoy even greater international esteem, Bernstein has always ploughed his own intellectual furrow. He has avoided aligning himself with fashionable positions just for the sake of invoking totemically potent authorities. His research and publications remain unmistakably his own. His own recurrent ideas were not borrowed from elsewhere; they embody a very personal—even idiosyncratic—set of themes. The breadth of his interests and the style of his theoretical discourse have, perhaps, marked him out as too dangerous—intellectually speaking—for some Anglo-Saxon colleagues, who have been all too suspicious of "theory." Worse still, he defies easy classification: He escapes the classificatory practices of lecturers and textbook authors. He is *sui generis*. Mary Douglas (whose own thought has been an influence on Bernstein and has been influenced in her turn) noted in this context:

> Some tribes reject and fear anomalous beasts, some revere them. In sociology Professor Bernstein is to some extent a fearsome scaly monster, cutting across all the tidy categories. The light he sheds on thoughts we would prefer to keep veiled is often cruel. No wonder he holds an anomalous place in his profession. (Douglas, 1975, p. 174)

Others, more open to theoretically sophisticated social thought, may have been reluctant to recognize a theorist of substance from among their own number. It is too easy to be enthused by exotically "foreign" authors rather than to acknowledge a "home-grown" theorist of stature. It is elsewhere (viewed from Bernstein's own London) that academic publics have been more ready to acknowledge his position as an "intellectual" (itself a somewhat alien concept for British academics and educators).

As the title of this collection implies, whatever the diversity of Bernstein's own writings, and the variety of other work he has inspired, there are clear continuities in his work. He has consistently addressed and developed a coherent set of themes throughout his career. He and his collaborators have of course addressed them in different ways over the years; and Bernstein's own treatment of them has grown more sophisticated and complex since his early essays. Nonetheless, one can trace the recurrent motifs quite clearly. In the early days Bernstein was known by a wide readership for his work on language and social class. Indeed, he became notorious in some quarters as a consequence of vulgar misrepresentations of his work as the embodiment of a "linguistic deficit" position. His work was erroneously assimilated to a crude caricature of language variation. But even in the earliest years, when "vulgar Bernsteinianism" was current, his true interests were apparent. His sociology was always grounded in classic problems. Most notably, he embarked on the ambitious attempt to produce a general sociology that could encompass the *reproduction* of social life. His emerging theory of "codes" (which replaced his earliest formulations of the sociology of language) represented a major intellectual undertaking. It was nothing less than a sustained attempt to comprehend the systemic relationships between social class, culture, and socialization. Codes were used to express general principles of structuring and reproduction that linked together an array of analytic levels: the division of labor, the distribution of roles and identities, the construction of messages and meaning, the exercise of social control. These were not ideas to be encapsulated within simple formulae, and in retrospect if is easy to see how and why they escaped so many readers. For Bernstein suffered the fate of many original thinkers—he was best known for things he had never said or written. Many could not see beyond their own limited horizons to understand the scope of Bernstein's work.

The periodization of Bernstein's life and work is not straightforward. The continuities are more important than the chronological differences in emphasis. A rough-and-ready categorization is possible, however. Before 1971, the work primarily focused on language, but important publications also addressed the *rituals* of schooling and their implications for social integration. Nineteen seventy-one saw the publication of the famous paper "On the Classification and Framing of Educational Knowledge," in which the Durkheimian preoccupation with "boundaries," and the sacred/profane divide, became especially prominent. This was coupled with the discussion of "visible and invisible pedagogies." Both revisited the theory of codes as regulatory principles in systems of reproduction. These in turn were supplemented by equally important statements on the systemic relations between education and *production*. Finally, from the early 1980s onward, Bernstein's work developed through several interlinked conceptual schemes. This included the significant addition of analyses of "pedagogic discourse": Bernstein addressed educational transmission itself (rather than as a medium for the expression of other things such as class, race, or gender differences) and the circulation of pedagogic *texts*. It is thus possible to trace a series of continuities and developments, marking a shift from a Durkheimian sociology of collective representations, to a structuralist preoccupation with regulatory principles, to a poststructuralist focus on discourse and texts. Our authors here engage with and depart from various facets of that entire output.

Several of the chapters in this volume identify and explore some of the implications of Bernstein's insights into language and identity. Hymes provides an important discussion of narrative, in which he constructs a major analysis of the poetics of everyday speech. With deliberate irony, he bases his discussion in part on speech analyzed by Labov (with whom Bernstein has been compared unfavorably by linguists unappreciative of Bernstein's sociology). In a parallel—but very different—chapter Silverman uses Bernstein as a reference point in a discussion of talk and social interaction. Silverman's comparison is with Harvey Sacks and the conversation-analytic approach. Likewise, Dickinson and Erben draw on Bernstein's insights into narrative, biography, and identity. Although all three papers stress very different influences and convergences, they all draw attention forcibly to the power of

Bernstein's work on language, speech, and narrative. Indeed, given the centrality of those topics to so much work in contemporary social science, it is remarkable—and regretable—that more scholars have not recognized the potential of Bernstein's work in this area. Bernstein's early and later work on language, socialization, and social control drew attention to the social construction and reproduction of the *child*, in sites of social reproduction (the family and the early years of schooling). One of our chapters addresses this theme. Jenks draws not so much on the construction of children but on the construction of "childhood."

The continuities in thought are, of course, more obvious in retrospect. It is easier now to see how the earlier and later formulations of his sociology reflect one another. It is perhaps in his formulations of school knowledge that his most fundamental interests became apparent to a wide readership. His continued use of the vocabulary of "codes" was no accident; nor was it a lazy carryover from his work on language. The theory of codes, whether applied to language or to curriculum, inscribes the same set of underlying analytic themes. It articulates the social distribution of principles of meaning and structure. It regulates the reproduction of social forms, including the reproduction of identities. It underlies the production and reception of message types and meanings. Whether Bernstein was writing about social class and family types, or curriculum and institutional organization, he was attempting to develop a general and systematic sociology or anthropology. He has continued to develop his general theory of cultural transmission with his most recent publications on pedagogic discourse. Cazden's chapter here also directs attention forcibly back to some of Bernstein's fundamental concerns. Writing on literacy education, Cazden presents important empirical material and raises important questions about the "invisible" pedagogies practiced in various "progressive" programs. Cazden's chapter draws together several of Bernstein's most important ideas in the context of contemporary pedagogy. Cazden's contribution provides an important link between work on language and on pedagogy, and so with Bernstein's papers on educational knowledge and transmission.

It is Bernstein's work on educational knowledge—its forms and contents—that also provides the stimulus for several of our chapters. Walford directly draws on Bernstein's conceptual apparatus of "classification and framing" in describing the boundaries of curriculum and pedagogy. Likewise, Grace stresses the significance of the forms of schooling. Walford and Grace discuss research from schools of very different character: A comparison of their respective contributions highlights the value of Bernstein's sociology in providing formal conceptual frameworks that are applicable to a wide range of institutional settings. Goodson locates his own contributions and the emergence of a sociology of school disciplines in relation to Bernstein's inspiration. Goodson emphasizes the role of a contemporary history of school subjects and the analysis of teachers' biographies in this field. The control of knowledge provides a theme addressed by both Apple and Ball. Apple writes of "official knowledge"—knowledge production and the state. Ball writes of the struggles over the National Curriculum. In a similar vein, Edwards writes of educational policy in terms of a struggle over the "pedagogical device." All three authors address the ideological character of educational forms and contents, drawing on Bernstein's classic work on classification and framing, on the one hand, and on pedagogic discourse on the other.

The reader will note that a recent development in the state education system of England and Wales—the National Curriculum—preoccupies several of our authors. This innovation, imposed by law in 1988 on state schools, remains controversial among teachers, administrators, parents, politicians, scholars, and pundits of both left- and right-wing persuasions. The background to this major change in the education system of England and Wales can be found in Ball (1990). Readers in other countries need to know all state schools in England and Wales have to cover the same curriculum with children ranging in ages from 5 to 16, that there is more emphasis on science and technology than was common before, and that the previous pattern of specialization into arts or sciences at age 14 is now restricted if not eliminated. The wider implications of these changes, especially the ideological implications, are analyzed in several of the chapters (especially Ball, Edwards, Goodson). The fact that fee-paying schools (discussed by Walford) do not have to follow this curriculum—so that the children of the richer sections of the middle and upper classes can continue to learn Ancient Greek and learn no science at all—is a matter of some sociological concern. Scotland and Northern Ireland are also beyond the scope of the legislation, so its very name—National Curriculum—is an interesting misnomer.

Although several common themes from Bernstein's work are apparent throughout this collection, there are others that have not been addressed by the majority of our contributors. Bernstein has dealt extensively with the family (especially the mother-child link) and often implicitly with gender. Those themes are not prominent in our collection. Although Jenks focuses on the construction of childhood, none of our authors deals centrally with the family, and only Chisholm addresses gender. Elsewhere (Atkinson, 1985; Delamont, 1989, 1995) we have expanded on Bernstein and gender, especially on his challenge to Goldthorpe's insistence on the irrelevance of women for class analysis. In this volume, however, the family and gender are less prominent overall than Bernstein's treatment of them deserves.

In this introduction we did not try to introduce and summarize the totality of Bernstein's intellectual contributions. Equally, we did not try to summarize the chapters that follow: They can speak for themselves. Rather, we tried to convey some of the reasons why we and our contributing authors wished to celebrate Bernstein with this collection of essays written for him and for others who may learn from his continuing intellectual contributions.

REFERENCES

Atkinson, P.A. (1985). *Language, structure and reproduction: An introduction to the sociology of Basil Bernstein*. London: Methuen.

Atkinson, P.A. (1995). From structuralism to discourse: Bernstein's structuralism. In A. Sadovnik (Ed.), *Basil Bernstein: Consensus and controversy*. Norwood, NJ: Ablex.

Ball, S.J. (1990). *Politics and policy-making in education*. London: Routledge.

Bernstein, B. (1990). *The structuring of pedagogic discourse: Class, codes and control* (Vol. iv). London: Routledge.

Davies, W.B. (1995). Durkheim, Bernstein and the British sociology of education. In A. Sadovnik (Ed.), *Basil Bernstein: Consensus and controversy*. Norwood, NJ: Ablex.

Delamont, S. (1989). *Knowledgeable women*. London: Routledge.

Delamont, S. (1995). Bernstein and the analysis of gender inequality. In A. Sadovnik (Ed.), *Basil Bernstein: Consensus and controversy*. Norwood, NJ: Ablex.

Douglas, M. (1975). *Implicit meanings*. London: Routledge.

Sadovnik, A. (Ed.). (1995). *Basil Bernstein: Consensus and controversy*. Norwood, NJ: Ablex.

1

Bernstein and Poetics

Dell Hymes
University of Virginia

In the introduction to his first book, Basil Bernstein (1971) described one of the experiments he undertook as a teacher at the City Day College in London. The students were on 1-day-a-week release from work as messenger boys or from various industries and the London Docks. Bernstein wrote:

> During the first two years I realized that the problem was, in Forster's phrase, "Only connect". Not being a born teacher, I had to learn by sensing that structure of meanings which were latent in the speech and writing. All this may seem to be an exaggeration. One day I took a piece of a student's continuous writing and broke it up into its constituent sentences and arranged the sentences hierarchically on the page, so that it looked like a poem. The piece took on a new and vital life. The gaps between the lines were full of meaning. I took a Bob Dylan ballad and produced a second version in which the lines were arranged continuously as in prose. I invited the students to read both versions. I then asked whether they felt there was any difference between the two versions. Yes, there was a difference. Poetry among other things has something to do with the hierarchical, and so spatial, ordering of lines. The space /6/ between the lines, the interval, allowed the symbols to reverberate against each other. The space between the lines was the listener or reader's space out of which he created a unique, unspoken, personal meaning. This may be bad aesthetics, but we experimented, putting together often weird or bizarre, sometimes unexpectedly beautiful series of lines, and exploring the symbolic nature of the space. I became fascinated by condensation; by the implicit. In my teaching I covered a range of contents and contexts, and yet, despite the variations, I felt that here was a speech form predicated upon the implicit. (pp. 5-6)

1

Bernstein went on to say that he wrote an account that eventually became the two papers (originally 1958, 1959) that began the volume being introduced. He further recalled discovery of Sapir, Vygotsky, and Luria, and the development of a conception of speech as orienting and regulative, as a starting point for his theoretical and empirical contributions.

The cited papers do not themselves present examples of the experiments with poetic form. I offer evidence that the intuition as to the presence of poetic form was correct. It appears that speakers of English, and of many other languages, have a tacit ability to shape what they say in terms of lines and groups of lines, in other words, in terms of poetic form. First, however, I say something about the conception of speech to which these experiences led, that of its implicit form.

SAPIR AND IMPLICIT RELATIONS

Bernstein's reference to Sapir points out the affinity of his work with a fundamental tradition in linguistic anthropology, as developed in the United States. Let me place it in that regard. The tradition is based on what might be called the "cognitive unconscious." Users of languages produce and interpret complex relationships of which they are mostly unaware. Two consequences follow: Being out of awareness, hence, out of reach of conscious manipulation, these relationships can influence their users in ways of which the users are unaware; others must discover what these relationships are.

The effective founder of the discipline, Franz Boas, singled out the unconscious character of linguistic phenomena as one of two reasons that linguistics was essential to anthropology (and the social sciences). One reason was that much of what people do cannot be grasped if one is unable to understand and analyze what they say (and write). The second reason he put this way:

> Language seems to be one of the most instructive fields of inquiry in an investigation of the fundamental ethnic ideas. The great advantage that linguistics offers in this respect is the fact that, on the whole, the categories which are formed always remain /71/ unconscious, and that for this reason the processes which lead to their formation can be followed without the misleading and disturbing factors of secondary explanations, which are so common in ethnology, so much so that they generally obscure the real history of the development of ideas entirely. (1911, pp. 70-71)

Whether Bernstein read Boas, I do not know, but Sapir, whom he did read, was recruited into anthropology by Boas and shaped by his outlook. Sapir's great book, *Language* (1921), still read and used in classes, refined and enriched the Boasian analytical conception of language in terms of the dimensions of grammatical categories and grammatical processes. Sapir's insightful essays on language and social life built on the thesis of unconscious patterning (cf. Sapir, 1927). He returned again and again to the antinomy between the relative autonomy of linguistic form and its inseparability from social life. He knew the lure of the study of linguistic form for its own sake, and he knew the need to understand what language is for those who use it.

Boas reconciled the tension by distinguishing between the short run and the long run. In the long run language responds to cultural need, but in the short run it can shape thought. That is a kind of autonomy for language, a mode of existence that makes it more than a pliable means, makes it a separate force. In the pioneering American Indian grammars that he wrote and guided, Boas stated the composite ideal of autonomous form and force: "the grammar has been treated as though an intelligent Indian was going to develop the forms of his own thoughts" (p. 81).

In his own career Sapir emphasized first autonomy, then insepar-ability. Whorf's thesis of linguistic relativity is a development of Sapir's, who coined the term, a development even more trenchantly phrased and intently pursued (see discussion in Hymes, 1966, 1970; Silverstein, 1981; and now the work of Lucy, 1992a, 1992b). It emphasized short and long run both. When a form of language and a form of life developed together over a period of time, patterns of language and conduct, of expression and expectation, would become congruent. The presence in a language of categories and of distinctions that must be made, if the language is used at all, the implicit patterning of so much of meaning, and the relative stability of language make language central to the transmission of such patterns to children.

Ideology and Equality

We have here what could be called an "ethnolinguistic theory of ideology." What Bernstein has developed in the course of his work can be called a "sociolinguistic theory of ideology." The ethnolinguistic tradition, as it developed before the World War II, thought in terms of a "language" and a "culture." The world was implicitly taken to be a horizontal map: here a people, language, and culture; there a people, language, and culture. Difference was difference between separate, autonomous groups.

Bernstein, a sociologist working in a complex society, recognized both linguistic form and social relations, but necessarily in terms of a plurality of styles and social positions. Styles and social positions are only sometimes side by side. More often, they are superimposed, stratified. Some control others.

I write in this almost childlike way because this simple idea did not enter into the thinking of most critics of Bernstein's work. They might work in the largest cities of the world. The conception of differences among peoples, languages, and ways of life remained the traditional anthropological one of equivalence. Class position might be part of placing people, but not of assessing them. Differential access to resources there might be, but so far as ability was concerned, class had no cost (cf. Labov, 1970).

Bernstein has independently pursued a path parallel to that of Bourdieu (e.g., 1991). Perhaps that is why Bourdieu has misrepresented Bernstein's work, stating (1991, p. 53) that Bernstein does not relate the elaborated code to social conditions of production and reproduction. Bernstein devoted at least 20 years of research to just such relations (Bernstein, 1990), and wrote the basis of his paper on "Class and Pedagogies: Visible and Invisible" (1973/1977b) while visiting the Centre de Sociologie Européenne directed by Bourdieu!

Bourdieu is frequently cited in linguistic anthropology and sociolinguistics in the United States, but Bernstein is not. One reason may be that Bourdieu's writings are in an international idiom shared with other writers who have come to the fore in the last two decades and address social life in a broader way. Bernstein deploys a terminology and conceptual framework that has remained much his own, and his written use of it can be formal and severe. (Bernstein's oral presentations may be as engaging as Exodus, but the written theoretical statements can resemble Leviticus.' Again, Bourdieu deals with issues of class in a way openly acknowledging Marxian tradition; Bernstein's Marx-like insights seldom mention that tradition. The fact that he places a fundamental analysis of social control in the context of Marx, Gramsci, and Foucault (Bernstein,1990, pp. 133-134) goes unnoticed (but cf. Hatlen, 1979). Neglect may be partly also because the immediate generation is in the habit of looking not to England, but to France, for social thought and writing about "language." The linguistic work of Michael Halliday and Ruqaiya Hasan, who have collaborated with Bernstein, has worldwide recognition but is almost never discussed in mainstream linguistics in the United States. If it were prominent, the relation with Bernstein would make his work better known to linguists as well.

The main reasons for neglect of Bernstein by linguists, and sociolinguists in particular, however, are two. First, he has been stereotyped, and misleadingly so. The fact that his work has steadily developed, that his theories have changed and grown, is not known. On the American scene he is understood (if "understood" can be used) as someone who divides the world into two kinds of people, one of which is irrevocably lingustically inferior and likely to be black (as in the account of his work in Crystal, 1987, p. 40). A young anthropologist recently told me that as a student she found Bernstein's account of restricted code to describe her own family but was told by a faculty member not to read him.

Indeed, it would be news to most of those who know his name to learn that much of his work has concentrated on the ideological role of the supposedly superior code, the elaborated code, and on the way in which pedagogy is central to reproduction of a social order, or that one of the most sensitive, well-balanced studies of white and black interaction is by a student he directed (Hewitt, 1986).

The case is like that of Whorf. A qualified and even nuanced view of the role of features and styles of language in shaping thought and behavior has been taken to be a simple-minded determinism. Neither Whorf nor Bernstein is ordinarily read carefully and completely. The case is like that of Whorf also with regard to the second main reason for neglect. If the view was properly understood, it would be not be welcome.

Both Whorf and Bernstein address the connection of language and social life in terms of constraint. The ways in which language is used constrain what is thought and done. That was plausible to a generation of anthropologists and associated linguists who understood differences among groups of people in terms of differences in culture. About 1960, however, the rise of transformational generative grammar to dominance carried with it, in Chomsky's formulation, a disdain of difference. The fundamental structures of language were considered to be innate, powerful, and operative early in the life of the child. Language was not "learned," but 'acquired'. Regularity came from within, not from without. There was no point to adding more data from different languages. The universal basis of all language was within reach, and introspection by the linguist as to his or her own language would suffice.

Whatever the degree of truth in this perspective, it has remained strong through various transmutations. It is not without rivals, now a number of them, but it has triumphed, if not in content, then in form. Formal, abstract analysis of the structure of language is identical with linguistic theory. In the 1950s, the linguists who had developed what has come to be called "American structuralism" had a sense of having reached a plateau from which it would be good to look around. There was a surge of attention to the study of paralinguistics, kinesics, the psychiatric interview, and cultural behavior. The kind of linguistic models being pursued were close enough to observable speech to be considered instruments of social and cultural investigation as well. That changed. The issues central to linguistic theory came to have to do with implicit rules and features, possibly innate. The issues were often internal to a model, only tangentially connected with behavior. The kinds of skill that would permit someone to transcribe speech and to analyze overt form in ways useful to others (including native speakers), became peripheral.

The goal of linguistic theory was stated to be an ideal speaker-listener member of a homogeneous community. In effect, linguistic theory adopted Feuerbach and rejected Marx. Language was to be understood in terms of human essence; members of a community were to be understood as related "naturally," through a linguistic equivalent of Durkheim's mechanical solidarity and what A.F.C. Wallace later called a replication of uniformity. Marx's understanding of a community as an ensemble of social relations, Durkheim's organic solidarity, and what Wallace called an organization of diversity were effaced (see discussion in Hymes, 1974, pp. 47, 121-122).

This turning away from diversity and social constraint was widely shared with cognitive psychology and what has become cognitive science. To be sure, the very extremism of Chomsky's position helped stimulate the self-conscious development of sociolinguistics. What had seemed too obvious to mention (the importance of diversity with respect to language) became a position to be defended and developed. Concern for the maintenance of minority and ethnic languages has come to see Whorf's respect for diversity as a positive precedent. Work on semantic patterning and metaphor has taken on something of the character of cultural anthropology. Social constraint with regard to language has come to the fore in both linguistics and elsewhere through feminist scholarship. And a large number of scholars in the social sciences, some of them concerned with language, have taken up a concern with power.

It remains that even linguists who study diversity and power may be unwilling to acknowledge inequality. External inequality, yes. Speakers of a certain variety may be discriminated against. A variety of speech may be restricted in its use. Perhaps the variety cannot now express certain meanings or be used in certain activities. It remains that it could be developed to do so. All normal human beings are equivalent in general linguistic ability, and all human languages can be developed to express new meanings and serve new needs.

There is a fundamental truth to that. It is the truth of the potential equality of languages. If English is now a world language, Anglo-Saxon was not. If circumstances had been different, Irish or Frisian or Catalan might have the place that English now has. This liberal position was enunciated by Boas (1911), that in the long run a language could do what its culture community required. It is a liberal position that stands against a variety of kinds of prejudice. In justifying respect for all languages, it also justifies attention to all by scholars.

The difficulty is that potential equality is taken as equivalent to actual equality (see discussion in Hymes, 1993a). It is as if history, like class, had no consequences. Let one language become an instrument of technical invention and research, explicit logic, schooling, and a multitude of metalinguistic activities. Let another language be restricted to the home and life in a local area. What can be done in the two will not be the same. But fear of giving aid and comfort to prejudice has inclined many linguists to ignore the obvious. What if only some languages are now world languages of science, and few if any will join that club? If country after country relegates some of its languages to a permanently local, limited role, though decisions as to what will be used and taught in different levels of schooling, and what money will be available for development of materials? What if even many users of a world language do not acquire much of its resources? If even where a language of marvelous structure survives, no one can perform myths and rituals, use it in once elaborated ways? What if children of immigrant workers end up with only impoverished comand of two languages; that of their parents and that of their present country (e.g., Moroccan children in The Netherlands)?

The practice of most linguists in the United States is not to draw conclusions from such facts. The notion of effective equality of all languages and speakers is too highly valued as a weapon against prejudice and a justification of uniform practice. To be sure, exceptions increase. Adequate study of pidginization and creolization must take for granted that languages, and those who use them, change in what they are able to do (see Hymes, 1993a; Mühlhäusler,1986; Romaine 1988). The subject of obsolescent languages has been opened up, and an important literature is emerging (see Dorian, 1989).

The study of oral narrative can extend understanding of potential equality and at the same time deepen understanding of forces at work in shaping actual competence. The attractive result of discoveries in ethnopoetics is that human beings generally have ways of giving shape and point to narratives, ways that seem almost inherent in having language (cf. Hymes, 1991b). At the same time opportunity for developing and using such patterning is dependent on social circumstance. It may not be recognized and, in a given language, it may not survive. The patterning is mostly out of awareness, and it is different from kinds of patterning to which speakers, teachers, and scholars attend. It is a matter of relations among lines.

It is commonplace in social science today to present what speakers say in lines. What is almost never attempted is to look for relations among the lines. Again and again, however, what speakers say in recounting experience can be found to be given shape by patterns of relations among lines. Much of local meaning and larger significance are implicit in

such patterning. Yet such accounts are usually heard or read as newspaper articles and prose stories are read. Information is sought; examples of
already determined categories are sought. What is uncommon is to look
for signals of form, to expect what has been said to display a close covari-
atioń of form and meaning, to be an expression of a narrative competence
that can be said to be poetic in the sense of implicit form. (An exception
is Hatlen [1979, p. 154] who argued for the poetic character of working-
class speech in terms of a high degree of concreteness and perceptual
precision, an important cognitive and stylistic trait that is missed by
those who argue that such speech is as abstract as any other. Hatlen saw
himself as building on Bernstein [and Whorf] in this regard).

A TEXT FROM SOUTH-CENTRAL HARLEM

Let me show how Bernstein's early insight into the poetic character of
line-by-line oral expression can be realized by this perspective. I do this
by considering a text analyzed by Labov. In the course of his pioneering
research into sound change in New York City, Labov studied narratives as
well, notably (although not exclusively) narratives by young African
Americans, and developed an influential framework for narrative analysis.

Labov's Approach

Labov defined narrative first of all in terms of clauses that are temporally ordered. A change in the order of the clauses would change the
temporal order. Not every way of recapitulating past experience is narrative, but only that way in which the order of inferred events is
matched by the order of clauses (p. 360). Labov mentioned syntactic
embedding and the past perfect as alternatives.

What we are to call stories that use other ways is not said, but
the problem does not really arise. Use of "narrative" for temporally *oriented* stories of whatever kind has prevailed, and the purely temporal
order singled out by Labov requires a modifier. Perhaps "linear narrative" would serve.

A minimal narrative is a sequence of two such temporally
ordered clauses (Labov, 1972, pp. 360-361). Narratives might consist
only of temporally relevant clauses, but of course many do not. Labov
focused on a contrast between narrative progression and "evaluation"
(in which narrative progression is suspended) (p. 374). There may be an
absence of evaluation, that is, of personal relation to what is recounted. There may be a richness of evaluation, as in the story studied here,
such that devices conveying evaluation occur in a variety of places.

All this is part of an adaptation and extension of categories from traditional rhetoric. A famous text of the time (Brooks & Warren, 1949, p. 312) distinguished four categories: Exposition, Complication, Climax, and Denouement. Labov and his co-workers recognized six categories: Abstract, Orientation, Complicating Action, Evaluation, Resolution, and Coda. These six are said to constitute a fully formed narrative.

Briefly put, an Abstract summarizes the story; an Orientation identifies time, place, participants, and activity or situation; a Complicating Action evidently need be no more than a second action following a first. (That is the only way to make sense of the remark made by Labov [1972, p. 363] that "complicating action has been characterized in the preceding section 1," and the remark that "Only c, the complicating action, is essential if we are to recognize a narrative, as pointed out in section 1" (p. 376). (The term *complicating action* itself is not used in section 1.)

Evaluation has to do with point; Codas signal a close and bridge the gap between the time of the narrative and the present.

The five main dimensions can be seen as answers to questions (Labov, p. 370):

Abstract:	What was this about?
Orientation:	Who, when, what, where?
Complicating action:	Then what happened?
Evaluation:	So what?
Result:	What finally happened?

Whose Questions and Answers?

Labov presents these categories as universal, as in effect a universal description or definition of fully formed narrative. They have often been accepted as such. A recent book concerned with literature for children accepts them in just this way (Hurst, 1990, pp. 95-97). The categories and the questions to which they are taken to be answers are taken to be in effect a definition of narrative as an ideal type.

The general difficulty with such definitions has been stressed by a leading folklore scholar (Ben-Amos, 1992). In the Native American and English language narratives I have analyzed, it is true that something usually can be found to fit these categories. That is not the same as finding the categories illuminating. Finding something to fit the categories is not proof that the associated questions fit. A story may answer questions specific to a tradition of which it is a part.

For example, many Native American stories of the trickster-transformer are not answers to these abstract questions, but meditations on the question: What is the nature of this fundamental figure? In Chinookan narratives and some others, the narrative answer is in terms of two cultural dimensions—being smart and being proper. To be smart is to be alert to what is happening and to interpret it realistically. To be proper is to know norms and maintain them. What happens is to be understood in terms of the relation of a principal actor to these dimensions: one who is both smart and proper succeeds, thus giving the story a happy, perhaps heroic ending; one who is neither fails, usually a numskull held up as a comic object lesson; one who is proper, but not smart, invites tragedy; or one who is smart, but not proper, can at best return to what had been before or start again.

When the trickster-transformer is both smart and proper, in the sense of serving the nature and interests of others as well as himself, he succeeds for both. When what he takes to be an interest is against the nature and interest of others, he fails. Sometimes a narrator chooses sides, as it were, underscoring respects in which Coyote is to be condemned, or highlighting respects in which Coyote is to be condoned and enjoyed. Occasionally one discovers a set of narratives in which aspects of Coyote's nature seem to be explored for their own sake (cf. Hymes 1987, in press-a, in press-b).

Let me indicate two ways in which effects associated with evaluation in Labov's analysis work differently in narratives from the Chinookan-speaking peoples of the Columbia river in Oregon and Washington, and many other Native American peoples. These narratives do usually begin with a conventional form of orientation: Someone (or more) was somewhere. In Chinookan often a second element says that someone always did a certain thing. That element tags the character in question as good or bad and thereby predicts the corresponding element of the outcome. A woman who is always out digging roots (obtaining food) will not come to ill. A boy described as mean to his playmates will in the end be deprived. Such initial evaluation is not emotional and is not embedded in the narrative proper (cf. Labov, 1972, pp. 372ff.). It does not suspend the action, but occurs before it begins.

Suspension of action is identified with evaluation in Labov's material. In Native American narratives a line of action may be suspended without evaluation, and without a break in succession of temporal clauses. What happens is that realization of a formal expectation is delayed. The main line of action is amplified.

In Simpson's "The Deserted Boy" (Hymes, 1981, pp. 142-183), the boy fishes five times. The outcome of the first four times is given succinctly. Each time there is one more fish. Each time is parallel in form: a single set of lines, or verse, beginning "Now then . . . , Now again . . . , Now again . . . , Now again . . ." The fifth time parallel form is maintained, but the lines do not say what is caught.

Now again did he go to fish for the fifth time,
now five times the boy had fished,
now he had become a grown man."

This fifth verse, concluding the scene of which it is a part, uses "now" in a summative way, not only about fish, but about the deserted boy. Now he had become a grown man. That implies some power had taken pity on him and entered into a relationship. Who it is, and what he receives, are both held over to a separate scene, a double outcome to be resolved there.

The boy examines his line and finds a cooking trough brimful with special food, huckleberries, and salmon. The daughter of a power who lives in the river has taken pity on him and has given it, implying there are other blessings to come. He sings again and again in celebration (cf. Hymes, 1981, chap. 4).

I call this device *extraposition*. What is expected at one point is extracted and placed outside that sequence. Another example occurs in a Zuni narrative. Coyote learns a song from Old Lady Junco, loses it, and comes back for it. The fourth time (the Zuni pattern number is four) she sees him coming, and at the point in the scene at which one would expect the outcome of the fourth time, the narrator says instead that Old Lady Junco put a rock inside her blouse. The outcome of the fourth time is a scene in itself, a fourth scene longer than any of the others. In it Coyote's fourth request is made six times. When twice Old Lady Junco does not answer at all, he threatens her and counts out loud four times, then jumps at her and breaks his teeth on the rock. Again, immediate outcome is delayed for sake of an extended finale. This is dramatic suspense—evaluation, one might say—of the dramatic importance of what happens, but there is no break in succession of temporal clauses (cf. Hymes, 1982).

Examples such as these show that oral narratives have more than a single level of successive action, and have groupings of lines that answer to expectations of form other than those posed by Labov's questions. Still, many have accepted the Labov model, as if in order to grasp the meaning of a narrative it is enough to grasp it as an answer to the questions cited earlier. Acceptance of the model sometimes has carried with it an assumption that in order to grasp the form of a narrative it is enough to segment it according to these categories. Hurst (1990) appears to act as if this were so.

The difference between categories such as those developed by Labov and the approach taken here is one of being both more inductive and more theoretical. Finer relations and further architecture are both sought and expected. The seeking can involve several stages of attention to the verbal details of the story, such that one seeks not only to segment it, but also to discover its rhythms and repetitions. The expectation is grounded in a body of experience in the last two decades as to the range of formal relations and resources narrators may deploy, in finding again and again that the deployment constitutes a coherent whole, and in discovering unanticipated themes and concerns through the formal relations.

On such an expectation, two short narratives from Labov's (1966) monograph were found to have ethnopoetic patterning (Hymes, 1991a), one indeed having an evaluative point where none had been seen. (I shared these analyses with Labov some years ago.) The three stories presented in an important paper of 1982 (quoted later) also have such patterning. Here I examine a story from the major study of 1972—one prominent in it and the one used by Hurst (1990, pp. 95-97) to illustrate Labov's approach. I exhibit the story first, then say more about an ethnopoetic approach in connection with its characteristics.

John L's Story

> "Well, one was with a girl . . .
> Told by John L.

What was the most important fight that you remember,   [i] (A)
   one that sticks in your mind. . . .

Well, one was with a girl   (B)
Like I was a kid, you know,
And she was the baddest girl,   5
   the *baddest girl in the neighborhood*.
If you didn't bring her candy to school,
   she would punch you in the mouth;
And you had to kiss her when she'd tell you.

This girl was only about 12 years old, man,   (C) 10
   but she was a killer.
She didn't take no junk;
She shupped all her brothers.

And I came to school *one day*   [ii]
   and I didn't have *no money*.   15
My ma wouldn't give me *no money*.

And I *played hookies one day*
[She] put something on me.

I *played hookies*, man,
so I said, you know,   20
   I'm not gonna play hookies no more
   'cause I don't wanna get a whupping.

So I go to school   [iii] (A)
   and this girl says, "Where's the candy?"

I said, "I don't have it." 25
She says, powwww!

So I says to myself, (B)
    "There's gonna be times my mother won't give me money
        because a poor family
    And I can't take this all, you know 30
        every time she don't give me any money."

So I say, (C)
    "Well, I just gotta fight this girl.
    She gonna hafta whup me." 35
    I hope she don' whup me

And I hit the girl, powww! (D)
amd I put something on it.
I win the fight.

That was one of the most important. (E)

Profile

Scenes/Stanzas/Verses/Lines				Features	Contexts
[i]	A	a	1-2	*Turn*	|Framing question|
	B	abcde	3, 4, 5-6, 7-8, 9	*Well*	|the girl|
	C	abc	10-11, 12, 13	*man*	|the girl|
[ii]					|ma and me|
	A	ab	14-15, 16	*And, one day, no money*	
		cd	17, 18	*hookies, one day*	
		ef	19, 20-22	*hookies, man, said*	
[iii]					|girl and me|
	A	abc	23-4, 25, 26	*So+turn; turn; turn*	|first round|
	B	a	27-31	*So+turn*	|deliberation|
	C	a	32-5	*So+turn*	|decision|
	D	abc	36, 37, 38	*And I. . .*	|second round|
	E	a	39		|answer|

Italics are as in Labov's presentation. Underlining is added to indicate significant repetition that is not line-initial.

Labov, W.A. *Language in the inner city* (pp. 358-359). Philadelphia: University of Pennsylvania Press, with discussion in the following pages. Given in Hurst, M.J. (1990), *The voice of the child in American literature. Linguistic approaches to fictional child language* (pp. 95-97). Lexington: The University Press of Kentucky.

ANALYSIS OF JOHN L'S STORY

Labov (1972) identified the lines of the story with successive letters of the alphabet; each such line was a narrative clause. He analyzed the story as having all five of his categories, except the first (abstract), to which no identifying letter was given: orientation (a-p), complicating action (q-t), evaluation (v-y), resolution (z-bb), coda (cc) (p. 375).

The summary of the assignment of lines to parts has what must be an inadvertent slip: "John L.'s narrative therefore fits the paradigm of Fig. 9.1, with a long orientation section *a-p*, complicating action *q-u*, evaluation *v-y*, resolution *z-bb*, and coda *cc*" (p. 375).

The discussion preceding this identifies a sequence of narrative events with *q, r, s, t,* and a set of five evaluative clauses with *u-y*. The evaluative section is also identified as u-y (p. 372). In the quoted sentence *q-u . . . v-y* must be a slip for *q-t . . . u-y*.

Letters correspond to line numbers in my presentation as follows:

a-p (orientation)	3-22
q-t (complication)	23-26
u-y (evaluation)	27-35
z-bb (resolution)	36-38
cc (coda)	39

Here is a profile of the story as analyzed in terms of relations among lines and groups of lines, revealing an implicit architecture of several levels. (The reasons for inferring these relations are given later.)

Scene/Stanza		Verse	Line
i	A	a	1-2
	B	abcde	3, 4, 5-6, 7-8, 9
	C	abc	10-11, 12, 13
ii	A	ab	14-15, 16
	B	cd	17, 18
	C	ef	19, 20-22
iii	A	abc	23-4, 25, 26
	B	a	27-31
	C	a	32-35
	D	abc	36, 37, 38
	E	a	39

The lines are taken from Labov, and indeed predicate clauses are often distinct lines in narrative traditions. The differences result from the kind of competence narrators are assumed to have. Narrators are understood to proceed in terms of expectations as to content (Labov's questions) and expectations as to form. The narrative that results may be understandable as an answer to the question Labov posits as fundamental: So what? It will be also be understandable as an answer to the question: What is satisfying (interdependence of) shape? In a word, And how? A narrator is understood to proceed in terms of a two-sided competence, integrating knowledge of a sequence of incident, event, and image and knowledge of sequences of appropriate form.

What Happens First?

Note that Labov did not assign a letter to the initial remark. The narrative, however, responds to that question. There are indeed three responses: an immediate answer, "Well, one was with a girl"; a summative answer at the end, "That was one of the most important'"; and the whole account of which these are a part. The opening question and summative answer enclose the rest.

   The event itself includes the talk of both participants, and the opening question appears to be a part of the pattern of the opening scene, the first of three sets of lines. To have three sets of lines is in keeping with the 3- and 5-part relations throughout the rest of the narrative. I conjecture that John L. sensed the question as part of the evolving discourse and that it entered into the shape he gave what he himself said. (On the shape that stories take in conversation as interactively organized, see Goodwin, 1990, pp. 236-237, 279; cf. Duranti & Goodwin, 1992. On conversational narrative generally, see Goodwin, 1990, pp. 231ff).

Where Does Narrative Begin?

If what John L. said had ended with line 13, indeed, one could consider the opening question as having been answered. The most important fight, one that sticks in the mind, does so because it was with a girl, and not just any girl, but the girl described.

   Labov (1972) assigned these lines and the rest of the lines through 22 to a single category and section: Orientation. On the present analysis, it has two sections. If the first is background to what happens, the second is certainly use of temporal clauses to enact past experience and as such a part of the story. Lines 3-13 are "an elaborate portrait of the main character . . . *the baddest girl in the neighborhood*" (p. 364), to be sure. But what about lines 14-22?

   Labov says that "the first *narrative* clause |line 23 brings John L.

and the girl face to face in the schoolyard" (p. 364; emphasis added). That is, the immediately preceding lines, 14-22, are *not* narrative claus-es, not part of the story proper. This is to overlook the fact that lines 14-22 do no follow directly on what has preceded. There is discontinuity with what has preceded, but continuity with what follows. Lines 23ff. follow directly on lines 14-22. Lines 14-22 explain why the narrator is at school, lines 23ff. what happens at school. The opening lines of each set (14, 23) are parallel; both have the narrator going to school. Change of location is a common way of indicating the opening a new narrative scene, and both sets of lines have it. And lines 14-22 twice have time reference ("one day" in lines 14, 17); time reference is also common mark of a beginning of action.

There is parallelism of ending point as well. Lines 14-22 end with desire not to get a 'whupping' from the mother. Lines 23-35 end with desire not to get a 'whupping' from the girl. Each three-step series is part of the point of the narrative, as an aspect of self-presentation. Each provides context for what happens next and support for the kind of person the narrator is, one who twice makes a courageous proper decision (not play hookies, just gotta fight this girl).

If line 23, bringing John L. and the girl face to face in the court-yard, is a narrative clause, so is line 14, bringing John L. to school in a preceding recounted event.

Such parallelism and proportion of words, theme, and place-ment is characteristic of oral narrative. It bespeaks an organization not reducible to sequences of clauses, propositions, or actions. The same sequence of clauses or actions may be shaped in more than one way, to more than one effect. Such "ethnopoetic" organization is marked by parallelism and repetition (cf. Tannen, 1989, pp. 97-97) and by implicit patterns of expectation.

Speech Acts Do Not a Difference Make

It should be noted that Labov (1982) subsequently revised his earlier conception. Much of previous work, he wrote: "focussed on the elabora-tion of narrative beyond the fundamental sequence of narrative claus-es. The main thrust of this discussion is in the other direction: to reduce the narrative to its skeletal outline of narrative clauses, and to outline the generating mechanism that produces the narrative back-bone" (p. 227). He concluded that:

> Though there are tying relations between sentences—anaphoric, ellip-
> tic—the coherence of discourse is not established at this level but a
> more abstract level of representation. Ultimately, the cohesion of the

three narratives that we are examining does not depend on the
sequence of narrative clauses but on the sequences of speech acts and
actions that the narrative presents. (p. 233)

Attention to a level of speech acts does not alter the basic conception of
a narrative as a composite of that which advances the narrative line (the
backbone) and that which does not. There is a single level of organization. There remains a limitation inherent in approaches, such as that of
Lévi-Strauss, that focus on the what of narrative and neglect the how (cf.
Hymes, 1985). Implicit architecture as a shaping of meaning is missed.

Ethnopoetic Dimensions

On what is this architecture based? Briefly put, on three considerations.
The first is that oral narrative begins not with sentences, but with lines.
One or more spoken lines are normally marked by certain intonation
contours or tone groups as units that can be called *verses*. When contours are not available, implicit relations and lines can often be
inferred from certain types of marker, repetition, and parallelism.
      The second consideration is that the relations among lines are
governed not by sequence alone, but by *equivalence* (Jakobson, 1960). In traditional poetry we are used to meter and rhyme marking lines as equivalent. In oral narrative, lines commonly do not have meter to mark them
internally or rhyme to match them. Rather, the verses that they constitute
are grouped according to a few implicit possibilities. In American English
the usual possibility is a sequence of three or five (cf. Hymes, 1991b,
1993a). In languages generally there appear to be two types of possibility;
three and five, on the one hand, two and four, on the other (cf. Hymes,
1987, 1991b, 1992). Against the background of one of these patterns, a
part of a narrative may be marked by recourse to the other, providing
emphasis or intensity. Sometimes the two types of pattern appear to have
social meaning, as when relations of two and four are associated with
women, three and five with men, as in the narratives from the Tillamook
Salish tradition of Clara Pearson (Hymes, 1993b). John L.'s narrative is
organized in terms of relations of three and five throughout, making use in
the section involving his mother of a common option, three pairs.
      When one has only a transcription with which to work, as in
this case, and not intonational contours, clauses, as noted, are close
equivalents to what are usually spoken lines. Turns at talk are always
verses (cf. the three verses of lines 23-26). Time expressions and parti-
cles, especially at the beginning of lines, commonly indicate verses. In
John L.'s narrative, the first stanza begins with a marker much used in
English, "Well." Three groups of the scene with the fight are marked initially by "So," which does double duty as a formal marker and a seman-

tically apt one, conveying consequence at this culminating point. Initial "and" twice indicates parallelism within a sequence (lines 14, 17, and 36, 37). The address term "man" is part of the signaling of lines 10 and 19 as new stanzas, and indeed "man" occurs in a parallel position within the two scenes: They are the third and last stanzas of their scenes. Notice also that the opening words of line 10—"This girl"— indicate a new sequence through explicit resumption of the subject. In this first scene each of the two stanzas by the narrator (3-9, 10-13) begin with "girl," succeeded by "she."

A set of verses that constitutes a stanza often enough has internal repetition. Notice the repetition of "no money" in the first stanza of scene ii (lines 15, 16) and the interlocking repetition in the first lines of each pair of verses in the scene: "one day" (14, 17) and "played hookies" (17, 19). Again, the three verses of scene iii A (21-24) are each a turn with a form of "say." (Labov remarked that objects that make noises are said to "say X," rather than "go X" (p. 372, n. 9); in this context "powww!," framed by "says," is evidently not only a noise, but a communication).

Change in location or participants commonly goes together with change of scene. There is close covariation of form and meaning in this regard in John L.'s story. Scene i introduces the girl at length, the narrator barely (line 4). Scene ii concerns the mother and the narrator. Scene iii tells the decisive encounter between the girl and the narrator. Scenes ii and iii each begin with change of location (came to school, go to school).

A stanza or scene may be marked internally by a grammatical feature, such as tense. Scene ii is in the past tense throughout. Scene iii goes into the present tense for almost all its first three stanzas (23, 24, 26, 27, 32; cf. Hymes, 1993a; cf. Wolfson, 1982). (Lines 23-26 might be taken to have four verses, one for each line, but the internal makeup seems to be controlled by the three steps marked by "says," "said," "says" (24, 25 26). The first line in each of the sequences introduced by "So" (22, 27, 32) appears to be introductory to what is said.)

A stanza can be expected to be coherent internally in terms of topic. It is no accident that the five verses beginning with "Well" develop the theme of the *baddest girl*, and no accident, perhaps, that the statement just quoted comes in the third verse. In a sequence of five units, the third and the fifth are the usual places of culmination. In this stanza the first three verses (1, 4, 5-6) appear to fit a common 3-step pattern leading to the emphatic culmination, the twice-repeated "baddest girl." At the same time this third verse can be seen as initiating a second, interlocking 3-step sequence, with the next two verses (7-8, 9) providing details. (cf. n. 1).

The next three verses are a separate stanza, indicated by the address marker "man" and ending with a point that recurs at the end of each of the first three sequences of stanzas, a boy being whupped: "She whupped all her brothers" (13), "cause I don't wanna get a whupping" (21), "I hope she don' whup me" (35). Often enough a narrator brings successive sequences around to share a theme as an ending point. John L. does this with dramatic effect. When being "whupped" comes around the third time, it is not a final ending point, but an intermediate one, followed by the fight and victory.

These kinds of effect are examples of the third consideration that informs ethnopoetic patterning—"arousal and satisfying of expectation" (Burke, 1925). Those who are party to a tradition of narrative form are sensitive to things coming around at a third or fifth step, if that is the tradition, or a second or fourth, in the other type. Some aspects of a tradition are consciously known. If there are a series of sisters, or a series of events, people will be able to remark that one can expect four, or five, as the case may be. People do not remark on such expectations at the levels of verse and stanza. These pervasive relations are like much of syntax in this regard.

DOUBLING

Labov introduced the story with these words (1972, p. 358): "Among the young adults we interviewed in our preliminary exploration of south-central Harlem, John L. struck us immediately as a gifted story teller; the following is one of many narratives that have been highly regarded by many listeners." I hope to have shown that the gift involves more than the disposition of the categories of orientation, complicating action, evaluation, or resolution (and abstract and coda). The gift involves a skill specifically linguistic and literary, a skill in the disposition of lines among local relations that enter into larger levels of organization. In particular, in addition to the shaping of stanzas and scenes, the story shows a pointed shaping of emphasis in terms of doubling.

The entire event is in a sense a sequence of questions and answers. Within that context John L. gives both an immediate and a summative answer. In the first and second scenes the third and final stanza of each begins with a line ending in the address form, "man." Within the second scene the three stanzas are linked by the overlapping doubling of "one day" and "I played hookies." The second and third scenes open in tandem with "And I came to school one day," "So I go to school." The third stanza of each ends with not wanting a "whupping."

Here John L.'s skill with larger form is especially evident. The third stanza of the third scene is a point of culmination, but only of local culmination. It is the end of one sequence of three stanzas and the beginning of another. (This interlocking within sequences of five is common in traditions that use relations of three and five. For an example from Philadelphia, see Hymes, 1993a). The first desire not to have a whupping was within the narrator's power; his decision was enough to avoid it. The second desire and decision was not in itself enough. The rest of the stanza, taking the desire now as the beginning point of a three-verse sequence shows the successful outcome in the fight.

In connection with the outcome, notice that doubling of the one expressive particle in the story underscores the question and answer to which the story may be seen as an answer, doubled from John L.'s standpoint: "Am I the kind of person who can make the right decision, even when it requires courage? Yes."

The first "powww!" is the girl hitting John (26), unanswered. It echoes, recapitulates (doubles), the long initial account of her prowess. The second "powww!" is an answer, a reversal, John hitting the girl. Labov noted in his analysis of the story that the two lines, 36 and 37, are not in narrative sequence. What they do, of course, is double the power of the blow, once with a particle, once with syntax:

> "And I hit the girl, powww!
> and I put something on it."

Perhaps in terms of a sequence of actions their order is indifferent, but I doubt that they could, expressively, have been reversed. Narratives answer to not one but two elementary functions of language, presentational as well as propositional.

CIRCLES

John L.'s narrative has yet another kind of relation. The question that prompts the story and the explicit answer enclose the rest. The question is followed by the account of the girl, and the answer is preceded by the fight with the girl, a second enclosure. At the center is the account of playing hookies and being punished by his mother. (I owe the observation that there are three circles to Scott Johnson).

These three spheres fit the three scenes of the story, an organization arrived at on other grounds. The center is the central scene. Moreover, this center is a center twice, another instance of doubling. In the sequence of three stanzas that opens the third scene, the first has the girl strike the first blow, and the third has John resolve to fight her. In between comes his reflection on the circumstances of the second scene, his mother and lack of money.

The centrality of the second scene is more than a matter of counting. It is this scene that groups verses in pairs. And it's this scene that has three pairs of verbal repetition (one day, no money, played hookies). Both are modes of intensification. John L. enhances his victory at the end by enhancing his opponent at the beginning, but the will to fight has his mother at its heart.

In terms of shape and artistry, then, John L.'s story is of course a sequence of actions, as Labov's method can show. It is also a sequence of doublings, and a series of enclosing circles.

CONCLUSION

Labov has done much to call attention to oral narratives and to urge that they be treated with respect. Ethnopoetics, understood as the study of the ways in which oral narratives are organized as culturally modeled groups of lines, makes it possible to connect oral narrative with linguistics in terms of the study of discourse markers and organization and competence generally. Such a conjunction is in the spirit of Labov's own efforts to connect his findings about variation with formal studies of phonology.

But if ethnopoetics is to contribute to an understanding, not only of stories, but of those who tell them and hear them and of what happens to narrative competence, to storytelling itself, it must draw on Bernstein's realistic grasp of the complex communities and institutions of urban life.

The range of what happens to stories in the Bible, for example, from Sunday School classes to sermons to scholarly exegesis, within and across groups, can be articulated in terms of Bernstein's dimensions of framing and classification. In some churches, the one who reads the lesson from the Old Testament or Epistles begins by framing in his or her own words the point of what the congregation is about to hear. In other churches, the one who reads does not, and may even take on the voice of, say, Isaiah. What is the distribution in region and class of the two practices? In what Sunday School classes do children hear the original story (in what translation?), and where do they hear a teacher's retelling? Where does the story remain a story, discussed as such? Where is it transformed into a set of questions and answers about isolated facts? Why are Fundamentalist churches and television the same in this regard? Neither trusting others with the words of their source; both feeling called on to make the shape of telling their own, transforming genres in the process.

Such mediation in terms of institutional culture by local personnel is the focus of Bernstein's book on pedagogy. We are probably all aware of the pervasiveness of such mediations. A number of linguists have come to recognize the necessity of studying them. It would be just and instructive to realize that Bernstein began exploring them more than 30 years ago and is a pioneer in the study of language in recognizing class as not just a diagnostic attribute, but an active, specifiable force.

REFERENCES

Ben-Amos, D. (1992). *Do we need ideal types (in folklore)? An address to Lauri Honko.* (NIF Papers 2). Turku, Finland: Nordic Institute of Folklore.

Bernstein, B. (1971). *Class, codes and control, Vol. 1: Theoretical studies towards a sociology of language.* London: Routledge and Kegan Paul.

Bernstein, B. (1990). *Class, codes and control, Vol. 4: The structuring of pedagogic discourse.* London: Routledge.

Boas, F. (1911). Introduction. In F. Boas (Ed.), *Handbook of American Indian languages* (Vol. 1, Bureau of American Ethnology, Bulletin 40, Part 1, pp. 1-18). Washington, DC: Smithsonian Institution.

Bourdieu, P. (1991). *Language and symbolic power* (ed. J.B. Thompson). New York: Harcourt, Brace.

Brooks, C., & Warren, R. P. (1949). *Modern rhetoric.* New York: Harcourt, Brace.

Burke, K. (1925). Psychology and form. *The Dial, 79*(1), 34-46.

Crystal, D. (1987). *The Cambridge encyclopedia of language.* Cambridge and New York: Cambridge University Press.

Dorian, N.C. (Ed.). (1989). *Investigating obsolescence. Studies in language contraction and death.* Cambridge: Cambridge University Press.

Duranti, A. , & Goodwin, C. (Eds.). (1992). *Rethinking context. Language as an interactive phenomenon* (Studies in the Social and Cultural Foundations of Language 11). Cambridge, NY: Cambridge University Press.

Goodwin, M. H. (1990). *He-said-she-said. Talk as social organization among Black children.* Bloomington: Indiana University Press.

Hatlen, B. (1979). The quest for the concrete particular, or, do poets have something to say to sociolinguists? In R.L. Brown, Jr. & M. Steinnman Jr. (Eds.), *Rhetor 78: Proceedings of Theory of Rhetoric: An Interdisciplinary Conference* (pp. 143-177). Minneapolis: University of Minnesota Center for Advanced Studies in Language, Style, and Literary Theory.

Hewitt, R. (1986). *White talk black talk. Inter-racial friendship and communication amongst adolescents.* Cambridge: Cambridge University Press.

Hurst, M. J. (1990). *The voice of the child in American literature. Linguistic approaches to fictional child language.* Lexington: The University Press of Kentucky.

Hymes, D. (1966). Two types of linguistic relativity: Some examples from American Indian ethnography. In W. Bright (Ed.),

Sociolinguistics (pp. 114-158). The Hague: Mouton.

Hymes, D. (1970). Linguistic method in ethnography. In P.L. Garvin (Ed.), *Method and theory in linguistics* (pp. 249-311). The Hague: Mouton.

Hymes, D. (1974). *Foundations in sociolinguistics*. Philadelphia: University of Pennsylvania Press.

Hymes, D. (1981) *In vain I tried to tell you. Essays in Native American ethnopoetics*. Philadelphia: University of Pennsylvania Press.

Hymes, D. (1982). Narrative form as grammar of experience: Native American and a glimpse of English. *Journal of Education*, 164(2), 121-142.

Hymes, D. (1985). Language, memory, and selective performance: Cultee's Salmon's myth as twice told to Boas. *Journal of American Folklore*, 98(390), 391-434.

Hymes, D. (1987). Anthologies and narrators. In B. Swann & A. Krupat (Eds.), *Recovering the word. Essays on Native American literature* (pp. 41-84). Berkeley: University of California Press.

Hymes, D. (1991a). Ethnopoetics and sociolinguistics: Three stories by African-American children. In I.G. Malcolm (Ed.), *Linguistics in the service of society* (pp. 155-170). Perth, Australia: Institute of Applied Language Studies, Edith Cowan University.

Hymes, D. (1991b). Is poetics original and functional?' *Language & Communication*, 11(1/2), 49-51.

Hymes, D. (1992). Using all there is to use. In B. Swann (Ed.), *On the translation of Native American literatures* (pp. 83-124). Washington, DC: Smithsonian Institution.

Hymes, D. (1993a). Inequality of language: Taking for granted. In J.E. Alatis (Ed.), *Language, communication and social meaning* (Georgetown University Round Table '92, pp. 23-40). Washington, DC: Georgetown University Press.

Hymes, D. (1993b). In need of a wife: Clara Pearson's "Split-His-Own-Head." In A. Mattina & T. Montler (Eds.), *American Indian linguistics and ethnography in honor of Laurence C. Thompson* (University of Montana Occasional Papers in Linguistics, No. 10, pp. 127-162). Missoula: University of Montana, Department of Anthropology.

Hymes, D. (1994a). Ethnopoetics, oral formulaic theory, and editing texts. *Oral Tradition*, 9(2).

Hymes, D.(1994b). Coyote, master of life, true to life. In B. Swann (Ed.) *Coming to light: Contemporary translations of Native American literatures of North America*. New York: Random House & Vintage Books.

Jakobson, R. (1960) Concluding statement: Linguistics and poetics. In T.A. Sebeok (Ed.), *Style and language* (pp. 350-373). Cambridge: MIT Press.

Labov, W. (1966). *The social stratification of English in New york City.* Washington, DC: Center for Applied Linguistics.

Labov, W. (1970). The logic of non-standard English. In J.E. Alatis (Ed.), *Report of the Twentieth Round Table Meeting on Linguistics and Language Studies* (pp. 1-29). Washington, DC. Georgetown University Press.

Labov, W. (1972). The transformation of experience in narrative syntax. In *Language in the inner city* (pp. 354-396). Philadelphia: University of Pennsylvania Press.

Labov, W. (1982). Speech actions and reactions in personal narrative'. In D. Tannen (Ed.), *Analyzing discourse: Text and talk* (Georgetown University Round Table on Languages and Linguistics 1981, pp. 219-247). Washington, DC: Georgetown University Press.

Lucy, J. (1992a). *Language diversity and thought. A reformulation of the linguistic relativity hypothesis.* (Studies in the Social and Cultural Foundations of Language 12). Cambridge and New York: Cambridge University Press.

Lucy, J. (1992b). *Grammatical categories and cognition. A case study of the linguistic relativity hypothesis.* (Studies in the Social and Cultural Foundations of Language 13). Cambridge and New York: Cambridge University Press.

Mühlhäusler, P. (1986). *Pidgin & creole linguistics.* Oxford: Basil Blackwell.

Romaine, S. (1988). *Pidgin and creole languages.* London: Longman.

Sapir, E. (1927). The unconscious patterning of behavior in society. In E.S. Dummer (Ed.), *The unconscious: A symposium* (pp. 114-142). New York: Knopf.

Silverstein, M. (1981). *The limits of awareness* (Sociolinguistic Working Paper No. 84). Austin, TX: Southwest Educational Development Laboratory.

Tannen, D. (1989). *Talking voices. Repetition, dialogue, and imagery in conversational discourse.* Cambridge, New York: Cambridge University Press.

Wolfson, N. (1982). *The conversational historical present in American English narrative.* (Topics in Sociolinguistics 1). Dordrecht: Foris.

2

Cultural Semantics: Occupations and Gender Discourse

Lynne Chisholm
University of Marburg

When I was young I little thought
That wit must be so dearly bought
But now experience tells me how
If I would thrive then I must bow
And bend unto another's will
That I might learn both care and skill
To Get My Living with My Hands
That So I Might Be Free From Band
And My Own Dame that I may be
And free from all such slavery.
Avoid vaine pastime fle youthful pleasure
Let moderation allways be thy measure
And so prosed unto the heavenly treasure.

By the 17th century, sampler verses such as this one, cited in Parker's (1984, p. 13) social history of embroidery and the making of the feminine, had begun to take up a distinct place in pedagogic discourse. Young girls quite literally worked the stuff of their gendered vocation, during which process they learned to express appropriate moral sentiments in material form and as perfectly as possible. This particular sampler verse is, however, "a curious mixture of piety and rebellion, resentment and acquiescence" (p. 13), in which not only accommodation but also resistance is expressed. In other words—in Basil Bernstein's terms—that which is voiced—here, visibly—carries with it the potential not-yet-voiced:

> Symbolic control, which inscribes the legitimate, translates power into discourse and discourse into modalities of culture, may well unwittingly also be the guardian of the new. There is a paradox at the heart of symbolic control. Control cannot control itself any more than discourse can control discourse. Symbolic control is always a condition for someone else's order, but it also carries within itself the potential for transforming the order of the imposing other. (Bernstein, 1988, p. 45)

In an essay for the fifth volume of *Class, Codes and Control* (1993), Basil Bernstein offered his readers a kind of retrospective natural history of the development of his ideas, during the course of which he referred to the well-known criticism that his theory can envisage neither the possibility of change nor active and autonomous subjectivity. He replied that the acquisition of codes that attempt to establish and maintain a particular modality of order necessarily incorporate the potential of disordering, and that the social power relations that govern access to and distribution of code positionings and usages necessarily generate struggles (presumably within and between subjects and groups) to dominate and to change the codes. He added that his work on pedagogic discourse, in which he distinguishes among the three fields of production, reproduction, and recontextualization of knowledge, demonstrates this: The recontextualizing field is by definition a site of struggle over the construction and relaying of discourse and its consequences for the positioning and the prospects of subjects. Hence, this field is defined precisely by contestation over the degree of openness and closedness of code production and reproduction (Bernstein, 1993, pp. 66-67).

In the case of the work I discuss in this chapter, it was the desire to find pointers for the shaping and the realizations of girls' contestations between resistance and accommodation to the terms of gender discourse, contestations that might indicate where and how openness—that is, the possibility for change—exists, that drove me to search for the social grammar of gendered occupational choice processes. It seemed that if I could understand at a deeper level more about what produces and reproduces legitimate outcomes at the level of surface realization (i.e., girls' voiced statements about what they "want" occupationally to be), then this ought to teach better recognition of (potentially) illegitimate outcomes, even though these might not yet be explicitly or fully voiced. In turn, such recognition skills ought to be useful in constructing more effective pedagogic strategies and practices of positive support for developing a more critically conscious openness in girls' own constructions of their transition biographies (Chisholm & Holland, 1987).

Understanding and explaining both continuity and change are ultimately indissolubly linked endeavors. On the other hand, it might be argued that the problematics one is particularly interested in pursuing may lead to a primary focus on tracing the former rather than the latter, or vice versa. On my reading of his own natural history account, it has been the determination to excise and display systematically the social processes effecting continuity—the production and reproduction of class-based power relations and their pedagogic consequences—that has constituted the driving force behind Basil Bernstein's theoretical and research biography. And yet, if my memory does not fail me, in discussions with him about this general problem in social theorizing, the conclusion has ever been that the difficulty lies less in explaining continuity, but much more in visualizing the possibility of change. I think it is unreasonable to project a problem that, as sociologists, we all have onto the work of one particular theorist, whatever its virtues and vices may otherwise be. If it is reasonable to conclude that Bernstein's theorizing is oriented in the first instance to understanding continuity and in the second instance to understanding change, then this is simply a descriptive statement about its chosen problematics and not about its intrinsic virtue.

My own interest has been, in the first instance, to understand more about change (or rather, the potential for it). To do so, it was evident that the starting point was to try to map aspects of continuity in the production and reproduction of gender relations. But equally, continuity really implies continuities: There is more than one way to skin a cat. So in studying gendered occupational choice processes it seemed important to identify more closely, for example, what differently positioned social and cultural fractions are held within the categories working-class girls and middle-class girls.

Within the empirical limits posed by the data (mainly working-class inner-London state comprehensive schoolgirls aged 11 to 16 in the mid-1980s), it turned out to be possible to tease out some of these finer patterns in the continuities of gendered transitions. In turn, these more subtle pattern descriptions—compiled over a 3-year period—released much information about the interplay of accommodation/resistance and their occupational realizations in relation to girls' social, educational, and gender locations. The most interesting aspect of the work was, however, that I think I can now see rather more clearly than before how what Bernstein termed the "pedagogic device" is able to field those challenges to the production and reproduction of gender relations that are potentially the most powerful.

A cultural semantics of gendered occupational choice underlies and frames these struggles and contestations; it provides sets of meanings with which girls juggle in coming to a decision about what they say they want to be. What they say is but part of what they mean; there is much they do not say, and sometimes what they might want to say cannot get out or is ignored when it does—and so fades away or becomes recontextualized. Returning to Parker's (1984) historical study, her account showed how girls' and women's professional and domestic involvement in the art/craft of embroidery symbolically expressed and concretely fixed their positioning and containment within a definition of femininity informed by a moral division of labor that prescribed virtue and obedience, chastity and humility as appropriate signifiers. At the same time, however, both the activity of embroidery and the content of its motifs offered space for resistance and the construction of alternative meanings, albeit ultimately nonproductive because without sufficient social power to assert their cultural validity:

> The manner in which embroidery signifies both self-containment and submission is the key to understanding women's relation to the art. Embroidery has provided a source of pleasure and power for women, while being indissolubly linked to their powerlessness. Paradoxically, while embroidery was employed to inculcate femininity in women, it also enabled them to negotiate the constraints of femininity. . . . Such overt recognition of the clash between individual ambition and the ideology of femininity (as in the 17th century sampler verse cited above) is rare indeed. . . . From our vantage point, it is all too easy to sneer at the Victorian embroiderer completing yet another pair of slippers stitched with a foxhead. . . . But rather than ridiculing them, or turning embarrassed from our history, we should ask why they selected such subjects, what secondary gains they achieved from absolute conformity to the feminine ideal, and how they were able to make meanings of their own while overtly living up to the oppressive stereotype. (p. 11)

The embroiderer no longer figures on girls' occupational horizons of aspiration or expectation, certainly not for inner-London 1980s girls, although the least well-placed among them might well find themselves as homeworker machinists in the years to come, especially once they have had children. Whether any of them will sew and embroider their children's clothes, as my mother was still doing for me in the 1950s, I do not know. But when I began this work in the early 1980s, it seemed important not only to find ways of widening girls' horizons and prospects, but also to take seriously the fact that, however we looked at it, the overwhelming majority of girls expressed classically gender-typed aspirations and stuck to them regardless of what they often, if hazily, knew about the pay, conditions, and prospects of the jobs concerned.

What might be going on here that gendered labor market structures of opportunity and constraint cannot, on their own, satisfactorily explain? In response to this question, cultural analysis has a great deal to offer to the study of gendered occupational choice processes. This does not have to be viewed as an alternative to a more straightforward materialist analysis of women's oppression, nor does it imply a denial of the importance of structural selection/allocation mechanisms that are directed toward the maintenance of a segmented, segregated workforce and thus toward the reproduction of social inequalities. On the contrary, it is manifestly so that occupational segregation by sex constitutes a fundamental feature of the objective social worlds in which all girls grow up. In constructing their own futures, girls must take this "fact of life" into account, even though they may resent it and/or present their aspirations as free choices.

However, it is rarely necessary explicitly to marginalize and exclude girls from wide sectors of the labor market. It is certainly rarely necessary to apply direct pressure and opposition, whether from school, family, or employers. In a variety of ways, girls generally come to exclude themselves, well in advance of the actual transition between education and paid work. They do so at least in part because the range of the possible is inherently delineated by gender, and so speaks intimately to identity. The range of the occupationally possible arises not only as a consequence of what girls see around them, but also as a result of what is culturally thinkable. The structuring of the channels of transition through secondary education, vocational training, job recruitment, and occupational socialization is by no means neutral in these respects. Its effects can be "read off" from the contraction in the range of girls' aspirations and expectations over time.

In studying gendered occupational choice processes, then, the aim was not only to show how girls' perspectives of the occupational world are shaped by what they see around them, but in particular to find ways of releasing the dimension of the thinkable. To do so, it was necessary to look more closely at the finer patternings of aspirations and to reach below the surface "monotony" of the dominant patterns. In my view, we shall progress no further in understanding processes of social reproduction and change unless we direct more of our attention toward hidden structures of cultural meaning in their relations with surface patterns of social origins and destinations. This requires seeking ways of empirically working at the surface level of cultural analysis without theoretically being restricted to it. In the case of this particular study, the task was very much oriented toward identifying potential for change where one would not immediately expect to find it. The subjects were groups of girls for whom, by and large, outcomes were virtually bound to be gender-appropriate, living and attending school in areas in which patterns of actual transitions to the labor market were, on the whole, depressed and depressing. Comparing occupational aspirations and expectations alone, as they stand, would never have been able to produce obvious and marked empirical contrasts. The strategy therefore lies in working to dig up and depict finely shaded and textured patterns; the ultimate intention, perhaps, to suggest that the picture is not quite so monotonous—and hence more hopeful—than it might appear.

OCCUPATIONAL WORLDS AND GENDERED FUTURES

The three state comprehensive schools from which the girls in this study came all had largely or wholly working-class pupil intakes, but were otherwise different in several respects (for full details of the sample and methods used, see Chisholm, 1990). Two schools were co-educational, of which the first (Wilhelma) was situated in an isolated, severely economically depressed part of inner London. Its pupil ethnic composition was mainly white indigenous; a large proportion of children came from socially highly disadvantaged backgrounds. Both the 16+ examination success rate and school-leaver employment prospects were poor. The second (Sternrise), a former selective secondary school, was located toward the boundaries of inner London and served a mixed-class clientele, primarily working-class but with some children from professional middle-class homes and relatively few from markedly disadvantaged backgrounds. Its pupils included a scattering of children from a wide range of ethnic minority backgrounds. Formal educational achievement levels were relatively good; there was a thriving sixth form, and transition prospects were as good as might be expected in the mid-1980s. The third school (Dame's Trust), a result of a merger between a grammar and a secondary modern, was for girls only. It was located in a solidly working-class "character" neighborhood, now suffering from the decline of traditional sectors and industries, that attracted a highly ethnically mixed pupil intake. The school was fighting hard to maintain the former grammar school's good examination and destinations success record, but under changed intake and labor market conditions this was proving difficult.

The employment status and occupational distribution of the girls' parents and, when present, elder siblings, indicated that gender and class relations were being intergenerationally reproduced in their families. The social origin differences among the three schools' intakes were effectively described by the spread of the fathers' occupations, so that Wilhelma fathers were employed in a narrow range of mainly lower level manual jobs and were also most likely to be unemployed. The spectrum of occupations in which Sternrise fathers were engaged was notably wider and extended into the self-employed professional category. Fathers of the Dame's Trust pupils fell in between, and they were the only group in which small proprietors (shopkeepers, publicans, building subcontractors, taxi drivers, etc.) were represented. These differences were invisible when mothers' employment only was considered: virtually all were distributed over the same few occupational sectors, and, predictably, these hardly overlapped at all with those in which fathers were employed. Apart from the odd teacher and secretary, employed mothers were almost wholly engaged either in lower grade service-sector jobs or worked in factories (manufacturing different kinds of products than factory-working fathers).

The extent of parental horizontal and vertical occupational segregation by sex was thus extreme, even at the broad level of occupational sector; at the more precise level of within-sector category and specific job, this segregation was virtually complete. Mothers were especially likely to be in part-time and often casualized employment (basically, cleaners and school dinner ladies), whatever occupations they may have had in the years before marriage and children, after which almost all had interrupted regular employment for some time. At the point of closest knowledge and experience, girls in all schools see a sex-segregated occupational structure and labor market, and parallel to that, a classic domestic division of labor between their parents.

As far as elder siblings are concerned, sisters had secured jobs of varying quality somewhere between routine nonmanual and casualized unskilled levels in the commercial and service sectors. Brothers had either managed to find skilled manual jobs (generally via apprenticeships) or they had experienced long-term or intermittent periods of unemployment punctuated by unskilled work. In other words, sisters and brothers were following in the footsteps of their parents, although sisters had not yet experienced the downward occupational mobility that marriage and motherhood characteristically brings. It is worth adding here that afterschool and weekend jobs were practically ubiquitous and regarded as wholly normal for girls aged 13+ at both Wilhelma and Dame's Trust, that is, from sometime during their second year at secondary school. They worked (more or less illegally) in local retail and service outlets; these frequently became full-time "fill-in" jobs upon leaving school. By the mid-1980s, this was a prime modality of education-employment transition for working-class young inner Londoners, one that was simply transferred across into the Youth Training Scheme via employer subsidies and still further depression of youth wages. Although most had no intention of staying in such jobs permanently, what happened was that, over time, young women tended to remain in them, whereas young men were gradually filtered into the adult male labor market into employment of varying quality and security.

The occupational universes within which the girls themselves worked in constructing their own gendered futures were clearly bounded, demonstrating that most were firmly positioned in their gendered, social, and educational milieux. Spontaneous job lists, in which first-year (11-12-year-olds) and third-year (13-14-year-olds) pupils of both sexes were asked to write down jobs that came into their heads (unaware of the purpose), confirmed research findings using similar techniques: The entries conformed to the gender and broad class positionings of the pupils. The lists well reflected the real world, in which the occupational structure and the labor market are male-dominated, in which women are found in a narrower range of occupations than are men, and in which men generally occupy higher level positions when employed in the same occupations as women. The girls "corrected" the male-dominated social world of occupations by drawing more heavily on the smaller range of female-staffed occupations, but unlike for the boys, who seldom included any female-staffed job (except for mother and prostitute, a sobering outcome), it was difficult for them to exclude male-staffed occupations altogether without quickly running out of ideas.

Some girls, however, produced significantly male-oriented or almost exclusively female-oriented job lists. The younger girls were more likely to do the former and less likely to do the latter; this supports the idea of processes of progressive gendered closure in occupational horizons in early adolescence, well before education-employment transitions take on an immediate practical significance. However, this age difference was not at all marked at Sternrise, where girls at both ages were more likely than those at Wilhelma or Dame's Trust to produce male-oriented lists, mainly because they included more professional-level jobs, many of which are male staffed. Particularly striking here were the (very few) girls at Wilhelma who returned male-oriented lists: These included not professional jobs but rather male-typed manual/technical occupations. Whereas especially Sternrise girls were registering an orientation toward educationally generated upward social mobility, in that the professional-level jobs they listed included their own subsequently elicited aspirations, this was emphatically not the case for the Wilhelma girls, whose aspirations later turned out to be classically gender stereotyped. In other words, these Wilhelma girls were spontaneously and indirectly describing the utterly male-dominated and socially depressed world in which they were growing up, as later and independently confirmed via in-depth interviews.

The various kinds of data on occupational perceptions, aspirations, and expectations point to the conclusion that it is the symbolic dimension of the gendering of occupations that positions girls in the first instance, but it is real labor-market factors that fix and realize these positions at the end of the educational day. The gap between aspirations and expectations opens up at an early age: Halfway into their first year of secondary schooling, over two-fifths of the 11-12-year-old girls in this study already definitely thought they would not get the job they then wanted. The first- and third-year girls whose expectations diverged from their aspirations were united in their view of the kind of job—if any—they would really get: most likely working as shop assistants, alternatively typing, working in a factory, working on a market stall, or working as a waitress or cleaner. On the one hand, they saw high unemployment rates and stiff competition for jobs as the reason for their fairly gloomy predictions. But equally, they judged themselves as lacking the talents and skills required for the jobs they really wanted (whatever the actual level of qualification demanded)—and these girls had no desire to continue their formal education beyond the minimum school-leaving age of 16.

The depressing aspect of the girls' aspiration patterns overall is that they were overwhelmingly gender stereotyped, whatever their level. On the other hand, almost a third of the interview study respondents mentioned a "nontraditional" aspiration at least once, in some way, at some point in the study. Most of these disappeared again, but they had existed. Similarly positive is the fact that two-thirds of the girls changed their aspiration at least once between 11 and 14, or 14 and 16 years of age. Unfortunately, these changes are prone to be of the scaling down and narrowing variety: in status and qualification level for the younger girls, in terms of what was realistically available on the local labor market for the older girls. The effect of (pre-National Curriculum) subject choice at 14 was to act as a key pivot to fix gendered transitions more firmly because most girls chose their subjects according to their then-current aspiration. Alternatives were thus closed in both status and gender terms; the only choice left was a further narrowing down toward that which was available at 16. Because choice forced nonreversible decisions, many girls expressly took a typing option as a safety net. And it became very clear that secretarial and bank work are fallback expectations, even when they are voiced as aspirations. The pinnacle of desirability that these two jobs appear to represent for working-class London girls is a masquerade: Desirability is the equivalent of accessibility in a labor market in which the alternatives are highly undesirable. The only, and significant, exceptions to all this were educationally successful girls—of whatever class or ethnic origin—who, quite literally, kept their options open: both occupationally and educationally. We return to these girls later because they are of some theoretical significance.

Overall, however, the data collected in this study gave little reason to suppose that girls would not, for the most part, reproduce the gendered and classed employment positionings of their parents, close relatives, and neighborhood networks. The processes by which they arrive there and the internal social and cultural differentiations that mark actual trajectories and destinations are not, however, all of a piece; nor are they free from signs of resistance.

OCCUPATIONAL SEMANTICS AND GENDER DISCOURSE

[I said to myself:] either you'll become a nun or a feminist, something radical in any event. (quoted in Borkowski,1992, p. 206)

In making the transition from education to employment and from youth toward adulthood, girls are working at their vocation of becoming women, a social identity informed by a differentiated culture of femininity in which the anchor feature is that of sacrifice. Within this context, occupational choice processes can be viewed as strategies for dealing with structured contradictions in personal and social circumstances, which provide a backcloth of resources that girls may use in constructing their transition biographies. The occupational aspect of this process of putting together social identity and practice works with the various strands of femininity as cultural doxa. These strands are selected and worked, in historically and socially specific ways, to produce variations on the motif of the gendered vocation. Any one occupational choice might then be viewed as a symbolic representation of one of the episodes in a work-in-progress narrative.

The symbolic boundaries between female-male and private-public are focal axes for the construction and expression of cultural meaning; the cultural field of femininity and its corresponding occupational translations are structured by a matrix of opposition and contradiction. Purity-pollution is a fundamental opposition through which women are positioned both within production and reproduction. At the same time, production-reproduction places women in a fundamentally contradictory position through the concept of vocation. At a deeper level of cultural meaning, there is a fundamental relation of equivalence between pollution and reproduction and hence between purity and production. Nearer the surface structures of meaning, these relations of equivalence are reversed: Production is polluting (materially and symbolically/morally "dirty"), reproduction is purifying ("clean").

The dimensions of these cultural semantics are contained in the relationships between the concepts of the madonna and the whore, or, occupationally, the nun and the prostitute. (If we recall that the madonna is a virgin mother and the nun a bride of Christ, then the fact that boys' job lists [as noted earlier] were singularly likely to include mother and prostitute—and little else—as representative of female occupations takes on an unmistakable symbolic significance.)

The term *vocation* implies "one's most important activities" or "that which is central in life" as distinct from what people engage in for the purposes of economic survival. In the term's origin as a calling, a vocation is not something one chooses for oneself, rather one is chosen. Women's paid work is linked, in various ways, with their "most important activity", that is, their vocation: being a woman, which means actively reproducing gender relations and struggling to find themselves in a web of ideological filters and material circumstances. A woman's paid work, her occupation, is a dimension of her femininity—its creation, recreation, and momentary expression. Moreover, this paid work takes a back seat—by definition, it must—in the scheme of things. It recedes in the service of the greater vocation, the reproduction of family life—and with this, the reproduction of patriarchal relations. After all, the vocation always implies elements of self-denial and sacrifice: In taking on the reproduction of femininity at home and at work, women are indeed—usually more or less knowingly—sacrificing themselves. The archetypal vocational expression is the holy life—the nun—and it was the nunneries that gave women a major exit route out of the social reproduction of gender relations, while at the same time exacting the price of a sacrificial version of the cultural reproduction of femininity—the brides of Christ, shrouded and secluded, their escape from femininity transformed into its caricature:

> Lady Carenza of the lovely, gracious body,
> give some advice to us two sisters,
> and since you know best how to tell what's best,
> counsel me according to your experience:
> Shall I marry someone we both know?
> or shall I stay unwed? that would please me,
> for making babies doesn't seem good,
> and it's too anguishing to be a wife.
>
> { ... }
>
> Lady Alais and Lady Iselda,
> you have learning, merit, beauty, youth, fresh
> colour, courtly manners and distinction
> more than all the other women I know;
> I therefore advise you, if you want to plant good seed,

to take as a husband Coronat de Scienza,[1]
saved is the chastity of her who marries him.

When nuns did not and do not conform to normative expectations (as
in the case of the embroidering medieval Beguines, a nonhierarchical
order ultimately officially dissolved by the Church), their resistance
threatens the social order precisely through the double rejection of sacrifice and femininity. In sum, the potential power of the vocation is kept
under control by sacrificial femininity.

The relationships of opposition between purity-pollution and
of contradiction between production-reproduction identified earlier
constitute elements of the doxic field of femininity; they can be linked
with (or translated into) equivalent social forms and cultural meanings
and ultimately into occupational expressions. Effectively, these elements make up a differentiated culture of femininity, each of which
plays a role as ideological representations of patriarchal relations.
Occupational choices can be seen as their surface realizations. Figure
2.1 orders these elements and their equivalents through to the surface
level of occupational expressions. The occupational examples included
are those that proved empirically to be the most popular aspirations
given by girls in the London study.

It is, of course, self-evident that cultural images and practices
(occupational choices) are not made up of one single element: The
occupations in Figure 2.1 were placed onto the semantic map on the
basis of an essentially intuitive judgment about which element of a differentiated culture of femininity seems dominant. And, just as has been
argued in the case of embroidery motifs, these expressions—as woven
into the dynamic trajectories that comprise transition biographies—
may contain elements not only of accommodation but also of resistance. This leads to a further crucial point: Although all women are
caught up in the implications of the culture of femininity as a whole—
that is, they position themselves and are positioned in relation to all its
elements—their positionings are not necessarily identically patterned.
We might expect that women are caught up with femininity in differently textured ways according to social and ethnic origin, for example. In
turn, we might expect to find that their struggles to negotiate transitions are also differentiated into a variety of combinations of positions
and strategies of accommodation and resistance. Most practically, we
might expect to find that the patterns of girls' occupational choices and
the processes of transition in which these are embedded both "hang
together" in plausible ways and express systematically their social, educational, and gender locations. The quotation at the beginning of this

[1]From a 12th-century poem in Bogin, 1976; cited in Parker, 1984, p. 33; *Coronat de
Scienza* is a name for God.

Culture of femininity: gender code structure			
Doxic elements	Social forms	Cultural meanings	Task functions
PURITY	MORALITY	RESPECTABILITY	REGULATORS
PRODUCTION	ECONOMY	SERVICE	EXECUTORS
POLLUTION	SEXUALITY	ATTRACTIVENESS	ATTRACTORS
REPRODUCTION	FAMILY	NURTURANCE	CARETAKERS

Culture of femininity: occupational realisations			
Core task functions	status/qualific. level 1	status/qualific. level 2	status/qualific. level 3
REGULATORS	BANK CLERK 9 SECRETARY 18	TEACHER 22 POLICEWOMAN 9	LAWYER 4
EXECUTORS	COOK 6	SHOPKEEPER 3	ENGINEER 3
ATTRACTORS	AIR HOSTESS 5 HAIRDRESSER 29	MODEL 4	DESIGNER 10 DANCER 4 ACTRESS 8
CARETAKERS	NURSERY NURSE 26	NURSE 9	VET 3 DOCTOR 4

Key
Questionnaire aspirations mentioned by at least 3 respondents are included.
The figure next to each entry indicates frequency of mention. The four most
popular aspirations are noted in bold type.

| elemental pairing | | elemental opposition | | elemental contradiction |

☐ occupational gender breaks here

Figure 2.1. Occupational semantics and the culture of femininity.

section comes from an educationally successful woman of working-
class origin participating in a workshop on upwardly mobile daughters
of working-class families. In the London study, this group was also one
of the most theoretically interesting with respect to looking for modalities of potential transformation, as we see next.

CHALLENGING THE TERMS OF GENDER DISCOURSE

As Kelly and Nihlen (1982) have remarked, the failure to confront
explaining "the ones who get away" has been the weakest point in theories of social and cultural reproduction. Clearly, some forms of resistance are powerful enough (and some personal and social circumstances favorable enough) to break through; but most are not quite
powerful enough, and they all entail costs as well as benefits.

In the study discussed here, the most complex and vibrant trajectories that emerged came from girls who were subject to a range of structurally framed cross-pressures associated with their gender, class, and ethnic cultural milieu, family situation and strategy, and educational environment. Such girls' transition biographies embody a strikingly exposed juggling of the tensions in which they were caught up. These girls were not, however, in the majority. Equally as striking was the extent to which many were trapped inside a world that did not succeed in releasing and fostering their potential or a positive, active subjectivity. Such girls had little opportunity to develop and exercise critical reflection and a sense of agency; they appeared to be passengers, almost flotsam, in the trajectory of their own lives. Additionally, of course, many more girls fell at neither of these two polar positionings between potential transformation and straightforward reproduction. There are also a number of interesting features in these "middle range" transition biographies that suggest possibilities for recognition of critical phases and turning points in negotiating between resistance and accommodation. However, in this discussion, the focus lies on considering girls' educational success in relation to potentially transformative transition biographies and, simultaneously, to their containment.

The broad sweep of research and writing on social origin, gender relations, and education suggests that working-class ideology and practice is somehow more traditional than that of the middle class. It is, of course, problematic to speak of these two groups as if they were self-evidently unitary and opposing social phenomena, but nevertheless, middle-class parents are typically characterized as practicing a more "egalitarian" (i.e., less strongly bounded) domestic division of labor; the degree of occupational segregation by sex is sharper in manual and lower level service sectors than in more highly qualified or professional sectors; working-class children, and especially girls, are still strongly underrepresented in higher education and hence in higher level occupations; marriage and childbearing occur sooner in working-class girls' lives; and so on.

Similarly, understandings of what might count as a transformative outcome as far as gender relations in occupation and employment terms is concerned tend to rest, rather simplistically, on two models. Either a girl is educationally high achieving, which (in theory) opens the door to greater financial independence, career development, and "controlling" functions; or, regardless of her educational performance, she enters a strongly male-typed occupation, in particular, scientific/technical or manual craft jobs. These two models are symbolically classed, at least to some degree: The former is a middle-class route, the latter a working-class route.

Although the parallel is not precise, educationally successful girls, that is, those with greater pedagogic capital—most of whom will be of middle-class origin—tend to move into occupations in what Basil Bernstein (1988) has called the field of symbolic control, but they will not frequently reach particularly controlling positions within it. In particular, they will be clustered into his categories of "repairers" (e.g., social workers), "reproducers" (e.g., teachers), and "executors" (e.g., administrators), which, it might be reasonably argued, are generally less powerful than those of "regulators" (e.g., lawyers), "diffusers" (e.g., advertising executives), and "shapers" (e.g., university professors). Insofar as they carry out these occupational functions, they function as agents of symbolic control, although they may be located, in terms of their employment, in the field of production (e.g., industrial scientists, architects, company administrators). Those girls who do not do well at school, that is, those with lesser pedagogic capital—and who will be disproportionately of working-class origin—are unlikely to become agents of any sort of control. In Bernstein's formulation (1977, 1988), they will occupy, in both fields, employment positions in which they are dominated (though not necessarily passively) by both production and discursive codes. All this poses an interesting question: How do educationally high-achieving working-class girls orient themselves occupationally, and what implications do their orientations have for challenging the terms of gender discourse, that is, for generating productive resistance to the reproduction of gender relations?

But first, looking briefly at the occupations shown in Figure 2.1, which were the most popular aspirations for the girls in the London study, it is clear that occupational agents of symbolic control, whether actually employed in the field of symbolic control or of production, are found only at the highest status/qualification level. But, in addition, the four elements of a differentiated culture of femininity included in Figure 2.1 might be reclassified in terms of their field orientation. It seems straightforward to conclude that the "executor" and "caretaker" functions belong in the field of production. "Regulator" functions obviously belong in the field of symbolic control. But where do "attractor" functions fall? Bernstein (1988) had a similar problem to resolve in the case of the occupational practices of agents of symbolic control operating in the private (as opposed to the public) sector. He distinguished between those offering a service to be hired (e.g., lawyers) and those creating a text to be marketed (e.g., designers). It is the latter group that interests us here. Bernstein argued that typically those holding power over a text are less those who create it, more those who market it—or, at least, there is an intrinsic tension here between two varieties of symbolic control agents: those oriented toward the production of physical resources (the marketers) and those oriented toward the production of discursive resources (the creators). In effect, the agencies in which they work have symbolic control functions, but they operate in the production field. To deal conceptually with this dual and tensioned field orientation, Bernstein proposed that those operating in agencies that market a text (such as publishers, theaters, films, television, cosmetic houses, fashion houses) could be said to be operating in a distinct, third field, which he called the *cultural field*.

Returning to the "attractor" occupations noted in Figure 2.1, it seems reasonable to suggest that these do, in fact, belong to the cultural field. They are all functions that involve creating a (cultural) text—especially, displaying or acting out texts. In some cases, the person physically "is" the text (as in the case of the model). Interestingly, however, none of these popular aspirations involves marketing the text: The model is hired to transform herself into a text created by someone else (usually, not always, male). So they fall toward the characteristically less powerful functional space in Bernstein's cultural field: They are creators—and perhaps only reproducers—of discursive resources. The occupation that does not quite settle happily into this account is that of hairdresser. Hairdressers certainly create texts (perhaps most clearly of all the "attractor" occupations in Figure 2.1, their function is to create the cultural text of femininity), but they not infrequently also *market* them. Hairdressing is one of the few craft trades in which women are both strongly represented and can potentially operate independently. It offers working-class girls a (apparently) realistic route into small-scale entrepreneurship. Earlier, we saw that the popular aspiration "secretary" was really only a safety net expectation for mid-1980s London working-class girls. This was absolutely not so in the case of hairdressing, which was consistently and overwhelmingly popular as a genuine first-choice aspiration among girls of whatever age.

In practice, hairdressing is well known to be highly exploitative of young women's labor; the girls themselves were not unaware of this, and certainly their mothers knew—several had strongly discouraged their daughters from going into the occupation. On the other hand, there were several cases in which girls' mothers had wanted to become hairdressers themselves, did not do so, and encouraged their daughters to "live out" this aspiration for them (and for no other mother's aspiration or occupation did girls relate similar stories). It would appear that, in some way, girls prefer the negative aspects of hairdressing to those of secretarial work, at least prospectively, before they have experienced it. In practical terms, hairdressing offers opportunities for self-employment and working from home. It is also one of the few women's jobs that traditionally offered a formally recognized apprenticeship, although entry to and practice of the trade has never been as strongly bounded by formal qualifications as male-dominated trades have been. It can be argued, however, that hairdressing equally offers quite a lot to girls in symbolic, cultural terms. It unquestioningly speaks to the most powerful dimension of femininity—sexuality/attractors—and it offers women the possibility to work with other women both as colleagues and as clients in a highly social, collective work context.

In other words, hairdressing expresses an intriguing complex of features that intrinsically hold and work with a series of tensions surrounding production/symbolic control relations and gender relations. On the surface, girls who say they want to become hairdressers appear to be straightforwardly accommodating to the terms of gender discourse. This might not, in fact, be quite as straightforward as it looks. Hairdressing might be the most common occupational expression of working-class female unproductive resistance (cf. McRobbie, 1978); it is undoubtedly a combination of resistance/accommodation that is not powerful enough to achieve potential "breakthrough" in terms of ideology or practice. But for working-class girls who either do not do well at school or who do not want to put up with schooling any longer than they have to (often for good reason, one might add), choosing hairdressing fits in with a strategy for constructing a livable transitions biography in a number of ways. Not the least of its positive aspects is, additionally, that it conforms to a "separate but equal" model of gender relations which, at least for some working-class fractions, is an important feature of, nevertheless, patriarchal cultural practice, both at home and in the workplace. In my view, it is this feature that has contributed to the widely held view that the working class is more traditional (by which is implied: old-fashioned, sexist, etc.) in these respects than is the middle class. It would be more accurate to say, perhaps, that there are class-specific modalities of patriarchy that are expressed in ideologies and practices in both private and public spheres, but that these modalities cannot in themselves be ranked against each other as "more" or "less" patriarchal.

This is possibly of some significance in turning back to the question of educationally successful working-class girls in terms of supporting versus containing the potential for challenging the terms of gender discourse. To begin with, Holland's (1986) research into adolescents' understandings of divisions of labor in the family and in the labor force included a comparison between middle-class girls' and boys' perspectives on gender relations (specifically, divisions of labor) according to their parents' occupations as located either in the field of production or in the field of symbolic control. She found the greatest difference in perspectives between girls and boys whose parents were employed in occupations in the production field. This arose because, on the one hand, the girls from both parental fields held relatively progressive views on gender relations, that is, all middle-class girls were disposed to support gender equality at home and at work. (This is in line with the broad sweep of research into girls' perspectives on this topic by social origin, referred to earlier. Whether it implies much more than the performance of a legitimated discourse about gender relations that bears only an imaginary relation to practice is another matter.) It was, however, boys whose parents were agents of production control who held by far the most conservative views on gender relations. Overall, the children of parents who were agents of symbolic control held less traditionally stereotyped ideas about the division of labor by sex.

Although these findings cannot suggest what the differences between working-class girls and boys are (and there remains the problem that working-class parents are positioned fundamentally differently in their fields of employment), they do prompt the thought that perhaps the fields of production and of symbolic control draw on different social recruitment bases. What, for example, is the social origin profile of engineers (perhaps of given generations and in given localities) compared with university professors? Might this make a difference in the ways their own children come to understand gender relations? In sum, it might well be that educationally successful working-class girls, for example, are equipped with particular kinds of resources that help them to struggle and persist that much harder. These resources might be a consequence of particular family histories in which disjunctions and cross-pressures play a significant role. Alternatively, we might simply propose that intersections between (working) class and (female) gender generate contradictions that foster the development of critical consciousness more effectively than for middle-class girls. To what extent this is so and, more importantly for our purposes, whether and how such critical consciousness can be translated into potentially transformative challenges to gender relations is sensitively dependent on a number of other factors, not the least of which must be the quality of educational experience. It might also be that educationally successful working-class girls' occupational field orientation is differently textured than is the case for middle-class girls. Specifically, might they be more disposed to choose occupations in the production field? Does this have implications for their understandings and perspectives about gender relations?

Bernstein (1977, 1988) argued that in European culture the fields of production and education are marked by a relation of strong classification, that is, their field boundaries are firmly insulated against each other. Whereas agents of symbolic control form an identifiable social class whose consciousness is directly constituted by education, the consciousness of both the ruling class (those who control physical resources and production codes) and the working class (those who are dominated by the same) is primarily constituted by production. This formulation leads to one way of decribing the characteristic quality of relations between teachers and their working-class pupils, of course. The tensions that are generated for working-class children who "defect" class membership to the symbolic control field via educational achievement need no exposition here. However, for working-class girls who are educationally successful, the Rubicon has already been crossed: Once having gone over to the other side, the onward journey is less onerous. Educationally successful working-class girls are, by definition, social marginals; marginals are disproportionately often innovators because they have less to lose. If, however, their consciousness has indeed been influenced by their social origin in the manner proposed by Bernstein, then they ought to be more open to occupations falling into the field of production, whatever the actual discursive location or hierarchical position they occupy within that field.

The London study does indicate that this may be so. The number of middle-class girls in the sample was small, as were the numbers of high-achieving working-class girls. Nevertheless, they were all studied intensively, over a 3-year period, using a variety of both quantitative and qualitative techniques. Some intriguing differences emerged between these two groups as far as their educational-occupational orientations were concerned. Those girls whose perspectives on gender relations were critically reflexive were also those who were doing well at school (at least initially and usually throughout the study); these girls were all regarded as occupying potentially transforming locations within gender discourse. All these girls reported a lively and varied history of past occupational choices when first interviewed, and their current aspirations were very likely to be at a professional level. However, the choices of the middle-class girls were more narrowly spread than were those of the working-class girls. The middle-class girls wanted to be journalists, lawyers, dancers in musicals, actresses, and teachers. In other words, they were primarily oriented toward occupations in the field of symbolic control or, alternatively, in the higher echelons of text creators in the cultural field. Such occupations are also wholly or relatively gender-appropriate choices. These kinds of aspirations were by no means absent from the working-class girls' choices, but they were balanced by a greater representation of less traditional jobs for women: archeologists, machine mechanics, laboratory scientists, and pilots. These occupations fall into the field of production, although their discursive function may be that of symbolic control within the field.

Fourteen-year-old Nadia's spontaneous job list is a particularly appo-
site example of this pattern: *astronaut*, astrologer, *lawyer, journalist*, miner,
politician, scientist, *space researcher*, gravedigger, author. The italicized
entries later turned out to be her aspirations at the time.

What was also interesting about Nadia is that she is of mixed
ethnic background, but her parents divorced when she was quite small.
Her father returned to his country of birth, and she grew up in a close-
knit working-class community among a support group of her mother's
female relatives. She identified wholly with her mother's indigenous
working-class Londoner culture and explicitly rejected any notion of
another ethnic and cultural orientation and identity (to the extent that
she expressed quite "nationalist" political views). In sum, Nadia's background and experiences contain characteristic indicators of discontinuities, fracturing, and conflicts to which other writers have pointed as
prompters of "innovative" lifestyles and values. An early example of such
research was the Rapoports' (1971, 1976) study of wives in dual-career
families. A contemporary example, of direct relevance to the London
study discussed here, is Safia Mirza's (1992) school-based ethnographic
study of young black London women, which underlines both their relative educational success and their high occupational aspirations that
were distinctively oriented toward nontraditional professions. In other
words, their choice profiles were similar to those for the working-class
high achievers here, whatever their ethnic origin. Ethnic origin, however,
was also of considerable importance in my own sample as a source of
the cross-pressures that generate more intensely experienced contradictions in relation to gender and transitions. In many cases, these tensions did not produce innovative and favorable educational-occupational trajectories. They simply produced a great deal of unhappiness and
anguish for girls who were "cornered" by the exigencies of their lives and
educational experiences. This was not always so, however: In combination with a middle-class background, in which both parents occupied
educationally achieved positions as agents of symbolic control themselves, ethnic minority status could very much play its part in turning a
double negative into a highly positive outcome.

Metz-Göckel (1992) has noted that apart from statistical census
data on educational and vocational training participation rates by social
origin, there are few sources of information and studies about working-
class girls' transitions between education and the labor market. There is
still less information on how the educationally successful among them
manage the transition and what they make of their lives in the longer
term. She took the view that working-class girls who are upwardly socially mobile via educational achievement can be regarded as an avant-
garde group, one that points to deeper social changes in women's roles

and self-identities and in gender relations overall. First and most importantly, she argued, paid work was always a taken-for-granted necessity in working-class women's lives. Hence, their social distance from their husband's social status and position was always narrower than in middle-class circles. On the other hand, gender relations in the home—as indicated by the domestic division of labor—are characterized by greater differentiation than is (at least) today the case for middle-class couples (by which she meant, in fact, "educated" couples). In other words, Metz-Göckel suggested, too, that working-class and middle-class women are differently positioned in gender discourse and that this differentiation is not simply a consequence of the rise of postwar egalitarian sex-role ideology among educated middle-class professionals. In considering the personal and social resources educationally successful working-class girls need in order to deal proactively with their life situation, she referred to features such as fractured familial traditions, supportive significant others ("chosen" role models), and the adoption of a self-made woman (i.e., highly individualized) orientation to life.

Rohleder's (1992) study of working-class girls who became doctors also pointed out that a significant proportion of respondents came from families who were in some ways not "standard" nor intergenerationally stable members of the working class, with the consequence that parents—especially mothers—had placed great emphasis on the importance of educational achievement as a means of (re)gaining social status. School success in itself had been an important motivator to continuing education, in that this had furnished the girls with a more positive sense of self-worth. Finally, the decision to study medicine had been centrally influenced by two factors: first, they felt they did not possess the appropriate habitus to study humanities. They felt that speech, manner, and so on, were not of so much moment in the natural sciences. Second, they judged that labor market prospects would be favorable (in comparison with the social sciences, to which several were initially more attracted) and that the practice of medicine is more closely related to manual male and female skills (such as mending pipes or sewing). In other words, medicine brought with it a sense of affinity, or at least less distance, in class and gender terms.

These findings are particularly interesting when set aside those of the London study. They point to the significance of contradiction and conflict as prompters for orientations toward nontraditional or innovative roles in both class and gender terms. They emphasize the critical role of education for working-class girls in developing their sense of self-worth and competence. By implication and in reverse, they similarly point to working-class girls' "hypersensitivity" to negative educational experiences, to which they are very vulnerable and for which they can seldom compensate by calling on educationally-focused support in family and community contexts, as a number of cases in the London study showed. Finally, they introduce, in embryonic form, an explanation for the popularity of medicine as a girls' occupational choice that speaks to cultural semantics as well as to material employment prospects. This explanation goes beyond the standard association of medicine with "caretaking" functions and specifically refers to the motivations of working-class girls as opposed to girls in general.

But, in fact, few working-class girls manage to make their way through formal education at the levels necessary to study medicine, or indeed anything else. The social reproduction of patriarchal relations for working-class girls is regulated through educational selection and allocation, in that the potential for resistance and transformation is progressively restricted and curtailed through elimination practices. At each hurdle, failure implies rerouting back into labor market sectors circumscribed primarily by gender. Success only implies the right to stay in the game for the next round. At every round the stakes are higher; fewer squeeze through, and the pressures toward gender-specific specialization become greater. In this context, gender discourse provides frameworks of orientations for the construction of personal biography. The potential challengers are thus reduced to more than manageable proportions.

In the process of educationally succeeding, however, girls (of whatever class background) acquire ideologies to explain that success, to legitimate their success in the face of other pupils' failures. Such girls in the London study, of both middle- and working-class origin, were fully aware of the nature of gender relations as far as vertical and horizontal divisions of labor between the sexes are concerned, and they were also able to make the crucial links between women's position in the family and in the labor force as, in tandem, ensuring the reproduction of gender inequality. They were, of course, all in favor of equal opportunities in employment, and they all hoped to establish as equal a domestic division of labor as possible in their own future families. Not a single girl self-identified herself as a feminist; in the interviews many girls expressly and spontaneously distanced themselves from feminism, which they judged as man hating and discriminatory, wanting to replace patriarchy with matriarchy. When it came to giving explanations for the patterns of gender relations that they could describe so well, these educationally successful girls all used ideas that essentially denied the contemporary relevance of structured social inequalities in the eradication of women's remaining disadvantage.

In other words, they emphasized equal opportunities (*not* equality) within a framework of meritocratic individualism. Serious gender inequalities were banished to an irrelevant past. This means that they were disinclined to politicize their insights via a collectivist program for social change. They preferred to place their trust in a progressive social evolution toward gender equality coupled with an individual responsibility to realize one's own potential. Women's continued disadvantage, in this account, becomes attributable to a degendered individual failure. In sum, these girls use the same kind of individualizing ideology that explains and legitimizes educational success and failure to explain and legitimize girls' and women's educational and employment positionings. Working-class girls, if they are to cope personally and socially with educational success and its implications, will almost inevitably make use of these ideas, too, even if later in life they come to a different view. It might well be argued that unless pupils (in general) are prepared to adjust their practices to fit the ideology of meritocratic individualism, they literally cannot educationally succeed because it is the principle of individualized selection and allocation that underlies the distribution of qualifications and credentials. If this is so, then there is little sense or justice in castigating girls for their lack of sisterly solidarity, howsoever one might wish things to be otherwise. But ultimately, the degendering of inequalities is more likely to lead to accommodatory rather than to potentially transforming resolutions as far as the reproduction of gender relations is concerned.

To feel that one can take one's fate into one's own hands is personally emancipatory, but it is not necessarily socially emancipatory. This is the contradiction and paradox at the heart of contemporary individualization processes, from which girls and women may well benefit, but which are nonetheless ideological motifs whose decoding is a more complex affair than ever. Taking one's fate into one's own hands in this individualized way also entails high risks because not only success, but also failure, rests with oneself. Partial autonomies are therefore always purchased at some cost. I would like to hope, however, that the consequences are not quite as gloomy as those Borkowski (1992) depicted. She viewed educationally successful, upwardly mobile, working-class girls and women as deeply injured individuals with deformed subjectivities, who as frequently as not end up running headlong into their own physical and psychic collapse in their struggles to live up to and exceed all expectations placed on them. She declined to find a higher goal to admire and celebrate in all this pain, but rather posed the question: For whom or for what do they destroy themselves?

The answer might be that the alternatives are worse; despite all the problems it entails, education has been for centuries and remains a relative haven for girls and women: as an intellectual activity in itself, as a professional location, and as an escape from personal and social oppression. This haven has not been available to working-class girls and women for very long; those who have been fortunate enough to stay the course know its value as well as its costs. Basil Bernstein has the last word:

> The pedagogic device which produces symbolic control and its modalities, in the very process of its transmissions makes available principles which both shape and can re-shape consciousness. The device itself produces a struggle for power over its realisations. . . . Normalising processes . . . are rarely free of the contradictions, cleavages and dilemmas they are set up to control. Socialisation . . . is then always both socialisation into another's voice and into one's own "yet to be voiced." (Bernstein, 1988, p. 45)

REFERENCES

Bernstein, B. (1977). Aspects of the relations between education and production. In Class, codes and control (Vol. 3, 2nd rev. ed., pp. 174-200). London: Routledge and Kegan Paul.

Bernstein, B. (1988). An essay in education, symbolic control and social practices [mimeo]. Revised version of a public lecture, CIDE, Santiago, Chile.

Bernstein, B. (1993). Code theory and research. In Class, codes and control (Vol. 5). Barcelona: EL Rouve.

Bogin, M. (1976). The women troubadors. London: Paddington Press.

Borkowski, B. (1992). Ausbruch und Aufbruch durch Bildung aus Milieu- und Geschlechtsrollen-Begrenzungen. Nachdenken über den Workshop "Arbeitertöchter und ihr sozialer Aufstieg" [Breaking out and up through education from milieu and gender constraints. Reflections on the workshop "Working Class Girls and Social Mobility"]. In A. Schlüter (Ed.), Arbeitertöchter und ihr sozialer Aufstieg. Zum Verhältnis von Klasse, Geschlecht und sozialer Mobilität (pp. 195-208). [Upwardly socially mobile working class girls. On the relationship between class, gender and social mobility]. Weinheim: Deutscher Studien Verlag.

Chisholm, L.A. (1990). Beyond occupational choice: A study of gendered transitions. Unpublished doctoral thesis, University of London Institute of Education, London.

Chisholm, L.A., & Holland, J. (1987). Anti-sexist action research in schools: The GAOC project. In G. Weiner & M. Arnot (Eds.), Gender under scrutiny: New inquiries in education (pp. 243-257). Milton Keynes:

Open University Press.

Holland, J. (1986). *Social class differences in adolescents' conceptions of the domestic and industrial division of labour.* Unpublished doctoral thesis, University of London Institute of Education. (Available in CORE, 10(1))

Kelly, G.P. & Nihlen, A.S. (1982). Schooling and the reproduction of patriarchy: Unequal workloads, unequal rewards. In M.W. Apple (Ed.), *Cultural and economic reproduction in education* (pp. 162-180). London: Routledge and Kegan.

McRobbie, A. (1978). Working class girls and the culture of femininity. In CCCS Women's Studies Group (Eds.), *Women take issue* (chap. 5). London: Hutchinson.

Metz-Göckel, S. (1992). Bildung, Lebensverlauf und Selbstkonzepte von "Arbeitertöchtern". Ein Beitrag zur sozialen Mobilität und Individualisierung von Frauen aus bildungsfernen Schichten |"Working class daughters'" education, biography and self-concept. An essay on social mobility and individualisation amongst women from social groups distant from education]. In A. Schlüter (Ed.), *Arbeitertöchter und ihr sozialer Aufstieg. Zum Verhältnis von Klasse, Geschlecht und sozialer Mobilität* |Upwardly socially mobile working class girls. On the relationship between class, gender and social mobility] (pp. 36-66]. Weinheim: Deutscher Studien Verlag.

Parker, R. (1984). *The subversive stitch.* London: The Women's Press.

Rapoport, R., & Rapoport, R.N. (1971). *Dual career families.* Harmondsworth: Penguin.

Rapoport, R., & Rapoport, R.N. (1976). *Dual career families revisited.* London: Martin Robertson.

Rohleder, C. (1992). Aus den Sperrsitzen in die höheren Ränge der Gesellschaft? Zum Prozeß der Studienfachwahl von Medizinerinnen aus Arbeiterfamilien und Momenten ihrer aktuellen beruflichen Verortung |From the back stalls into the front balconies of society? On the process of university degree choice amongst women doctors from working class families and their current occupational specialisms]. In A. Schlüter (Ed.), *Arbeitertöchter und ihr sozialer Aufstieg. Zum Verhältnis von Klasse, Geschlecht und sozialer Mobilität* |Upwardly socially mobile working class girls. On the relationship between class, gender and social mobility, pp. 36-66]. Weinheim: Deutscher Studien Verlag.

Safia Mirza, H. (1992). *Young, female and black.* London: Routledge.

3

Official Knowledge and the Growth of the Activist State

Michael W. Apple
University of Wisconsin-Madison

I must start my contribution to this Festschrift to Basil Bernstein in an odd way. Festschrifts are usually made up of essays in honor of someone, not essays about someone. My chapter takes the former path, not the latter, as is usual. However, I want to make a few prefatory remarks of a more personal nature. In a recent appreciative yet critical appraisal of some of Bernstein's work (Apple, 1992), I suggested that the lack of a substantive theory of the state and of state formation limited a number of Bernstein's more provocative insights. I also argued that the complex and at times contradictory intersections of multiple dynamics of power needed to be more integrated into our analyses if we want to capture the ways education functioned socially and discursively. At the same time, however, I argued that Bernstein's work was absolutely essential to understand even the areas I identified as partly problematic in his own efforts.

The following chapter—part of a larger project of mine on the relationship between official knowledge and cultural, political, and economic power (Apple 1993a, 1993b)—is indebted to Basil Bernstein in two ways. First, as you will see, it draws on his work to form part of the conceptual apparatus of its analyses. Second, it is partly a result of my attempt to think through the complex relations the state has to multiple axes of power, how state control itself is actually formed out of a complicated politics of social ferment and hegemonic alliances, and how "official knowledge" in the school curriculum actually gets to be declared officially legitimate knowledge in determinate situations.

My investigation here is historical and conjuctural. It takes one nation—the United States—at a major period in its history and interrogates its educational politics and the politics of wider social movements. It focuses on one "pedagogic device" (Bernstein, 1990), on the one artifact that is declared as official knowledge in so many schools in the world. I speak here of the textbook. And I do so in a way that employs and extends Bernstein's suggestive work.

INTRODUCTION

Behind Herbert Spencer's famous question, "What knowledge is of most worth?", lies another even more contentious question, "Whose knowledge is of most worth?" During the past two decades, a good deal of progress has been made on answering the question of whose knowledge becomes socially legitimate in schools. Although much still remains to be understood, and the very terms of how we are to understand it are subject to serious critical scrutiny, we are now much closer to having a clearer understanding of the relationship between school knowledge and the larger society than before. Yet, as I argued in both *Teachers and Texts* (Apple, 1988b) and *Official Knowledge* (Apple, 1993a), little attention has actually been paid to that one artifact that plays such a major role in defining whose culture is taught, the *textbook*. Of course, there have been literally thousands of studies of textbooks over the years. But, by and large, until relatively recently, most of these remained unconcerned about the politics of culture. All too many researchers could still be characterized by that phrase coined years ago by C. Wright Mills, "abstract empiricists." These "hunters and gatherers of social numbers " remain unconnected to the relations of domination and power that surround them.

This is a distinct problem because texts are not simply "delivery systems" of "facts." They are at once the results of political, economic, and cultural activities, battles, and compromises. They are conceived, designed, and authored by real people with real interests. They are published within the economic and political constraints of markets, resources, and power, with the state often playing a crucial role in all of this. Finally, what texts mean and how they are used are fought over by social groups with distinctly different commitments and by teachers and students as well. The text, then, becomes a door into nearly all of the power relations involved in education (Apple & Christian-Smith, 1991).

In this chapter, I take a piece of this complex story. I focus on how in the United States a situation has evolved in which the governments of a number of states have the right to declare which textbooks are to have the official imprimatur of state sponsorship. The story I tell, a story of conflict, struggle, and compromise inside and outside of education, is not a neat and tidy one. Neither is reality.

OPEN AND CLOSED TERRITORY

Nearly half of the states in the United States have some process by which curricular materials, usually textbooks, are evaluated and endorsed at a state level. Publishers differentiate between two kinds of states. In what is called "open territory"—most of the East, Midwest, and Far West—publishers sell directly to school districts or individual schools. In "closed territories"—mostly in the South and Southwest—centralized adoption policies prevail. Individual districts in the "closed territories" can usually buy nearly any book, but state funds can only be used to purchase approved texts. Of all the states in the "closed territories," Texas and California (and now increasingly perhaps Florida) have the most power.

The influence of such state adoption policies should not be underestimated. The sheer economics of it is very important. Take Texas as an example. Texas spends tens of millions of dollars on instructional materials and has a rather narrow policy of approving five textbooks or less (the minimum is two) for each subject. This puts it in an exceptionally strong position to influence the content of texts as publishers compete to gain their share of what is obviously a lucrative part of the market. This, of course, is one of the reasons right-wing groups devote so much of their attention to making an impact on text adoption in Texas (Apple, 1993a).

Texas has other characteristics that make it powerful besides the stringent limits it places on the number of texts it approves. Texas not only has a rapidly growing population that puts it second only to California in the "closed territory" in sheer numbers of students for which it buys books, but it adopts for both elementary and secondary schools. Furthermore, purchase contracts between the state and textbook publishers are for eight years, thereby guaranteeing that large market for a considerable length of time. Finally, and not unimportantly, Texas uses a method of payment that is in many ways a publisher's delight. It has a single-payment system in which one large check pays for the state's entire purchase of particular textbooks. To quote one publisher, "The money we get from sales in Texas is fast and clean" (Council on Interracial Books for Children, 1983, p. 17).

Although Texas may be the most visible economically, the recent choice by California to reject all of the submitted textbooks in one subject area—and the shockwaves that rippled through the educational and publishing communities—demonstrates its own considerable ability to exert pressure on the content and form of official knowledge. Along with Texas, it controls nearly 25% of the market in textbooks (Apple, 1988b; Apple & Christian-Smith, 1991). In the process, both have an immense impact on what gets published for schools in the entire nation.

In my discussion here, I begin by illuminating one major element in this process of making knowledge official, the complicated politics of the text that is seen in such state adoption policies. Part of my task here is theoretical. How do we think about this process? This requires that I make some arguments about the role of government (the "State")[1] in making some groups' "cultural capital" more legitimate than others'. And part of my task is political, historical, and empirical. What happens within this process? What are its roots in the past? What can we learn about this that can help us challenge the growing power of the conservative restoration in so many countries? This requires that we examine some of the previous and current conflicts over state adoption policies. I first turn to some initial theoretical points about the role of the State. However, for those readers who have less tolerance for such theoretical labors, you can turn to the section on "'Incompetent' Teachers, 'Unethical' Publishers" that follows the next three without jeopardizing too much of the historical story I now tell.

SYMBOLIC CONTROL AND THE STATE

Although there is a formal right for everyone to be represented in the debates over whose cultural capital, whose knowledge "that," "how," and "to," will be declared legitimate for transmission to future generations of students, it is still the case that as I noted earlier a selective tradition operates in which only specific groups' knowledge becomes official knowledge (Apple, 1990). Thus, the freedom to help select the formal corpus of school knowledge is bounded by power relations that

---

[1]I differentiate between the State and the state. The first signifies the assemblage of publicly financed institutions, meaning the government and the institutions it supports in general. The second refers to a geographical entity, 1 of the 50 individual states in the United States (see Dale, 1989).

have very real effects. Perhaps a sense of how this formal right operates in real material conditions can be best seen in another area of the cultural apparatus of a society—the press.

Freedom can be defined in two different ways—negatively and positively. Speaking specifically about freedom of the press, Mandel (1981) put the negative case this way:

> The negative definition of freedom means the absence of censorship and of institutions apriori denying average citizens (or organizations of citizens) the opportunity of printing and diffusing their opinions. In that negative sense, freedom of the press means the formal right of all to publish whatever they wish, at least in the field of beliefs, opinions, commentary on events, and general information. (p. vii)

Mandel continued, turning to the positive sense of freedom:

> The positive definition of a free press means the effective material capacity of individuals or groups of individuals to have their opinions printed and circulated. If it costs $10 million to found a daily newspaper, and many more millions to run it, the abstract "right" to do this— that is the absence of any law or institution prohibiting it—will be of little avail for the overwhelming majority of citizens. It will be like the right to become a millionaire, when in fact less than 0.5% of the population accumulate such wealth. (p. viii)

These points are significant. Notice that the positive sense of freedom is linked to existing relations of power. The right of cultural distribution is partly dependent on economic and political conditions. This means that one cannot simply assert that all parties have a "right" to make their knowledge public. The question of the right to determine what counts as legitimate content cannot be answered in the abstract. We need to focus on the actual economics and politics of regulation. What counts as legitimate knowledge and one's right to determine it is lodged in a complicated politics of symbolic control of public knowledge. Because it is public, that is, because it is declared to be "knowledge for all," it is subject to scrutiny by official bodies (and is subject to the drives and tendencies of a market). In most countries, this means that some level of government is officially charged with the duty of creating a selective tradition.

In fact, one of the most interesting historical dynamics has been the extension—gradually but still graphically—of the direct or indirect State authority over the field of symbolic control. Education has become a crucial set of institutions through which the State attempts to "produce, reproduce, distribute, and change" the symbolic resources, the very consciousness, of society (Bernstein, 1986, p. 230). These institutions have, of course, often been sites of intense conflict over whose symbols should be transmitted and whose principles should organize this transmission (Bernstein, 1977; Hogan, 1982). At the center of these conflicts, however, sits the State.

In the past, as critical work on the curriculum began to emerge as a serious force in educational research, all too many people assumed that the State would uniformly support only the knowledge of dominant groups. In a capitalist economy, only the knowledge required by economically powerful groups would become legitimate in publicly supported schools. However, as Carnoy, myself, and others have documented, this is far too simplistic and is historically inaccurate (Apple, 1988a, 1988b, 1993a; Carnoy, 1984; Carnoy & Levin, 1985). The State is *not* guaranteed to serve the interests of a unified dominant class. Instead of this "instrumentalist" view, like civil society the State is a site of *interclass* struggle and negotiation, "a sphere of political action where the interests of dominant classes [and gendered and racial groups] can be partially institutionalized and realized" as well (Freiberg, 1981, p. 13).

It is not only the case, however, that the State acts as an arena of *interclass* conflict and negotiation. It also, and very importantly, serves as a site for intraclass conflict and compromise. That is, there is a second logic that informs State action. The State tends to balance the opposing interest of different segments of dominant groups (Freiberg, 1981, p. 13).

To further complicate matters, but also to be true to the historical record, as I have argued elsewhere, because the State is the arena in which the conflict over the dominance of property rights versus person rights in government comes to the fore—the conclusion of which cannot always be known in advance—there will be times when State educational policy will be genuinely progressive (Apple, 1985, 1988a). Because the State is a site of conflict, compromises or accords will have to be formed that will sometimes signify at least partial victories for progressive or less powerful groups (Apple, 1993a).

In essence, historically there has often been something of a tradeoff between the meeting of State-sponsored goals and the wishes of groups outside the State itself. Economic, political, and cultural elites will seek a maximum amount of support from other groups for their educational policies "in return for conceding a minimum amount of diversification" (Archer, 1986, p. 31). Thus, there will always be pressure from above to gain support for decisions made by government bodies; but such support is very difficult to obtain if State policies do not also incorporate some of the other diverse perspectives both within other elements of elite groups and from those groups with less economic, cultural, and political power. The key is to form an accord that acts as an umbrella under which many groups can stand but which basically still is under the guiding principles of dominant groups (Apple, 1993a).

Yet, because of this, the content of curricula and the decision-making process surrounding it cannot simply be the result of an act of domination. The "cultural capital" declared to be official knowledge, then, is *compromised* knowledge, knowledge that is filtered through a complicated set of political screens and decisions before it gets to be declared legitimate. This affects what knowledge is selected and what the selected knowledge looks like as it is transformed into something that will be taught to students in school. In this way, the State acts as what Basil Bernstein would call a "recontextualizing agent" in the process of symbolic control as it creates accords that enable the creation of "knowledge for everyone."

This process of transformation, in which knowledge is taken out of its original social or academic context and "recontextualized" and changed by the political rules that govern its new setting, is elaborated on in even greater theoretical detail by Bernstein. Agents such as textbook publishing houses, content consultants, and state and local educational authorities—all those whose task it is to *reproduce*, not produce, knowledge—together act as recontextualizing agents. The original knowledge from academic disciplines, from differing social groups, and so on, is appropriated by those groups of people who have power in the new context. The "text," as Bernstein called it, "undergoes a transformation prior to its relocation" in the new context. As the text is "de-located" from its original location and "re-located" into the new pedagogic situation, the logic and power relations of the recontextualizing agents ensure that "the text is no longer the same text" (Bernstein, 1986, pp. 226-227). Political accords and educational needs can radically alter the shape and organization of the knowledge.

This occurs in three distinct ways. First, "the text has changed its position in relation to other texts, practices, and positions" (p. 227). It is no longer part of the professional discourse of researchers or part of the cultural discourse of oppressed groups, for example. This, thereby, alters power relations. In the new context, the knowledge re-producers have more power, and the knowledge is integrated around a different set of political and cultural needs and principles. Second, the text itself has been modified by "selection, simplification, condensation, and elaboration" (p. 227). Thus, for example, dominant pedagogical approaches and the economics of publishing will both influence textbook writers and adopters to order knowledge into bite-sized chunks that can be easily understood and mastered (and that are politically safe). In the process, the knowledge is transformed. Third, "the text has been re-positioned and re-focused" (p. 227). Not only is the knowledge organized around different principles, but its *use* changes. It may be there for socialization purposes now, not to expand our intellectual horizons, or as I demonstrate in the second half of this chapter, it may now signify a way to maintain the unstable equilibrium that has been established by the accord over whose knowledge will have gained the official imprimatur.

Thus, when knowledge is made into content for school, certain principles are embodied in identifiable agents who bring these principles into play. In Bernstein's words, "The de-contextualizing principle regulates the new ideological positioning of the text in its process of re-location in one or more levels of the field of reproduction" (p. 227). Of prime import here are agents in the State and agents in the economy, textbook publishers in particular. The decontextualizing and recontextualizing principles are built through the interaction of the political and educational needs represented in state adoption policies and by the need for profitable operation by publishers.

These points about the State and about how knowledge is altered by the politics of symbolic control may seem rather abstract, but although theoretical, their import is great. They do support my claim that curricula are rooted in differential power, in a set of social relationships that ultimately play a large part in determining whose cultural capital is made available and "re-located" in our schools. Only by understanding the interaction between the forces acting on government regulation and on the economics of textbook publishing can we determine how such decontextualizing and relocating works.

REFORM FROM ABOVE

The reasons for the increasingly powerful State regulation of symbolic control are tied up both with larger patterns of differential political and economic power as well as more specific issues that arise within the educational system itself. In understanding both these external and internal reasons, we need to be sensitive to the fact that not all parts of the United States are the same. There are different patterns of regulation; different class, race, gender, and religious relations; and different articulations between, say, the ways official knowledge is chosen and the textbook publishing industry. Perhaps the best way of demonstrating this is to delve more deeply into the history of state adoption policies and the conflicts and compromises that they generated.

Even given the interest by state governments in extending their control over what counts as legitimate knowledge, there were decidedly different plans for centralizing text selection and rationalizing adoption procedures. Not all plans gave power to the state. Thus, for instance, in 1933, although 25 states empowered the state board of education or a special textbook committee to select texts for use in the public schools, another group of 5 states left that decision at a county level. Still others did not intervene in local decisions at all (Henry, 1933, p. 19). Why the difference?

Why would the South be the area in which one finds most of the centralized state adoption procedures, as well as the longest history of rightist populism? This is a very complicated question because it requires not only that we think about the causes within education that could lead to the centralization of "re-contextualizing agents" at the top, but it requires also a firmer understanding of the larger relations of power in which educational "reforms" of this type took place. Even a brief glimpse at, for example, class and economic conditions that differed from region to region shows the significance of such power relations.

We need to remember some of the peculiarities of American political history. Unlike many European nations, for example, the United States educational system grew out of a federation of relatively independent states. Thus, the power of national controls, and the pattern of state control over curriculum and teaching, is dependent on this history. Although it is possible to speak of a national curriculum here currently—one whose content is determined largely by Texas and California and by the competitive market in textbooks—the situation is still one of a very different articulation between the power of the state and the school than in those nations with homogeneous school systems (Richardson, 1986, p. 36).

These differences can be readily seen in the politics of school governance. Historically, although the stereotype exists that all states had similar patterns of school governance, a closer look reveals clear patterns of regional variation:

> The model of state-level appointments and local-level elections characterized northeastern states and is reasonably defined as bureaucratic. Yet the southern model was the reverse, with state officers elected and local levels appointed. Both levels were elective across midwestern states. The divergence of southern and midwestern states from the bureaucratic model of the Northeast sufficiently jeopardizes the claim that there was a single, national model of school governance. (Richardson, 1986, p. 38)

Some of the political and economic reasons for these regional differences were noted by Richardson (1986) in his own discussion of the class and race relations underlying the different strategies used for "reforming" education:

> Although the architects of public school systems in the northeastern and southern states were from similar social backgrounds and were members of the weakly established new middle class, they differed significantly in the broader context of relations. The presence of a landed, planter class and its potential for antagonistic relations to poor white farmers underlay the essentially conservative intentions of southern educational reform. . . . "The small professional middle class that included a number of important southern reformers allied itself with the landed upper class that sponsored industrialization and, after 1900, expanded the range of state activity, thereby exchanging the right to rule for the right to teach school." For southern educational reform, the systematization of schooling was entrapped by the politics of class and race which led inexorably to the construction of dual systems separating whites and blacks. (p. 47)

It is not as if class and race dynamics were absent in other regions of the country. Of course they were present. Yet, because of the specific differences in the regional political economies and class structures, the power of the state was articulated in diverse ways. Richardson (1986) is again helpful here:

> While the design and content of both northeastern and southern school systems were motivated by pressing needs for social |and symbolic| control, the "universal educational movement" of the South spoke more openly of the need to design a common education in the service of industrialization. . . . In this respect, the content of school reform differed between the Northeast and the South. The absence of a landed class in the North enlarged the flexibility of school reformers. Educational systems in the Northeast originated from substitutive strategies where school reformers were able to erect an institutional structure upon already established *local instructional networks*. This enabled them to link more closely the conduct of instruction to the character and occupational futures of the new middle class, evident in curricula stressing a denial or escape "from the ethos of the industrial system and its traditional asceticism." . . . In contrast, southern educational reform originated from partial restrictive strategies, restrained by the continuity of political power based in a landed, planter class. Here educational reform was *"from above"*, defining the public realm by the extension of common schooling to the broad base of poor whites. (p. 47, emphasis added)

In the South, then, as I show in more detail shortly, an accord is formed between a somewhat less powerful but still emergent white middle class with its own professionalizing and rationalizing interests and those of the landed planter class in which the "needs" of poor whites are taken into account. "Reform from above" rather than a greater emphasis on "reform from below" is established because of different educational conditions (a longer tradition of local educational networks in the North, for instance) and because of both the class and race antagonisms and the perceived need by powerful groups for industrialization in the South. A tradition of state intervention and control, hence, is established very early on in the history of the accords that govern how and whose knowledge is recontextualized.

Even though I have focused my attention on the South and Northeast here, similar data are available on the Midwest and Far West regions of the country. Although I do not go into detail about this, there, too, specific differences emerge that help us explain the reasons behind centralized or decentralized models of curricular decision making (Richardson, 1986). The important point is to recognize not only the differences but the connections between these varied traditions and the specific conditions of economic and political power within each region.

Yet the attention one might give to such economic and political conditions is not sufficient. There were serious regional *ideological* differences as well that need to be taken into account and that also contributed to further regulation of the text. Historically, there was strong sentiment after the Civil War, for example, for textbooks to reflect the perspectives of either the North or the South; but in the South this became integrated more readily into "reform from above" strategies. Thus, in one instance, in Texas, Scott, Foresman was pressured to make certain that its arithmetic text included problems that featured "the victories of southern generals." In another instance, an advertisement in 1867 for books published by the New York firm of E. J. Hale and Son claimed that the publishing house printed textbooks that were specifically "prepared for southern schools, by southern authors, and therefore free from matter offensive to southern people" (Kline, 1984, p. 224). The power of the politics of adoption policies and the economics of publishing are already more than a little visible here as the principles of ideological screening become institutionalized.

CONTESTED REFORM

We need to be careful not to overextend these arguments. State control over the text may appear to be total and, from the outside, can seem to be an example of strong top-down power. Yet, this may not always be the case. It is not preordained that state institutions always influence others more than these institutions are influenced by them. The fact that a centralized administrative framework for making decisions exists "does not automatically make it the leading part" (Archer, 1986, p. 26; see also Tidwell, 1928). In fact, if my earlier arguments about the State being a site of conflict both within dominant groups and between dominant and less powerful groups is correct, then we should expect that even though such top-down mandates were instituted, they were undoubtedly subject to intense debate and conflict. When we look more specifically at the history of state adoption policies in these primarily southern regions, we see that this is exactly the case.

My discussion of the nature of the accord over knowledge and of the historical roots of state adoption policies has so far stressed the larger relations of power and the political/economic (and ideological) history of regions. Although these relations are important in that they provide the structural boundaries within which educational decisions were made, there were reasons internal to the educational system for such centralized policies as well. Here, too, these reasons were continually contested. As is shown later, such policies resulted not only from pressure from above but again from pressure from below. Furthermore, there were partly progressive elements interwoven with the more conservative bureaucratic tendencies in the actual policies that were instituted.

The conflict over state adoption policies that we are currently witnessing is not new by any means. The controversy over whether such policies are wise has had an extensive history, at least as far back as 1850 (Henry, 1933, p. 20). A deeper analysis of this is essential if we are to more fully understand how the politics of official knowledge—with all of its contradictory tendencies—has operated.

"INCOMPETENT" TEACHERS, "UNETHICAL" PUBLISHERS

As I noted, state adoption policies and the overall tendency to centralize control of educational policy and content in general that they represent did not spring full grown. They have a distinctive history and grew out of a multitude of social and educational conditions. Although my focus in this part of the chapter continues to be primarily on the larger sociohistorical conditions that led to such a tendency, it is important to first understand the overt educational arguments for such policies.

Historically, the arguments for state adoption policies and for statewide uniformity in texts centered around four basic points: (a) such policies tend to ensure that books will be purchased at the lowest price; (b) instead of the all too real dangers of selecting poor textbooks that are associated with local school district control, state adoption guarantees that selections will not be done by relatively naive people but by experts; (c) state adoption of uniform texts ultimately lowers the costs associated with a mobile population in which parents (often looking for work) move their children from district to district, each one with different textbooks; and (d) uniformity of textbooks at a state level enables the establishment of a minimum and standard course of study throughout the state (Whipple, 1930, p. 51).

Certain historical themes emerge here: the overpricing of texts due to what were seen as profit-hungry publishers, control by experts, a particular vision of school populations, and a statewide curriculum. As is shown here, each of these had its roots in wider social movements and conflicts.

Yet this history of internal problems does not exhaust the reasons for turning to statewide solutions in the South. The perception on the part of some government officials that teachers themselves were by and large incompetent played a part here as well. Speaking in 1874, the Superintendent of Schools of South Carolina, for instance, complained vociferously that county examiners awarded teaching certificates "to persons whose ignorance was glaringly apparent to the most careless observer" (Knight, 1930/1969, p. 80). As he went on to say, "our schools never will and never can become deservedly popular so long as the evil of employing so many incompetent, inefficient and worthless teachers continues" (p. 80). All too many teachers taught "from motives of personal convenience, and in many instances, from a consciousness of being unfit for anything else" (p. 80). Though similar complaints were heard throughout the country, its effects in the South were more powerful (p. 97).

This "incompetence" of teachers was a continuing concern that supported the power of state textbook commissions. As one educator summarizing decades of criticism of teachers and reviewing the status of the state adoption policy in Kentucky put it, "We must recognize that our teachers are not . . . well prepared professionally." Given such a "poorly prepared corps of teachers," there is only one hope if we are to improve instruction. We must place the best textbook possible in the hands of the students. "The poorer the teacher, the better the textbooks need to be" (Donovan, 1924, p. 31).[2] (Does all this sound familiar in the current calls for more rigorous national curricula?; see Apple, 1993b).

We need to be careful about accepting this interpretation of teachers as largely "incompetent and worthless" at face value, however. Most teachers were neither stupid and uncaring nor were they passive "victims" of this situation with no voice. In fact, one of the first inter-

---

[2]It would be important to know whether the majority of teachers being attacked here were women. Often, gender relations underpin the mistrust of teachers' autonomy (see Apple, 1988b).

preters of the origins of state adoption plans understood that in earlier periods of schooling in the United States it was not unusual for teachers to have to rely either on whatever books students might have available at home or whatever books or texts a local store had in stock. Because of this, pressure to institute state laws that required uniform textbooks also *"had its origin in the complaints of disheartened teachers against this incongruous situation"* (Henry, 1933, p. 19, emphasis added). Teachers' pressure, based on the conditions they faced every day, takes center stage here.

Yet, although I want to stress the importance of teachers' self-formative activity here, this did not seem to have an effect on those who saw teachers as a major part of the problem. In many ways, they intensified their attacks. Thus, to the claim that teachers were so poorly prepared was added the claim that teachers could be too easily influenced by textbook agents who worked their way through the state. A new group of recontextualizers—"disinterested" experts, not naive teachers—was required.

Commenting on the situation in 1918, when state adoption policies adopted in the late 19th and early 20th century were being questioned, Judd (1918) described this part of the case for statewide adoption:

> It is because teachers are showing so little wisdom in the selection of books that the public has in many states safeguarded the situation by laws removing from the teacher all power of choice. The writer recalls a letter from a public official responsible for the choice of text-books who was moved by criticisms made of his selections to a sharp retort. He said that there was no justification for criticisms of the state selections, that school people were for the most part wholly unreliable in their choices. He asserted that it was entirely possible to map out the route followed by certain book agents through the state by the stream of letters recommending certain books that came to the state textbook commission. (pp. 145-146)

Teachers were not the only ones who were focused on. Linked to the distrust of teachers was a concern that is of great significance here—the vision of textbook publishers as more than a little rapacious and corrupt. Money motivated them, not educational issues. And although many publishers expressly argued against such stereotyping (Brown, 1919, pp. 382-388), this view of textbook publishers was still widespread even as late as the 1930s. It had its beginnings much earlier.

For example, throughout the later part of the 19th century and the early decades of the 20th, serious questions were raised about "the control of text-books by private individuals and commercial publishing houses" (Judd, 1918, p. 143). As long as the textbook was produced by commercial concerns whose motive was profit, and as long as teachers had such limited educational experience, the textbook unfortunately was "removed from institutional control" (p. 143).

Of course, many publishers disputed the arguments about their rapaciousness, preferring to be seen as "constructive workers in the field of education" who were partners in enhancing the cultural life of the nation. A representative of one of the largest textbook publishers waxes eloquent about just this point:

> |The publisher| is not merely a manufacturer of and distributor of books for material gain. He is an idealist, a constructive worker in the field of education, ambitious to do his share in putting into the schools of the nation the ideas and ideals which express the nation's best thought now and which should later be wrought into the national life through the influence of schools. (Brown, 1919, p. 388)

Publishers did not deny they were a business, but they were organized in fact to act as the agents that would test out and improve American life:

> |The publisher| represents a large business organization, which he is ready to place at the service of any author who can convince him that he has a message for the schools, and through the schools for the nation. And, finally, he stands ready to risk his reputation and financial resources to test the validity of approved ideals and methods in textbooks as a means to the constant improvement of the nation's educational life. (p. 388)

Not all people agreed with such a positive portrayal of textbook publishers. For many people, they were still not to be trusted. That such concerns about the motives of publishers continued to be widespread and influenced the development of state adoption policies can be readily seen in a questionnaire that J. B. Edmonson sent out to school superintendents and other educators and representatives of textbook publishers in preparation for his chapter on "The Ethics of Marketing and Selecting Textbooks" in the famous NSSE Yearbook on the textbook. Among the questions that seemed important to ask about the ethics of publishing and publishers' representatives were the following (Edmonson, 1931, pp. 208-215).

1. Would it be ethical for a representative to try to influence the election or appointment of persons to teaching or administrative positions in order to secure adoptions of certain books?

2. Would it be ethical for a representative to try to stimulate dissatisfaction among teachers with the textbooks adopted for use in schools?
3. Would it be ethical for a representative to bring to the attention of a board of education unethical practices of a superintendent in the selection of textbooks?
4. Would it be ethical for a representative to bring to the attention of the superintendent unethical practices of a committee in the selection of textbooks?
5. Would it be ethical for a representative to try to secure confidential information regarding secret committees for textbook adoption?
6. Would it be ethical for a representative to circulate criticism of superintendents who have made decisions adverse to the representative's company?
7. Would it be ethical for a representative to take an active interest in the election of school board members in a community other than his own?
8. Would it be ethical for a representative to circulate petitions among teachers calling for changes in textbooks?
9. Would it be ethical for a textbook company to employ attorneys to influence the adoption of textbooks?
10. Would it be ethical for a representative to influence the appointment of persons to selecting committees?

The fact that questions such as these had such prominence documents the fear that the politics and economics of textbooks had been and still could easily get out of control. The answer across the South was to regulate and centralize to keep this from happening (Tidwell, 1928).

However, there are a multitude of responses that could be made to this situation. One response could be to heighten accountability through enhanced local control as many northern and midwestern states did. Another would be to simply bring the sales practices of publishers under the ethically regulated codes of State Departments of Commerce and Industry or leave it up to the Better Business Bureau. These and other solutions may not be adequate, but it is not preordained that the *state* should set up an elaborate machinery to specifically "police" the practices of publishers and the content of the textbook. Yet this is exactly what many southern states did.

What conditions caused such a response? The roots lie not in the immediacy of decisions to regulate texts, but further back. As I argued in the discussion of regionalism in the first part of this chapter, these roots lie in the establishment throughout many areas of the South of strong centralized regulatory dynamics that set the South off historically from the North. Without a more thorough understanding of these dynamics we will miss the larger social movements that generated such centralizing responses, for as I show, these regulatory urges—as in the case of the teachers who wanted less random and better curriculum material—again came not only from above but from *below* as well. Finally, we will miss the role that the government has played in forming accords or compromises that incorporate certain progressive tendencies over knowledge and power while at the same time recontextualizing them so that they do not threaten the overall basis of power over culture and economy.

TOWARD A REGULATORY STATE

From the late 19th century to the early years of the 20th century, American governance went through a fundamental transition. As Wiebe described it, what emerged was "a government broadly and continually involved in society's operations" (Wiebe, 1967, p. 160). Instead of a government dominated by the legislature, the executive branch enlarged its power. Even more importantly, increasing power became vested in what was essentially a new branch of government made up of administrative boards and agencies. Through these administrative mechanisms, government agencies became increasingly involved in mediating clashing interests. These agencies assumed greater responsibility for mitigating conflicts through planning, administration, and regulation. Toward the end of the 19th century, government was not deeply involved in "recognizing and adjusting group differences." Yet by the time the second decade of the 20th century closed, "innumerable policies committed officials to that formal purpose and provided the bureaucratic structures for achieving it" (McCormick, 1981, p. 251).

Scandals at local, state, and national levels had created a furor against politico/business corruption. Among the most glaring offenses that were uncovered were the many ways corporations corrupted politicians to secure government subsidies, public privileges, and benefits (McCormick, 1981, p. 255). In California, legislative hearings uncovered fresh scandals. In many southern states, the divided Democratic party and the other less powerful parties and alliances brought their rivalries into the public eye by extolling their own virtues and telling tales of each other's corruption by business interests (p. 262). Muckraking helped, of course, to bring these scandals center stage, and business corruption of politics soon became a leading theme in public halls (p. 260).

Out of this situation emerged a commitment to a particular type of government, one that would restrain privileged corporations, protect the weaker elements of the community, establish formal mechanisms for new interest groups to have a voice in government, and "acknowledge and adjust group differences" (p. 259). At the state level in particular, the late 1890s and early 1900s were years that were characterized by experiments with a variety of methods of regulation and administration (p. 259). These experiments soon solidified into a body of practices and a particular approach to reform.

Although these types of scandals were not new to the American political and economic system by any means, and many people had a vague understanding of the pervasiveness of some of the corrupting practices, something important was very new here. A new understanding had begun to emerge, one in which an awareness of the *process* of corruption was central. No longer was corruption seen largely as the result of a few "bad men." Rather, the problem was *systemic* and could only be solved by enlarged government action that altered the system itself (p. 265). An onslaught of legislation ensued, regulating lobbying, outlawing special favors given by business to public officials, and establishing and/or strengthening the regulatory and administrative arms of government in a wide array of areas from commerce and transportation to health, welfare, and education (p. 267).

In the process, government involvement and direction shifted. The forces of localism and opposition to government authority (forces that were very strong in the South) slowly but surely lost ground to the forces of centralization, bureaucratization, and expanded governmental authority (p. 268). This had a special impact on education in general and ultimately on the state regulation of texts. Throughout the South, a coalition of businessmen, professionals, and the urban middle class— assisted by turmoil and pressure from below as will be shown later— formed an important element in the push for greater state responsibility, one that combined efficiency with limited social reforms in education and social welfare (Grantham, 1983, p. 416).

For "progressive" reformers from dominant economic groups and within the upwardly mobile new middle class, one succeeded in bringing more efficient and effective schooling throughout the South by relying on objective information, on "the facts," and by employing experts in public administration for dealing with social problems (Grantham, 1983, p. 275). Industrialization, economic development, material progress, the transformation and conservation of elements of southern culture, the "race problem," and the social conflicts that were threatening stability throughout the region—all of these could be solved through limited social reforms (Barrow, 1990; Grantham, 1983, p.

276). The public sphere must be organized around knowledge, expertise, and efficient administration. The disinterested expert could be counted on to promote the general interest. Although municipal and countywide reforms were focused on as well, it was in the growth of state functions that one saw the largest changes. As a commentator argued in 1912, "A realization of the greater efficiency that central state departments have . . . has, during the past decade, caused the people to delegate all new functions, and some old ones, to state departments or commissions" (Grantham, 1983, pp. 301-302). In all of this, however, the most striking development of state services and state authority occurred in education.

Other actors were important here besides the spokespeople for the "new South" including modernizing businessmen, professionals, and the urban middle class. Given the largely agrarian nature of the South, movements among farmers were also significant in focusing attention on areas that were crying out for reform, from credit and monetary policy to elections and education. The "old South," with its history of a powerful, landed, planter class, had already established a tradition of educational reform *from above*, and the newer calls for reform by small farmers and others often moved in that direction as well (Richardson, 1986, p. 47).

Small farmers in the South, who were being squeezed by sagging prices, mounting interest charges, and unfavorable laws, joined together to form organizations such as the Farmers' Alliance which soon began searching for answers to their problems (Mitchell, 1987, p. 25). With their way blocked by policies within the resurgent Democratic Party in southern states such as Texas, agrarian movements spawned calls for reform (Mitchell, 1987, p. 40). Although radical about class politics, the Alliance consistently focused on the resolution of differences through the ballot (p. 88). The individual sovereignty of a more *politically educated* public electorate would vote into office a government whose actions would serve "the greatest good for the greatest number." Armed with feelings of the political and moral superiority of the small farmer, they stressed a vision in which the State was to be used as an instrument supporting the weak against the strong (p. 88). Although adult education centering around radical political and economic issues played a very strong part in their program, public education and the kinds of knowledge taught (and not taught) to farmers and their children in schools were important areas of interest and political work for the Alliance (Mitchell, 1987, p. 46; see also Lufkin, 1968). For Alliance members, what was going on was *miseducation* in which "those who labor are educated to be abject slaves and the rich are educated to be tyrannical, presumptuous, and vicious. . . . All the people have been educated to bow submissively at the feet of Mammon" (Mitchell, 1987, p. 70).

Some of the reconstructed lyrics to the song "My Country tis of Thee" gives a good indication of their anticorporate sentiment.

> My Country tis of thee
> Land of lost Liberty,
> Of thee I sing.
> Land where the Millionaires,
> Who govern our affairs
> Own for themselves and heirs,
> Hail to thy King. (Mitchell, 1987, p. 52)

Because the capitalist, "Mammon," also controlled "the channels of information," only miseducation could result. In opposition to this, Alliance spokespersons mounted attacks on newspapers, the publishing industry, and the public schools (Mitchell, 1987, p. 71).[3]

Leaders of the Alliance were not loath to criticize the public schools as being controlled by the exact same "plutocratic" groups that dominated the other elements of government. They argued against both monopolies in textbook publishing and partisan political control of educational governance. At the same time, they supported creating a more effective system of public education in Texas and in other southern states (Mitchell, 1987, p. 23).

In 1890, the national leadership of the Alliance leveled charges against a group of textbook publishers. They accused the publishers of "conspiring to consolidate markets, control competition, and raise prices in the schoolbook market through the creation of a holding company, the American Book Company" (Mitchell, 1987, p. 128). For the Alliance, this had the effect of raising the prices of texts, a cardinal sin for the hard-pressed farmers of the South. Just as bad, however, was the fact that the textbooks themselves seemed to teach exactly the ideological perspectives the Alliance so strongly opposed, the virtues both of industrialization and the industrial giants. At the same time, the Alliance argued that this publishing "trust" had guaranteed its economic and ideological power "through an intricate and secret system of kickbacks to local and state superintendents" (pp. 128-129).

The Alliance's arguments about education and about the economic and political situation small farmers and workers found themselves in struck a responsive chord throughout the region. The fact that many of the economic, political, and cultural interests they fought

---

[3]In the process, the Alliance also built its own educational materials, in essence, a series of "countertexts," organized around its own sense of class politics. For further examples of such "countertexts" in, say, the socialist movement, see Teitelbaum (1993).

against originated in the North helped bind their supporters together, but it also helped bind otherwise opposing groups within the South together as well.

The strength of sentiment against the North was something that united most white southerners of all stations. The waving of "the bloody shirt"—the traditional symbol of white southern solidarity— wrapped race, party, and region tightly together as the wounds of the Civil War and the Reconstruction period proved very slow to heal. This left a scar across the southern landscape uniting many southerners in a dislike and distrust of things northern (Mitchell, 1987, p. 74). What happened in school content was not immune from these emotions.

The issue of race plays an important role here. Racism and racial antagonism helped determine a significant part of the cultural politics of the entire region at the same time as it so effectively shaped the consciousness of southerners (Kielbowitz, 1986; Mitchell, 1987, p.76; Wood, 1984), including the small farmers. Racism and racial politics helped split the Populist movement and the Alliance in the South. It divided people against each other and helped to hide their common interest against dominant economic groups (Mitchell, 1987, p. 77). The ultimate result, as will be shown, was limited reform and a strong State dominated by conservative and "moderate" interests.

Other factors too split the Populist and Alliance forces, a split that enabled centralizing reformers to take up some of the educational and social issues they raised and to transform these issues into problems to be solved not by the more radical proposals coming from the Alliance but by the methods of "experts."

The defeat of the Populists in 1892 "broke the spirit of the Alliance" (Mitchell, 1987, p. 170). As it became more and more difficult to maintain its status as a mass-based, grass roots organization, in later years many of its members were easily recruited into the educational crusade of the late 19th and early 20th century to rebuild southern schools and to bring them under the more centralized governance of a strong network of experts sponsored by Rockefeller and other northern industrialists and strongly supported by many southern industrialists, a rising new middle class who also were interested in southern economic development, university intellectuals, and others. The Alliance's faith in education later led many of its members to support policies that they would have been more than a little skeptical of earlier (p. 148). In the process, they too became actors in the historic dynamic to centralize and bring education under the control of recontextualizing "experts."

"Expert" regulation and administration had a number of advantages. It appeared sane and moderate at the same time that it transferred responsibility out of the hands of the business and political figures who seemed to be at the root of the problems. It gave a (*limited*) voice to varied factions of the public. Even more important perhaps, it primarily focused on the *state* level, thereby effectively removing politically volatile elements from possibly exercising power. Thus, by shifting the passion for reform from the local, and often more insurgent, level, it isolated groups that might have called for more radical solutions (McCormick, 1981, pp. 272-273). As McCormick put it, "In gaining a statewide hearing for reform, the accusations of politico-business corruption actually increased the likelihood that conservative solutions would be adopted" (p. 273).

How and why did this happen? What were the deeper economic, political, and ideological conditions that led to centralization in the South? This requires that we look again at the more general context in which education and the politics of symbolic control functioned.

THE CLASS AND RACIAL ROOTS OF CONSERVATIVE COMPROMISE

We need to understand that in the late 19th century, despite a regional trend toward diversification and industrialization, the South still retained important elements of what can only be called a colonial economy. It was characterized by undeveloped resources and an abundance of unskilled labor, low-wage industries, outside domination by railroads, and large timber and mining interests, as well as external control of much of its banking and industrial wealth. Class resentments and racial antagonisms were exceptionally strong (Grantham, 1983, p. 4). Poverty became increasingly institutionalized on both the farm and in the cities. And the schooling system in many states was more than a little underdeveloped and underfinanced. It was an inherently unstable and tense situation, one that fostered a concern for social order, stability, and efficiency among many groups (p. 7).

Because of this, across the South during the period, the state was increasingly looked on as the source of regulatory action and as an important provider of new services (Grantham, 1983, p. xxi). Throughout the South, the crusaders to improve schooling were influenced by the belief that it was essential to try to create a situation in which educational leaders were less vulnerable to pressure from an electorate and legislatures that were often less than enthusiastic about spending large sums of money for education (Mitchell, 1987, p. 186) or who would interfere in decisions better left to experts.

The reformers were bound together by a set of assumptions that favored increasingly centralized control to "balance" the tradition of local autonomy that was so powerful in the South. First, the educational reformers believed in the very correctness of their vision. Their own success as individuals gave them the right to lead. As Dabney, one of the leaders of the educational crusade put it, "The people need leaders to show them the way" (Mitchell, 1987, p. 190). In Mitchell's compelling words, these reformers "saw public opinion as a mass to be shaped and molded, convinced to accept their notions of education and schooling" (p. 190). Second, their vision combined a progressive commitment to "clean government," one that was unpolluted by the taint of scandal and political interference, with an equally strong commitment to social control. The role of the public school in both its content and pedagogy was to "develop a broad and efficient system of drilling the children . . . to the habits of discipline and the customs of obedience which make for the public order" (p. 190). Sound moral training and obedience were to be combined with the third element—the reformers' belief that the South would only grow economically with the help of an enlarged and efficient school system, but again one that was insulated from political parties and politics in general (Mitchell, 1987, pp. 190-192).

This was to be a society that was "democratic," but for whites only. However, although seeking to preserve white solidarity in the face of tensions and conflicts, not all whites were seen as being equal. All too many well-to-do and middle-class white southerners, including the bulk of the reformers, held a profound mistrust of the masses of people they were seeking to help. Because of this, mechanisms were developed that "cleansed" the governance of education and other services and at the same time limited participation in decision making to include only "those who were prepared for responsible citizenship" (Grantham, 1983, pp. xvii-xviii). State-level experts who could stand above the corrupt or overly political processes of educational governance and text and curriculum selection were clearly more "responsible" than others.

The evolving class structure of the South—"the presence of a depressed mass of rural and urban working people and an emerging middle class increasingly conscious of the need for social control and restraint"—is not an inconsequential element in this equation (Grantham, 1983, p. 176). Yet, as I hinted at earlier, educational efficiency experts and reformers did not ignore the black population in their plans for centralization of authority over schools and texts. Their approach to what was called the "race problem" mixed paternalism, social efficiency, guidance, and protection in separate schools in exchange for the values of the new South that were emerging—thrift, industriousness, "self respect for the 'good negro,'" and continued subservience (Grantham, 1983, pp. 231-233; Harding, 1981).

There were differences between states, of course. Texas, for instance, had a smaller black population and somewhat less of a tradition of corruption common to many southern regimes (Barr, 1971, p. 74). Yet, it is quite clear that behind certain reforms that the Democratic Party enacted in the first decade of this century was a concern with the Latino/Latina and black citizens of the state (pp. 241-242). Thus, as with all movements for reform in the South, the racial undercurrent here undoubtedly played no small part in the growth of centralized control over schooling and the text.

Both whites and blacks were focused on by the reformers. For the more liberal reformers, a more efficient and effective school system—one organized by reformers and experts—was essential not just to "elevate the inferior race," but also to "save whites from the blighting influences of narrow mindedness, intolerance and injustice" (Grantham, 1983, p. 31). Rigid racial separation could be guaranteed by the state and could be fostered by state regulation and inspection of education and texts. Furthermore, by educating the masses of poor whites and instilling in them "appropriate" morality and codes of behavior, it would make them more tolerant of blacks. Order and tranquility would reign supreme (pp. 125-126).

All of this was not only due to the politics of class and race. Gender politics played a role here as well. Although white women in the South may seemingly not have been as overtly militant as in other areas of the country, in part because of the particular ways patriarchal relations operated in the South, they did actively seek educational reforms and organized around a variety of issues of social justice. One women put it this way, perhaps more than a little wryly: "We have to go slow in the South. . . . We may not at first do very big things and we are perfectly certain not to do spectacular things, but . . . *we are not dead!*" (Grantham, 1983, p. 213). Thus, importantly, added impetus for the educational crusade came from the involvement of women. Organized groups of mostly middle-class white women became deeply involved in social reform movements including prohibition, women's suffrage, the regulation of child labor, and the expansion of education (Barr, 1971, p. 230; Grantham, 1983, p. xx; Reese, 1986). These all required an expansion of the role of the state. And although the women's movements ultimately helped spawn processes that over the next decades solidified state control over education and the text, they also led to major gains in the self-formative power of women.[4]

---

[4]This is an important point. There were contradictory results from the movement to centralize authority. What may have often been retrogressive in class and race terms could at one and the same time have been partly progressive in gender terms (see Apple, 1993a; McCarthy & Apple, 1988).

I do not wish to slight the immense accomplishments of African-American women, especially women teachers, here. Their struggles with the local State over

Given these kinds of contradictory class, race, and gender pressures, in the largely one-party politics of the region, southern Democrats in many states themselves increasingly accepted what had originally been an idea generated out of the Populist movement—the concept of the positive State in which government played a much more active role in promoting growth and stabilizing and protecting the economic, cultural, and moral fiber of society (Grantham, 1983, p. 13). And these movements dovetailed easily with some of the anticorporate and proregulatory sentiments I mentioned earlier in this chapter.

When the anticorporate attack came as expected from farmers and labor, it also included small manufacturers, warehousemen, local merchants, and others who supported public regulation of large business concerns (Grantham, 1983, p. 145), thereby creating quite complicated alliances among groups. Texas provides a good example of the complicated social alliances and ideologies that stood behind the movement toward more state regulation and control in a number of areas. It also shows how regional differences and antagonisms played a crucial role in the State's activity as a recontextualizer.

As in other Southern states, funding for schools had always been a problem in Texas. Class, ideological, and ethnic differences made it an even more difficult situation. A relatively decentralized system, but one in which railroads, land sales, and school funding were tied together, evolved that favored church and private schools and often left little resources for public schools. After the devastation of the Civil War, with the economics of railroads and land in disarray and with reformers from the North holding greater control of state governments, a more centralized system was established.

One early commentator who was sympathetic to "the cause of the South" pointed to the increasing power of the state board in this context:

> The reformers from the North in 1881 established an autocratic, centralized system of schools with a state board and districts in charge of local trustees under the direction of a state superintendent of schools assisted by thirty-five supervisors. . . . The lands for the school fund were donated and put under the control of the state board, the lost funds were reappropriated, one-fourth of the state's annual revenue from general taxation was appropriated. . . . The state board invested school funds and allotted income according to law, made the regulations for the control of the schools, examined and appointed teachers, laid down the courses of study and selected textbooks. (Dabney, 1936/1969, p. 417)

---

respect, resources, and even schooling itself is a crucial part of the history of the African-American battle for freedom. For further analysis of black teachers, see Perkins (1989).

These centralizing tendencies were enforced by a state superintendent of schools who, while he served in the Federal Army, had not taught school. Over a good deal of conservative opposition, he often overruled school district decisions, appointed inspectors, set up schools, appointed teachers, and selected textbooks, many of which, according to Dabney's early history, were "written by Northern authors, made statements and expressed opinions offensive to southerners" (Dabney, 1936/1969, p. 418).

Whatever Dabney's sentiments, there can be no doubt that this system did in fact generate considerable controversy, and soon the state, now under the control of Democrats, in the mid-1870s returned to a more locally oriented model of governance and funding in which central guidance was almost "nonexistent." This soon led to frequent and bitter controversies and rivalries over political favoritism, incompetence, inefficiency, and racism (Dabney, 1936/1969, p. 421). A slow return to a somewhat more centralized system began. By 1900, or so, pressure for an activist state had grown again.

In Texas, the major campaign in the early years of the century concerned efforts to deal with corporate wealth and with the fact that the foremost corporations were of "foreign" (i.e., northern) origin. The rapaciousness of capital and the influence of "foreign" corporations fed into the other concerns. Not only was there "foreign" control of the economy through northern railroads, banks, and so on, but anger at "foreign" ideas—an anger that had been simmering since the Civil War—was unleashed against northern publishers as well, not only by the Farmers Alliance but by many groups. The same regulatory impulse that was now impacting on banking, food, medicine, and so many other areas again ultimately worked its way out in the state regulation of textbooks (Grantham, 1983, p. 155).

In Texas, organized labor and farmers unions were more influential than elsewhere and for a time at the beginning of the century were able to work together to try to influence the state to support their cause. Support for increased state power again came from professional groups and organized businessmen whose own influence grew as well (Grantham, 1983, pp. 99-100). Texas reforms, probably to a greater extent than other southern states, represented a response to the state's very diverse economic, physiographic, and cultural interests. Its very diversity fostered the formation of groups to pressure the state. The pattern of Texas reforms was highlighted by "well-organized urban middle class pressure groups loosely coordinated at times with farmer, labor, business, or professional organizations" (p. 103). Thus, this newly emerging middle-class group played a major part. It was this group from which experts employed within the state would be drawn. Support for increased state intervention in education and elsewhere would guarantee their own mobility and give them a controlling interest in an expanded State. Motivated by a contradictory bundle of sentiments including altruism, optimism, expanding economic opportunity, social control, and a search for order and efficiency in a time of very real uncertainty, they provided important support for the power of "the expert." As members of a reforming coalition, their increasing power within the emerging state bureaucracy helps explain the historic pattern of tight state control of texts in Texas.

Politicians were not blind to these issues. In fact, in many states they were quick to sense the advantages that could be gained in supporting (and leading) campaigns against corporations. No matter what their commitments, which may or may not have been quite laudatory, many state politicians were talented enough "to capture the liveliest issues in sight" (Grantham, 1983, p. 146). In the first decade of the century, campaigns to establish regulatory commissions quickly grew. They soon spilled over into the borders of transportation and commerce and extended into other areas such as education. In the context of these concerns, the state assumed more and more of the functions of resolving and regulating conflicts, business practices, and social behavior (p. 14).

Yet it is important to realize that many southern conservatives feared that the anticorporate sentiments would discourage northern economic and cultural investment in the region. The answer was not to drive northern corporations out, but to regulate them so that they helped economic development in the South (Grantham, 1983, p. 157). Education was part of this program of economic development, and textbooks—recontextualized and organized around southern but less overtly regional and more modernizing themes—were essential to such progress.

Grantham (1983) provided one of the most coherent summaries of the ideological tendencies that lay behind much of the centralizing movement. The southern reformers that ultimately led the movement for state control:

> shared a yearning for a more orderly and cohesive community. Such a community, they believed, was a prerequisite for economic development and material progress. Its realization depended upon the effective regulation of society in the interest of ethical business practices and good government, and in the elimination of political corruption, machine politics, and the insidious power of large corporations and other special interests. This meant that the regulatory power of the state must be expanded. Social controls were also indispensable for the preservation of moral values, for the purification of social institutions, and for the protection of men and women from their own weaknesses. Underlying this coercive

reformism was a substantial vein of self-righteousness and moral apprehension. Optimistic about future prospects but alarmed by the tensions
and conflicts that pervaded the South in the late nineteenth century,
southern |reformers| looked toward the creation of a clearly defined com-
munity that would accommodate a society differentiated by race and
class, but one that also possessed unity, cohesion, and stability. (p. xvii)

The result was what I have earlier called an *accord*, an historic
compromise in which dominant groups maintain much of their economic, political, and cultural power by incorporating under their own
leadership parts of the perspectives of competing or dispossessed
groups (Apple, 1988a, 1993a). Top-down models would incorporate
greater public control. They would offer new services to the poor, the
farmer, and the laborer. They would "cleanse" the government in general, would cleanse the control of education and texts from the taint of
corruption, and would expand schooling extensively. Yet, they would
also effectively depower the more democratically inclined movements
for public control of economic, political, and educational institutions
by keeping them in the hands of "experts" and elites. The underlying
politics of the accord or compromise that developed is nicely summarized by Grantham (1983):

> There was room in this |compromise| for material progress, efficiency,
> ethical standards, social order, a more vigorous regulatory state, social
> justice, public services, and especially the vision of a revitalized south-
> ern community. The |reformers| were able to effect a synthesis of the
> antithetical approaches of the Bourbons and populists. They attracted
> support from diverse social elements, including the section's civic-
> commercial elites and upwardly mobile urban groups. But |they| also
> drew on the swirling protest of the 1890s, and agrarian radicalism
> flowed in a somewhat attenuated but distinct current into the politics
> of the progressive era, helping to account for the anticorporation senti-
> ment, party insurgency, and morality oriented campaigns that fol-
> lowed. In the early twentieth-century setting the |reformers| were able
> to function both as agents of modernization and as guardians of south-
> ern tradition. (pp. 418-419)

There was progress to be sure. But the reforms were still characterized by paternalism and a hierarchical view of society, by a class consciousness that distrusted the masses of people in the South, by basic
acceptance of racial stereotypes and a racist social order, and by a search
for social consensus and social stability that would be guaranteed by a
"disinterested" state (Grantham, 1983, p. 421). The politics of state regulation, then, is—in a microcosm—the politics of the South as a whole.

OLD PROBLEMS RENEWED

Although I have painted a picture of the social, ideological, and educational context out of which state control over official knowledge emerged, of how the state became the prime recontextualizing agent, it would be wrong to assume that the growth of state intervention completely dealt with the problems they were meant to solve. Accords are compromises. As I argued in *Official Knowledge* (Apple, 1993a), they provide *temporary* "solutions" at a variety of levels; but almost always they also spawn further conflicts at the level of the State or in the daily practices and policies involved in the politics of school knowledge. The example of state textbook adoption provides a case in point here. Although it did establish "expert" mechanisms for partially dealing with the complicated ideological differences concerning class and race in the South (again, usually on the terrain favored by dominant groups), it also created an arena for older conflicts to emerge again in a new form.

Take the case of the accusations of governmental corruption and the rapaciousness of textbook publishers, issues that had been among the important internal educational reasons for the adoption of state control in the first place. Even after the adoption of state control, this controversy continued nationwide, especially over questions of expertise and political/economic favoritism. Thus, in the 1930s, Edmonson reported that a considerable number of people throughout the country thought "baleful influences" that could "undermine standards of good practice in the selecting of textbooks" were most likely to occur in connection with state adoption policies. The possibility of "scandal" was enhanced "when political appointees who are laymen are able, directly or indirectly, to influence the selection of texts for the public schools, and thus control the distribution of considerable sums of money" (Edmonson, 1931, p. 218).

This situation was not lost on textbook publishers. Many publishers also recognized both the politics and the economics that may have lay behind some of the original state adoption models. One textbook publisher, reflecting on the history of state adoption policies, argued that "bookmen" wanted to "salt down" business for a number of years at a time, especially in those geographical areas in which "schools gave all of their business to their favorite bookman" (Henry, 1931, p. 182). Some superintendents and boards of education "were not above sharing in the profits of the adoption" (p. 182). In the process, state officials and legislators were turned to in order "to 'sew up' the business for five year periods, and finally the state adoption was conceived" (Henry, 1931, p. 182; see also Tidwell, 1928). Here, state control was specifically *used* as a mechanism for guaranteed profits and to squeeze out competition, even at the same time that it was meant to protect schools from some of these same problems.

The pressure local districts, administrators, and teachers, and later state textbook boards were put under became legendary. Even as late as the 1920s, what was called an "insidious form of bribery" was practiced to insure the adoption of particular texts by state boards. Here, the textbook agent retained a well-known attorney who was located in the state and attempted to exert influence on board members through the intervention of the attorney, interventions that would be prohibited on the part of the publisher's representative. Numerous reports surfaced of attorneys having direct relations with the board. More egregiously, other reports indicated cases in which the attorney had so much political clout that his entreaties for particular books were hard to resist because of "cronyism" or in other cases because of "the most brazen threats of political or personal punishment to members of the adopting board or their agents" ("Political attorney," 1927, pp. 162-163).

Again, publishers responded to this criticism. Although admitting that there was corruption in textbook publishing, the situation had gotten considerably better according to them. Although they did not totally approve of many of the existing programs of state adoption, even they did not want a return to a totally unregulated system. One of their major criticisms of those who put the blame totally on publishers was that the critics failed to see that it was often not the publishers' supposed hunger for profits that was at fault. Often, it was the profit motive behind local business concerns within states that had uniform adoption policies that was at the root of the problem:

> We do not find uniform adoptions in the states that are most progressive educationally but rather in the states which are far distant from central sources of supply. The laws inaugurating these state adoptions were in most cases engineered by a concern in the capital city in the state which hoped to profit by being assigned the distribution of the books in that state . . . which means 10 percent more out of the pupils' pockets into the pocket of the unnecessary middleman. ("State adoption," 1928, p. 403)

This comment is fascinating because it points to the multiple uses of state power over official knowledge. In a compromise among old and new elites, experts from the emerging middle class, and populist forces such as the Alliance, multiple agendas are brought together, some internal and some external to educational policy and practice. Yet, somehow out of this complex set of relations and even with the growth of the regulatory state, "Mammon" enters in again through the back door. Thus are the seeds of conflict and even further state intervention sown again.

CONCLUSION

In this chapter, I explored what is seemingly a simple question—Why the South? What made this region more inclined to accept state-centered solutions to the regulation and control of textbooks in particular and education in general? How did what is usually the most conservative region of the country come to be so powerful in the politics of official knowledge, in the political economy of the textbook? In answering these questions, I purposely focused our attention on larger social movements and on economic, political, and ideological forces that differentiated the South from other areas, rather than on the internal educational justifications given by educators at the time.[5] Not that I believe that such internal arguments had no weight. Of course they did. However, they would not have been made or accepted if these larger social movements and race and inter- and intraclass forces had not been so powerful. The justifications for state educational control and recontexualization did not stand alone, isolated either from the conflicts in the larger society or from attempts to solve these conflicts on terms acceptable to groups with power.

Although I have highlighted the complex nexus of historical forces out of which the centralizing tendencies arose in the South, this story should be of interest not only because it is a fascinating part of the history of the growth of educational regulation in this country. The story says something of great import to those interested in the politics of official knowledge and of educational policy in general. It was large-scale social movements, organized groups, stimulated from above and below, that made a difference. State regulation and control, the very processes of recontextualization, came about because of a complicated politics of social ferment. *Altering what we now have will undoubtedly require the same.* This is something that the "authoritarian populism" of the New Right has clearly recognized (Apple, 1993a, 1993b).

How something becomes "official knowledge" is always a political process. If we are to understand how the primary carrier of such official knowledge—the textbook—comes to look the way it does, and if we are to understand how to alter it, we cannot afford to ignore the historic politics of social movements. History has a way of not always remaining in the past, especially if we rely only on waiting for the State to act in a time—like now—of the conservative restoration.

---

[5]Although I pointed to it earlier in this chapter, I realize that I have not gone into the role played by organized groups of teachers here in the debates over state regulation. This would be essential if we were to more completely understand the internal dynamics and the political movements that determine the context in which the processes of state regulation and recontextualization are formed. A further discussion of the complex politics of race and region, and a much more detailed analysis of the constant attempts by African Americans to use the State (and transform it), would be essential as well.

REFERENCES

Apple, M.W. (1985). *Education and power*. New York: Routledge.

Apple, M.W. (1988a). Social crisis and curriculum accords. *Educational Theory, 38*, 191-201.

Apple, M.W. (1988b). *Teachers and texts*. New York: Routledge.

Apple, M.W. (1990). *Ideology and curriculum* (2nd ed.). New York: Routledge.

Apple, M.W. (1992). Education, culture and class power. *Educational Theory, 42*, 127-145.

Apple, M.W. (1993a). *Official knowledge*. New York: Routledge.

Apple, M.W. (1993b). The politics of official knowledge: Does a national curriculum make sense?" *Teachers College Record, 95*, 222-241.

Apple, M.W., & Christian-Smith, L. (Eds.). (1991). *The politics of the textbook*. New York: Routledge.

Archer, M. (1986). Social origins of educational Systems. In J. Richardson (Ed.), *Handbook of theory and research in the sociology of education* (pp. 3-33). New York: Greenwood Press.

Barr, A. (1971). *Reconstruction to reform: Texas politics, 1876-1906*. Austin: University of Texas Press.

Barrow, C. (1990). *Universities and the capitalist state*. Madison: University of Wisconsin Press.

Bernstein, B. (1977). *Class, Codes and Control* (Vol. 3). Boston: Routledge.

Bernstein, B. (1986). On Pedagogic Discourse. In J. Richardson (Ed.), *Handbook of theory and research in the sociology of education* (pp. 205-240). New York: Greenwood Press.

Bernstein, B. (1990). *The structuring of pedagogic discourse*. New York: Routledge.

Brown, J.F. (1919). Textbooks and publishers. *The Elementary School Journal, 19*, 382-388.

Carnoy, M. (1984). *The state and political theory*. Princeton, NJ: Princeton University Press.

Carnoy, M., & Levin, H. (1985). *Schooling and work in the democratic state*. Stanford, CA: Stanford University Press.

Council on Interracial Books for Children (1983). The textbook selection Process. *Interracial Books for Children Bulletin, 14*(5), 17.

Dabney, C. (1969). *Universal education in the South* (Vol. 1). Chapel Hill: University of North Carolina Press, Arno Press reprint. (Original work published 1936)

Dale, R. (1989). *The state and education policy*. Milton Keynes: The Open University Press.

Donovan, H. (1924). How to select textbooks. *Peabody Journal of Education, 2*, 1-11.

Edmonson, J.B. (1931). The ethics of marketing and selecting textbooks. In G. Whipple (Ed.), *The textbook in American education* (pp. 199-234). Bloomington, IL: Public School Publishing.

Freiberg, J.W. (1981). *The French press: Class, state, and ideology.* New York: Praeger.

Grantham, D. (1983). *Southern progressivism.* Knoxville: The University of Tennessee Press.

Harding, V. (1981). *There is a river: The black struggle for freedom in the United States.* New York: Vintage.

Henry, N. (1931). The problems of publishers in making and marketing textbooks. In G. Whipple (Ed.), *The textbook in American Education* (pp. 175-198). Bloomington, IL: Public School Publishing.

Henry, N. (1933). Value of state textbook adoption is debatable. *The Nation's Schools, 12,* 19-20

Hogan, D. (1982). Education and class formation. In M.W. Apple (Ed.), *Cultural and economic reproduction in education* (pp. 32-78). Boston: Routledge.

Judd, C. (1918). Analyzing textbooks. *The Elementary School Journal, 19,* 143-154.

Kielbowitz, R. (1986). Modernization, communication policy, and the geopolitical news, 1820-1860. *Critical Studies in Mass Communication, 3,* 21-35.

Kline, M. (1984). Social influences in textbook publishing. *Educational Forum, 48,* 23-34.

Knight, E. (1969). *The influence of reconstruction on education in the South.* New York: Teachers College, Columbia University Contributions to Education, no. 60, Arno Press reprint. (Original work published 1930)

Lufkin, J. (1968). *A history of the California state textbook adoption program.* Unpublished doctoral thesis, University of California, Berkeley.

Mandel, E. (1981). Foreword. In J.W. Freiberg (Ed.), *The French press: Class, state, and ideology* (pp. iii-xiv). New York: Praeger.

McCarthy, C., & Apple, M.W. (1988). Race, class and gender in American educational research. In L. Weis (Ed.), *Class, race and gender in American education* (pp. 9-39). Albany: State University of New York Press.

McCormick, R. (1981). The discovery that business corrupts politics. *American Historical Review, 86,* 247-274.

Mitchell, T. (1987). *Political education in the Southern Farmers' Alliance 1887-1890.* Madison: University of Wisconsin Press.

Perkins, L. (1989). The history of blacks in teaching. In D. Warren (Ed.), *American teachers* (pp. 344-369). New York: Macmillan.

"Political attorney and textbook adoption. (1927). *The Elementary School*

Journal, 28, 162-163.

Reese, W. (1986). *Power and the promise of school reform*. New York: Routledge.

Richardson, J. (1986). Historical sequences and the origins of common schooling in the United States. In J. Richardson (Ed.), *Handbook of theory and research in the sociology of education* (pp. 35-63). New York: Greenwood Press.

"State adoption of textbooks. (1928). *The Elementary School Journal*, 28, 403.

Teitelbaum, K. (1993). *Schooling for good rebels*. Philadelphia, PA: Temple University Press.

Tidwell, C. (1928) *State control of textbooks with special reference to Florida*. New York: Bureau of Publications, Teachers College, Columbia University.

Whipple, G. (1930). The selection of textbooks. *The American School Board Journal*, 80, 51-53, 158.

Wiebe, R. (1967). *The search for order 1877-1920*. Cambridge: Hill and Wang.

Wood, J.P. (1984). The Evangelical origins of mass media in America, 1815-1835. *Journalism Monographs*, 88, 1-30.

4

Culture, Crisis and Morality: The Struggle Over the National Curriculum

Stephen J. Ball
King's College London

Education in the United Kingdom is in the throes of fundamental change. Everything from funding, to teachers pay, to examinations and assessment, to parental choice of schools is subject to the reform process. In large part the effects of this process are a deregulation of the education system and a dismantling of the universalist principles that have unsteadily underpinned the system since 1944. But at the center of the reforms, acting as a kind of policy glue that holds everything else together, is the National Curriculum—a 10-subject compulsory prográm of study (plus Religious Education and Welsh in Wales) divided into 10 levels of attainment (with a related system of National Testing).

   The National Curriculum proposals (leaving aside for a moment controversies over the content and orientation of particular subjects) were met on the whole with a sense of grudging acceptance, mixed with suspicion of the range of new powers that left the final determination of the detailed content of each subject area firmly in the hands of the Secretary of State for Education. Writing in an ironic tone, one commentator summed up the positive interpretation of the new curriculum as follows:

> As well as being broader and more relevant, the new education is effi-
> cient. It specifies far more clearly than its predecessors the levels of
> attainment that students should reach. Through regular assessment of
> students, the work of schools can be carefully monitored. Standards
> will rise—but not by means of a return to a teacher-centred classroom,
> with student activities firmly controlled by the undemanding exercises
> of textbook and worksheet. The best of existing education has been
> assimilated to a new project, which is being pursued with a degree of
> will and organization previously missing. The Conservatives have done
> what the left could not, and harnessed educational energies to a
> coherent programme for national renewal, that at the same time pro-
> vides the individual student with a sense of satisfaction and achieve-
> ment. (Jones, 1989, p. 118)

Now I do not want to underplay the essential conservatism of
the post-1988 National Curriculum—its monoculturalism, its traditional divisions of subject knowledge, its overbearing system of assessment—but to a significant extent (in some subjects at least) the development of the programs of study recognized and utilized the perspectives and concerns of established educationalists. Importantly, the orientation of the new curriculum, particularly in the key subjects of mathematics, science, and Technology, was driven by the affinity of interest
between, what I have called elsewhere, vocational progressivism and
new progressivism, and their "discourse of competence and inclusion
and response to change" (Ball, 1990, p. 113). The relationship of contents, pedagogies, and assessment in these subjects to post-fordist
modes of production was clear (Ball, 1990, pp. 100-132; Rustin 1989).
"The post-Fordist mode of accumulation places a lower value on mass
individual and collective consumption and creates pressures for a more
differentiated production and distribution of health, education, hous-
ing and transport" (Jessop, Bonnett, Bromley, & Ling, 1988, p. 142). New
progressivism, although essentially apolitical, and although not totally
unified and coherent, "gives emphasis to skills, processes and methods
rather than content, and to applications and problem solving rather
than abstract knowledge; the teacher is facilitator rather than pedagogue" (Ball, 1990, p. 136). The learner (and learning) is conceptualized
in constructivist terms as a unique and active meaning maker. It is not
unreasonable to argue that a new form of correspondence was being
forged between the requirements of capital accumulation and the
reconceptualised forms and processes of schooling. In Bernstein's
terms, we were seeing a shift in the principles of social control underpinning the curriculum—a shift from collection to integration, from
submission to conformity. He also related this to changes in the principles of control operating in the economy:

Changes in the division of labour are creating a different concept of skill. The inbuilt obsolescence of whole varieties of skills reduces the significance of context-tied operations and increases the significance of general principles from which a range of diverse operations may be derived. In crude terms, it could be said that the nineteenth century required submissive and inflexible man, whereas the twenty-first century requires conforming but flexible man. (Bernstein, 1971, p. 67)

For the sake of argument, I talk about this orientation of curriculum development as being part of the Mark I National Curriculum (MkIC). (I do not suggest that all subjects can be analyzed in this way.) The Mark I phase lasted from 1988 through 1990. From 1990 on, the orientation of curriculum began to change. Under Prime Minister John Major and Secretaries of State Clarke and Patton, the progressivist/vocational orientation has undergone significant deconstruction, and cultural restorationism is very much in the ascendent. The restorationist agenda consists of a regressive traditionalism applied to all facets of educational practice (see Ball, 1993); it is a hard-line, old humanism based on a discourse that links education strongly with traditional social and political values and with social order (Ball, 1990, p. 24). In political terms, the shift in orientation has come about (been achieved) by the wholesale replacement of the representatives of the educational establishment in key contexts of influence within the educational state by representatives of "cultural rightism." (The replacement is discussed in detail in Ball 1993.).

[Cultural rightism] could trace its philosophy back to Hobbes and the political ideology of Burke. It emphasizes the importance of a strong state to control the evils that an unregulated society is prey to. It regards custom and tradition as vital properties of an established order. Without them, the state is weakened, and subversion can grow in strength. Thus, it regards cultural cohesion as an essential prop of state authority. (Jones, 1989, p. 32)

Interestingly and significantly, the heart of the restorationist project lies not in science and mathematics but in english, history, geography, and music. However, the impact of the reassertion of traditionalism post-1990 has been felt in all subjects. The Mark 2 National Curriculum (Mk2C) rests even more heavily (than MkIC) on heritage, nationalism, and canonical knowledge, on transmission modes of teaching and the deference of the learner, and on the competitive, formal testing of students.

Let me be clear, the shift I am trying to identify here is a relative one. The MkIC was already established on conservative and traditionalist principles in many respects. It was already subject to criticism from representatives of industry suspicious of its regressive structure. "They are concerned that he (Secretary of State, Kenneth Baker) has given 'too much importance to narrow academic knowledge and too little to the fostering of transferable skills and learning ability' (Jackson 1989)" (Whitty, 1990, p. 29). As I see it, the MkIC was a kind of political compromise, although a compromise unstably founded on terms set by the Conservative government. Each subject in turn was struggled over in private (see Ball, 1990) and debated in public. The Mk2C is much more uncompromising, much more a curriculum by fiat, an authoritarian curriculum (although some private struggles continue, see later discussion). The shift might be seen in the latest stages in what I have described as a "series of ratchet steps, each one based upon a firmer, more clearly-defined and more clearly determined curriculum. Attempts are made to mobilise acceptance at each turn of the ratchet—a process of climate building" (Ball, 1990, p. 147). Each turn relates to a change in what is politically possible. Viewed in this way we should understand the political beginnings of the National Curriculum not as occurring in and around 1987-1988, but in 1976.

One of the most recent in a series of shifts from the MkIC to the Mk2C was the rewriting of the documents for National Curriculum English. The *Independent* newspaper (February 3, 1993) ran a page-one headline: "English curriculum rewritten: Traditionalists win return to emphasis on grammar, punctuation and spelling." The article also explained that "teachers will have to correct six- and seven-year-olds who speak dialect and persuade them to speak 'standard' or grammatically correct English." Further, "The present curriculum, which became law three years ago, mentions only one author, Shakespeare. The new one says 14-year-olds must also have read works chosen from a list of authors, including two written before 1900." And the article noted that "Ministers believe the original working party on national curriculum English, chaired by Brian Cox, professor of English at Manchester University, was hi-jacked by members of the educational establishment and failed to address the need to improve pupils' basic skills." The creation of the MK2C English is seen by the defenders of "comprehensive" English as a hijacking of a different kind: "rising above the chaos are the names of John Marks [see also later], Sheila Lawlor, John Marenbon and Martin Turner—a group connected with the Centre for Policy Studies [see Ball, 1993]. In short, there's been a coup" (Rosen, 1993, p. 42).

This is a second and decisive step in the anglicization of the "English" curriculum, a sort of literary "ethnic cleansing," the invention of a "state" culture:

> Marenbon and co assume that "literature" in schools should be "English" and that "English literature" is in essence "English". So the Authorized Version is recruited into Eng. Lit and his canon implies that English literature simply recreates itself down the centuries within the national boundary. He admits only one influence, or "special connection"—Latin. (Rosen, 1993, p. 42)

The Mk2C in English is to be accompanied by a system of National Tests for 14-year-olds. The testing proposals have also sparked controversy, with considerable numbers of schools, with support from the teacher unions and parents organizations, boycotting the tests. The tests have also highlighted dissension within the government-appointed agency, the School Examinations and Assessment Council (SEAC). Under the headline "Council accused of 'paranoia' over tests," *The Times Educational Supplement* (January 22, 1993) reported on its front page that:

> Peter Harding, a member of the committee appointed to advise the School Examinations and Assessment Council on English testing, has accused it of being obsessed with secrecy verging on paranoia. He also says SEAC failed to seek advice from its English committee members, preferring to conduct its business in ad hoc sub-committees.

Mathematics continues to provide another area of contention in the National Curriculum, but in this case the struggles over what is to count as school mathematics have been less public and more esoteric than the struggles over English. The points at issue between the new progressive math educators and the *dirigiste* cultural restorationists focus specifically on AT1 (Attainment Target 1 in the Programme of Study for Mathematics). AT1 contains three elements of mathematics work to which the original working party attached great importance. They are: applications of mathematics (a politically inspired euphemism for mathematics problem-solving processes in both pure and applied contexts); mathematics communication; and logic, reasoning, and proof. These represent what some critics call "soft" math. They have their origins in the progressivist Cockcroft Report (Cockcroft, 1982), specifically the recommendations that "mathematics teaching at all levels should include . . . problem-solving, including the application of mathematics to everyday situations [and] investigational work" (p. 71). Ernest (1989, p. 5), with perhaps some exaggeration, asserted that "the mathematics teaching community in Britain is virtually unanimous in its support for a more problem-solving orientation to mathematics teaching, incorporating discussion, practical and investigative work." All of this is contrasted to "hard" math which gives primary emphasis to exposition and the practice and reinforcement of basic procedures.

(The point is that the "softliners" want to give emphasis to both basic procedures and investigations; whereas "hardliners" want to exclude investigations *and* applications from school mathematics.) Significantly, within the testing regime of the National Curriculum (in the Mk1C), the investigatory activities required by AT1 provided the basis for the 1990 and 1991 pilot Standard Assessment Tasks in mathematics (National Testing). These tests were then described by the then Secretary of State Kenneth Clarke as "elaborate nonsense," and the tasks have been replaced by short written items for all the content attainment tasks; with AT1 left to be assessed only by teachers. In the pilot run of assessments at Key Stages 1 (7 years olds) and 3 (14 year olds) the Teacher Assessment elements of mathematics testing were found to be unreliable. This provided further fuel for the hardline attack on AT1. Additionally, if AT1 should go, then Teacher Assessment will go, and with it the rationale for investigatory and real-world problem-solving work in the mathematics classroom.

The struggles over AT1 are currently again enjoined within the interstices of SEAC. In the hardline/restorationist corner are among others Professor Sig Prais and Dr. John Marks; in the softline/restorationist corner among others is Professor Geoffery Howson. The role of Sig Prais here is particularly interesting in that he was an initial member of the original Mathematics National Curriculum Working Party, but resigned, saying, according to press reports, "that drill and rote-learning, including long division, were the only way to bring English school-leavers to the same standard as the Germans, Japanese and French" (*Observer*, August 14 , 1988, p. 4). The reappearance of Professor Prais on the Mathematics Committee of SEAC is itself indicative of the reassertion of the restorationist position. The restorationist argument involves both treating mathematics as a set of methods and solutions (right answers) and delocating mathematical practice from its real-world setting. (This is central to the contradiction between the restorationist and modernizing tendencies within conservatism; see later]. Again it is important to emphasize the point that the Mk1C in Mathematics was already subject to ministerial interference (based on powers acquired by the Secretary of State in the 1988 Education Reform Act). AT1 is the most recent focus point in an ongoing struggle in a series of rearguard actions by defenders of the softline. Thus, earlier, ground had already been lost. The final Report of the original (Mk1C) had been amended by the then Secretary of State. "Plans for maths in the National Curriculum have been revised extensively to put more emphasis on basics, despite overwhelming opposition for the 2,286 people and organisations who responded during consultations" (*Times Educational Supplement*, December 9, 1988, p.9). Again the restorationist ratchet is in evidence.

All of this is also tied closely to the form and weight of the assessment of mathematics. In November 1991, SEAC advised the Secretary of State that coursework (as opposed to examination style) assessment in mathematics for GCSE should be limited to 20%. Again this would limit the possibility and worthwhileness of investigatory work in the classroom. However, this advice did not emanate from the expert mathematics committee within SEAC. Indeed, the committee members (or some at least) were angered by the "advice," having prepared a paper recommending up to 70% coursework assessment. The Times Educational Supplement (December 6, 1991, p. 1) reported that:

> The authors of the paper that will go to the SEAC council next week include Dr Peter Alderson, an IBM manager and the CBI's nomination on the committee. It has been endorsed by all but Dr John Marks, the chair of the committee, and one other member. The view of the 16-strong committee, which is made up of teachers, lecturers and maths advisers, is that coursework assessment allows pupils to demonstrate what they know and has led to an improvement in standards.

The SEAC proposal was similarly attacked by The Royal Society. And as with the case of Professor Cox, quoted earlier, the criticisms were spear-headed by one of the architects of the Mk1C: Professor Roger Blin-Stoyle, the first chair of the Mathematics National Curriculum Working Party. (nb. Professor Blin-Stoyle is not a mathematician, he is a physicist. It was considered "too dangerous" to have the Working Party chaired by a mathematician.)

> Pupils cannot be tested properly under the Government-imposed rules for GCSE maths, says Britain's leading society for mathematicians and scientists.
> Professor Roger Blin-Stoyle, president of the Royal Society and a former chief schools curriculum adviser, has written to John Pattern demanding a change in assessment arrangements. (Times Educational Supplment, January 22, 1993, p. 8)

In Bernsteinian terms, these are struggles over the strength of the classification and framing of the school curriculum. But this struggle is multidimensional. What is at stake is not simply the discourses of the curriculum, but also the relations of power for the reproduction and legitimation of the strength of insulation and principles of classification:

> Any attempt to change the classification necessarily involves a change in the degree of insulation between categories, which in itself will provoke the insulation maintainers (reproducers, repairers, surveyors) to

restore the principle of the classification and themselves as the dominant agents. In order for this to be accomplished, the insulation maintainers must have power and the conditions to exert it. (Bernstein,
1990, p. 24)

Here, Bernstein captured perfectly the contemporary politics of
education in the United Kingdom. The National Curriculum is founded
on the invention of a new set of powers and conditions within which
the work of the new insulation maintainers can be achieved. In this
sense the NCC and SEAC provide sites (if somewhat discordant sites)
for the articulation of power and the creation of new or renewed educational discourses. And the "coup" referred to earlier (see also Ball,
1993) involves the replacement of one set of reproducers, repairers, and
surveyors (modernizers and progressives) with another set (restorationists). The restorationists have asserted control over key primary and
recontextualizing contexts within the state. "It is the recontextualising
field which generates the positions and oppositions of pedagogical theory, research and practice" (Bernstein, 1990, p. 61).

The use of investigatory pedagogies and related coursework
assessments in mathematics can be seen as key points in the realization of a classificatory principle in and for mathematics. They provide a
particular form of the communicative context in and through particular
pedagogical practices. The interactional/temporal and locational/spa-
tial principles of and within an investigatory pedagogy are weakly tied
and weakly insulated, and the relation between objects and attributes
in the investigatory classroom are loosely related and can be relatively
nonspecialized. I do not have the space here to ground or illustrate the
specifics of this analysis. But a shorthand representation of the complex relationships between principles and practices adumbrated earlier
is provided in the following extracts from a paper on mathematics
investigations by Lerman (1989, pp. 77-78):

Mathematical knowledge de-reified, seen as a social intervention, its
truths, notions of proof, etc. relative to time and space, has to be seen
as integrally involved with the doing of mathematics, and indeed cannot be separated from it. Mathematics is identified by the particular
ways of thinking conjecturing, searching for informal and formal contradictions, etc., not by the specific "content" . . . We are working in
education in a time when our students may be faced with a lifetime of
unemployment and uncertainty; with threats to the ecology of the
planet: an increase in disparity of wealth between rich and poor in
society and between nations; and even the threat of total annihilation.
Traditionally these have not been issues that have been thought of as
having any relationship to mathematics. We have always rested safe in
the knowledge that mathematics is value-free, non-political, objective

and infallible. . . . Quite the contrary, we have a particular responsibility, since so many political, moral and other issues are decided using
"mathematical" techniques, to enable pupils to examine situations,
make conjectures, pose problems, make deductions, draw conclusions,
reflect on results, etc.

Similar shifts in classificatory principles, in the move from the
Mk1C to the Mk2C, can be traced in virtually all other National
Curriculum subjects. In each case, complex contradictions and dilem-
mas inherent in the principle of classification as being supressed
(Bernstein, 1990, p. 25) are left for individual teachers to deal with in
their classroom practice.

A CULTURAL CRISIS IN EDUCATION

The prior discussion adumbrates the grounds of struggle and debate
with which I am concerned. But in this section of the chapter, I address
the question of not how but why this shift from the Mk1C to the Mk2C
has occurred. How can we begin to explain the resurgence of traditional
forms of curriculum practice that appear to be divorced from and anti-
thetical to the requirements of capital accumulation during a time of
international recession when the state of industry and the economy
occupy the center ground of politics?[1] Interestingly, Aronowitz and
Giroux (1991) noted a similar policy turn in the United States during
Reagan's second presidential term: "The importance of linking educational reform to the needs of big business has continued to influence
the debate, while demands that schools provide the skills necessary for
domestic production and expanding capital abroad have slowly given
way to an overriding emphasis on schools as sites of cultural produc-

---

[1]Writing in early 1993, the center ground of politics is as much about the social as
the economic. Rising crime figures, juvenile and child crime, crimes against the
police, social unrest in areas of economic distress have begun to generate a reactive
discourse of public morals that makes the current politics of school and family much
less surprising than I am perhaps presenting it in the main text. The tensions
between Thatcherist competitive individualism and the concern with the decline of
moral identity and the decline of deference have never been so clear-cut as now
(Minogue, 1993). Guilt, shame, and virtue do not sit easily alongside challenge, initiative, and self-interest. This is pointed to by recent interventions in the moral
panic over juvenile criminality by Prime Minister John Major and Archbishop of York
John Habgood. The former had called for society "to condemn a little more and
understand a little less." The latter retaliated, arguing that "the government, with its
strong emphasis on competitive success, feeds the notion that in our society, in a
sense, we are against each other and one does need some countervailing forces to
show that actually true human life is about cooperation. . . . I am not saying that
people aren't bad but often badness is brought out of them by circumstances, by
upbringing, by the sense of boredom and by a sense of hopelessness."

tion" (p. 24). This suggests that generic political, rather than economic, causes may underlie the shift toward cultural rightism.

We might usefully begin by returning to Bernstein's (1971) concern with the principles of social control:

> I suggest that the movement away from collection to integrated codes symbolizes that there is a crisis in society's basic classifications and frames, and therefore a crisis in its structures of power and principles of control. The movement from this point of view represents an attempt to declassify and so alter power structures and principles of control; in doing so to unfreeze the structuring of knowledge and to change the boundaries of consciousness. From this point of view integrated codes are symptoms of moral crisis rather than a terminal state of an education system. (1971, p. 67)

Bernstein's *crisis* in effect points to a fundamental contradiction within education and within the relationship of education to the modern state and the modern economy. The integration of education and work, although serving the requirements of capital accumulation, threatens (or at least fails to concern itself with the reproduction of) the established social order and fails to achieve the requirements of social legitimation. For the cultural restorationists (or neoconservatives as they are also called), education has become implicated in what Habermas (1985) described as "the so-called inflation of expectations and the lack of willingness to acclaim and obey, which is based on tradition" (p. 80; emphasis in original). And again this is articulated in the language of *crisis*: "The current crisis is above all a cultural crisis. . . . The problem is that our convictions are full of holes, our morals and our manners corrupt" (Steinfels, 1979, p. 55). Again, writing of the U.S. education system, Aronowitz and Giroux (1991) described a similar restorationist impetus as militating around a "cultural crisis" in education. They see the work of U.S. restorationist writers such as Bloom (1987) and Hirsch (1987) as representing "a frontal attack aimed at providing a programmatic language with which to defend schools as cultural sites, that is as institutions responsible for reproducing the knowledge and values necessary to advance the historical virtues of Western culture" (p. 25).

In their analysis, Aronowitz and Giroux saw textual authority and political authority as tied tightly together with restorationist education. The aim of these "aristocratic traditionalists," as they call them, is "to restore knowledge as a particular form of social authority, pedagogy and discipline" (p. 39). This is central, I suggest, to the project of the Mk2C.

What I have called vocational/new progressivism in education is an aspect of, in Habermas's terms, *social modernism*. Although such social modernism is not unwelcome itself to the cultural restorationists, its apparently inevitable association with cultural modernity—the changing boundaries of consciousness—is most certainly unacceptable.[2]

> Danger lies in cultural transformations, motivational and attitudinal changes and shifts in patterns of values and identities, which are attributed to the entry of cultural innovations into more or less traditional forms of life. Therefore, the legacy of tradition has to be preserved as far as possible. (Habermas, 1985, p. 87)

What Habermas called "the programmatic dismissal of cultural modernity," which "should make room for a *healthy sense of tradition*" (p. 91), captures the essential features of the Mk2C perfectly: "It concentrates on a 'courage to educate', i.e., an educational policy which tailors elementary education to basic skills and secondary virtues (industriousness, discipline and cleanliness). Simultaneously it emphasises a 'courage of the past' in schools, the family and the state" (p. 91).

All of this is well evidenced in recent British writing on the theory and practice of conservatism. Thus, in one example, Willetts (1992, p. 65) contrasted "our modern image of the human condition [is of] a soul stripped bare of all haphazard ties of place and time, of culture and society" with the conservative celebration of:

> those specific ties to places and people, being part of a culture, which give life its meaning. This is not just culture in the sense of high culture. "It includes all the characteristic activities and interests of a people: Derby Day, Henley Regatta, Cowes, the twelfth of August, a cup final, the dog races, the pin table, the dart board, Wensleydale cheese, boiled cabbage cut into sections, beetroot in vinegar, nineteenth century gothic churches and the music of Elgar." [Quoted from T.S. Eliot, "Notes towards the definition of a culture," in *Selected Prose* (Faber, 1975, p. 298). (pp. 66-67)

It is almost unnecessary to highlight the quintessential "Englishness" of much of Eliot's list, or to suggest the structural significance of food, religion, and sporting encounters as "dividing practices." Willetts continued to argue that "this conservative account of what it is to be a person offers a powerful explanation of the origins of moral

---

[2]Even the commitment of U.K. Conservatives to social modernity can be questioned. The politics and organization of the National Curriculum, for example, are primarily Taylorist rather than post-fordist. There is little evident of attempts to achieve negotiated consent from, or Kalmarist autonomy for, teachers. Rather, schools and teachers are caught between the raw disciplines of market and state.

obligations" (p. 68). Culture and identity are tied to morality, obliga-
tion, and duty. Place and self articulate, in the conservative version of
culture, an unself-conscious commitment to "the deeper traditions and
values of our society" (p. 76). The subtext of Willetts's exposition is one
of order and deference based on a firm moral identity and traditional
vigorous virtue.

Key elements of cultural restorationism, which tie together the
family and the state with the past, are national language and national
identity. As Aronowitz and Giroux (1991) commented, again about the
writing of Hirsch, "the national language, which is at the centre of his
notion of literacy, is rooted in a civic religion that forms the core of stability in the culture itself" (p. 42). Thus, in the United Kingdom the
English curriculum is crucial terrain in the culture wars. Via struggles to
control the form of the language and to set firm boundaries around the
definition of the literary canon markers of national and ethnic identity,
a basis for moral and social regulation are established. "For language
lies at the root of human identity, and to tamper with that is either
poetry or treason" (Eagleton, 1993, p. 35). And "literature . . . is the concrete correlate of that abstract political unity which we share as formally equal citizens of the state" (p. 32). The Mk1C and more profoundly
and blatantly the Mk2C are attempts to magically recreate a mythical
past of English cultural unity. Ethnic and cultural diversity are made
invisible by the recomposition of Englishness within the National
Curriculum. An imaginary past of glories and civilizing influence is to
serve as model and guardian for the future. "The neo-conservatives see
their role, on the one hand, in the mobilization of pasts which can be
accepted approvingly and, on the other, in the neutralization of this
pasts, which would provoke only criticism and rejection" (Habermas,
1985, p. 91). Culture is made over into an artifact; history becomes a
"museum of information" (Aronowitz & Giroux, 1991). "We are dealing
here with ideologues for whom language is essentially an elocutionary
affair, poetry a kind of metrical patriotism, and English literature a
semantic Stonehenge" (Eagleton, 1993, p. 35). In Bernstein's (1990)
terms, the National Curriculum establishes a set of "insulations":

> Punctuations written by power relations that establish as the order of
> things distinct subjects through distinct voices. Indeed, insulation is
> the means whereby the cultural is transformed into the natural, the
> contingent into the necessary, the past into the present, the present
> into the future. (p. 25)

(An analogous set of insulations are employed in the increasingly fine
definitions of Britishness enacted through immigration legislation.) A
new category of Englishness is thus forged, or at least attempted,

through the media of speech, grammar, and literature. "Imaginary sub-jects" are created "whose voices are experienced as real, as validating and constituting the specialized category" (p. 25). Here the "voice" is both metaphorical and eminently real. The breaks and dislocations that the Mk2C seeks to establish insulate literary from popular culture, received from demotic pronunciation, "proper" language from language "in use," national identity from origin and ethnicity, history from poli-tics, and social consciousness from social experience (see Ball, 1993). The objective here is "depluralisation"; the articulation of a classless and mono-ethnic society with a common, transcendent culture.

The assertion of tradition, of morality and literary history in the face of "declining standards," cultural heterogeneity, and a fragmented modernity is not simply an abstract trend. The opposition to progres-sivism, in art as well as in education, is a political project. Some indica-tions of this have been offered already in the struggles within the edu-cational state. So let us look a little more closely at the articulation of "the programmatic dismissal of cultural modernity." Two recent political texts will serve the purpose: one a lecture by former Secretary of State for Education Kenneth Clarke (1991), the other a speech by the then Chairman of the National Curriculum Council, David Pascall (1992).

CLASSLESS CULTURE

Both texts, significantly, initiate their attacks on progressivism with a set of opening shots toward Rousseau and specifically *Emile*. Rousseau's emphasis on experience and useful practical knowledge as the basis for education and his "rejection of the humanist and classical heritage in favour of the present and the scientific" (Pascall. 1992, p. 1) establish the basic polarization across which both texts range: the cul-tural over and against the social, the past as against the present, instruction as against experience. Rousseau and Dewey are portrayed as cultural luddites whose ideas underpin child-centered progressivism and legitimate repudiation of "the canons of western civilisation in favour of multiculturalism" (Clarke, 1991, p. 5). For Clarke and Pascall, diversity and struggle are irrelevant to culture; "the culture of a society is defined by its political and social history, its religious and moral beliefs, and its intellectual and artistic traditions" (Pascall, 1992, p. 4). These are taken to be unitary and coherent and constituted by fixed truths, unchanging values, and universal virtues. There is a "dominant culture," and its "important strands" can be listed: "the Christian faith, the Greco-Roman influence, the Liberal enlightenment, romanticism, the development of modern humanism" (p. 5). And the links among

culture, heritage, and social order are made very clear so that "such traditions are profoundly important in their own right and because this
teaching will develop that intelligent perspective on the past present
and future upon which our democracy, ultimately, depends" (p. 6). Here
culture is insulated entirely from the practical realities of the immediate, from conflict, from doubt, and from inequality. It is reified as "a
process of intellectual, spiritual and moral development" (p. 7).

Culture is "handed down by instruction and learning" (Clarke,
1991, p. 5): "If new generations are to participate," they "must be initiated into their cultural heritage so that, in due course, having assimilated
what they can of the wisdom of the past, they can make their own contribution to the development of human understanding" (Pascall, 1992,
p. 9). The new is always contingent and subordinate. History is a seam-
less trend of human improvement. We are to face the future by always
looking backwards. Furthermore, our appreciation and contemplation
of "man-made and natural things" must be learned, thought, and spoken through heritage and history. Pupils "need to be taught how to
think critically about art so that they learn how to make choices and
identify works which have genuine merit" (p. 11). Merit is simply inherent, clear to those of discernment (dominant agents), the arbiters of
taste (that is, of classification). This is based on what Bourdieu (1986)
called "the denial of the social." Taste exists here outside of society. The
"antagonistic relations to culture" that Bourdieu examined are
supressed. History is constructed by the learning of "successive generations." There are no revolutions, ruptures, or dislocations in this history. And these "generations" are genderless, classless, and raceless, their
"great works" and "cultural tradition," "stir the memories of a shared
past and point to a shared future" (Pascall, 1992, p. 12). The participation and contribution of those whose "shared past" is distinctly different is clearly problematic here. They stand outside of culture, marked
off as different, as, in effect, "uncivilized."

These texts mark a profound rearticulation of the National
Curriculum in cultural rather than social terms. The use of forms of
legitimation based on arguments of modernization and economic
necessity have been virtually swept away (despite Clarke's incoherent
attempt to roll the two together; "the founder of Gulf Oil, one of the
most successful businessmen of this century, has gone on record as
saying that he got most benefit in his education from majoring in poetry at Harvard," Clarke,1991, p. 7). The curriculum is interpolated into
the past and via a discourse of stability and civilization. "Any domination of popular and temporary cultural movements in our approach to
the curriculum will only serve to separate our children from their inheri-
tance which has shaped our society today" (Pascall, 1992, p. 18). The

past tense is interesting. Society is shaped rather than being shaped. And literature and art, rather than being part of politics and social struggle, are the touchstones that define humanity and social consciousness and the restorationist curriculum: "it is important for children to understand why Shakespeare or Mozart has lasted. This is not just a statement of belief that such artists are good for you—behind their works lie essential truths about our understanding of humanity" (p. 15). And, despite the odd caveat, the image of the classroom is one in which locational and interactional principles are strongly tied, fixed, and specialized, through a pedagogy of "awe and wonder" (p.14).

It is tempting to relate this articulation of the "cultural curriculum" back to the invention of the modern school curriculum in the 19th century and to the political and cultural crises that were the driving forces of the development of state education. Focusing on the key role of "literature," Davies (1981, p. 253) wrote that:

> following the semantic shift in the word itself, I want to argue that, faced with a crisis of ideological dominance and unable to resort either to the classics or to a science increasingly feared as the voice of soulless materialism, education discovered and therefore created literature as the principal material and object of its institutions and practices.

What literature offered and continues to offer, as Eagleton (1985/86) argued, is a basis for intransitive morality, a moral technology. It provides a cultural and moral naturalism, a lexicon of essential values, identities, and meanings. It thus obscures and defies difference, heterogeneity, and struggle. Struggles over class and race, over inequality and oppression, are displaced by common heritage and the classless society. Insulations disappear from view; they are naturalized. "The paradox of the imposition of legitimacy is that it makes it impossible ever to determine whether the dominant feature appears distinguished or noble because it is dominant" (Bourdieu, 1986, p. 92). The other paradox here is that all of this insulation work, and the Kantian distinctions and positions that underlay it, are intended to ensure and underpin classlessness, an apparent absence of insulations and distinctions.

CONCLUSION

The Mk2C is about the politics of depoliticization, it is about the assertion of symbolic control—ways of relating, thinking, and feeling, and forms of consciousness (Bernstein, 1990, p. 135). It is about drawing the discursive resources that constitute school knowledge more tightly inside and to the state. It is about the suppression of opposing posi-tions. It is also about contradictions, specifically, those contradictions within the state between the need to create the conditions for capital accumulation and the need to maintain social legitimacy, and those con-tradictions within conservatism between restoration and modernization and between the cultural and the social. As such it is inherently unsta-ble. Eagleton (1993) summed up these contradictions in dramatic terms:

> No government can afford its people to be at once idle and well-edu-cated; and if it can do little about the former, given the grave economic crisis of the system under which we live, then it is highly probable that it will try even more strenuously than it has already to do something about the latter. (p. 4)

I suggest that the Mk2C is the government trying "even more strenuous-ly than it has already."

The National Curriculum is a fantasy curriculum. It is intended to conjure up and reproduce a fantasy of Englishness, classlessness, authority, legitimacy, moral order, and consensus. Such a fantasy, founded on a mixture of class nostalgia and ethnic mythologizing, speaks powerfully about order and rationality to the fears and desires of beleaguered teachers and politicians and of many middle-class par-ents. But this is essentially a political and oppressive curriculum. The positionings, forms of thought, and exclusions and insulations inscribed within its texts and practices are part of a continuing struggle over what it means to be educated.

REFERENCES

Aronowitz, S., & Giroux, H. (1991). *Postmodern education: Politics, culture and social criticism*. Minneapolis: University of Minnesota Press.

Ball, S.J. (1990). *Politics and policy making in education*. London: Routledge.

Ball, S.J. (1993). Education, Majorism and the curriculum of the dead. *Curriculum Studies*, 1(2), 195-214.

Bernstein, B. (1971). On the classification and framing of educational knowledge. In M.F.D. Young (Ed.), *Knowledge and control* (pp. 47-69). London: Collier-Macmillan.

Bernstein, B. (1990). *The structuring of pedagogic discourse*. In *Class, codes, and control* (Vol. 4). London: Routledge.

Bloom, A. (1987). *The closing of the American mind*. New York: Simon and Schuster.

Bourdieu, P. (1986). *Distinction: A social critique of the judgement of taste*.

London: Routledge.

Clarke, K. (1991, June 12). *Education in a classless society*. Westminster Lecture to the Tory Reform Group.

Cockcroft, W.M. (1982). *Mathematics counts!* London: Her Majesty's Stationery Office.

Davies, T. (1981). Education, ideology and literature. In T. Bennett, G. Martin, C. Mercer, & J. Woolacott (Eds.), *Culture, ideology and social process* (pp. 251-260). Milton Keynes: Open University Press.

Eagleton, T. (1985/86). The subject of literature. *Cultural Critique, 2,* 95-104.

Eagleton, T. (1993). The crisis of contemporary culture. *The New Left Review*, No. 196, 29-42.

Ernest, P. (Ed.). (1989). *Mathematics teaching: The state of the art*. Lewes, UK: Falmer Press.

Habermas, J. (1985). Neoconservative culture criticism in the United States and West Germany: An intellectual movement in two political cultures. In R.J. Bernstein (Ed.), *Habermas and modernity* (pp. 78-94). Cambridge: Polity Press.

Hirsch, E.D. (1987). *Cultural literacy: What every American needs to know*. Boston: Houghton-Mifflin.

Jackson, M. (1989, March 24). CBI struggles to "save" curriculum from Baker. *The Times Educational Supplement*, 1.

Jessop, B., Bonnett, K., Bromley, S., & Ling, T. (1988). *Thatcherism: A tale of two nations*. Oxford: Basil Blackwell.

Jones, K. (1989) *Right turn*. London: Radius.

Lerman, S. (1989). Investigations: Where to now?'. In P. Ernest (Ed.), *Mathematics teaching: The state of the art* (pp 73-80). Lewes, UK: Falmer Press.

Minogue, K. (1993, February 16). *Is conservatism at last developing a theory?* A Lecture at King's College London.

Pascall, D. (1992, November 20). *The cultural dimension in education*. A Speech to the Royal Society of Arts.

Rosen, M. (1993, February 12). Clean the floor, maltworms. *New Statesman and Society*, 42.

Rustin, M. (1989). The politics of post-fordism: Or the trouble with 'New Times'. *New Left Review*, No. 175, 54-78.

Steinfels, P. (1979). *The neo-conservatives*. New York: The Free Press.

Whitty, G. (1990). The new right and the National Curriculum: State Control of Market Forces. In M. Flude & M. Hammer (Eds.), *The Education Reform Act 1988: Its Origins and Implications* (pp. 21-36). Lewes, UK: Falmer Press.

Willetts, D. (1992). *Modern conservativism*. London: Penguin.

5

Changing Pedagogic Discourse

A.D. *Edwards*
University of Newcastle

Bernstein's analysis of the structure of pedagogic discourse is highly formal in its presentation. There are few empirical illustrations, the "unit of analysis" being neither particular teachers and pupils nor particular instructional contexts, but the "social relation of transmission and acquisition" (Bernstein, 1990, p. 7). In this chapter, I explore aspects of that relation at a much lower level of abstraction, thereby rejoining the ranks of critics, recyclers, interpreters, and other "secondary servicers" whose distortions of his work he deplores. They are regarded as especially deplorable when they break up "the unity of the original corpus" for their own academic convenience, treating a part as all that matters and subjecting the rest to "discursive repression" (p. 8). Yet it seems unreasonable to expect complex theoretical formulations to be used only in their entirety and strictly within their terms of reference. In this case, and despite Bernstein's reluctance to make such parochial appplications, I consider some of the restructuring of pedagogic discourse being attempted and contested in British education from the "interesting" viewpoint which those formulations offer. For my own current research into modes of teaching and learning across the academic/vocational divide in postcompulsory education, they are proving an invaluable heuristic.

AUTHORITATIVE TEACHING

The relationship between transmitters and acquirers of knowledge is described by Bernstein as being "essentially and intrinsically" asymmetrical. The asymmetry may take complex forms, and it may be softened by various mitigating devices, but the form of the pedagogic relationship is hierarchical because it is for the transmitter to determine what is to be learned, in how much time and in what sequence, and how that learning is to be appropriately displayed. Bernstein therefore takes as normal pedagogic practice what many on the Right see as needing urgently to be restored.

"Real" education, they argue, is inherently undemocratic because its transactions are properly between those made unequal by relative mastery or ignorance of a body of established knowledge. It has been undermined by a subverting of subjects through excessive regard for "relevance" and immediate appeal to pupil interest, and by a deference to the ignorance of pupils which replaces facts with "easygoing discussion and opinionated vagueness" (Hillgate Group, 1987, p. 3). Progressive child-centerdness is attacked with particular fervor because "until the self is situated within a cultural tradition, there is nothing to explore, no direction to any discovery, and nothing to express or articulate" (O'Hear, 1991, p. 20).

The pamphlet from which that last quotation is taken belongs to the neoconservative strand in New Right polemic and is unusual only in the explicitness of its antidemocratic stance. What is required, O'Hear argued, is an education system that is "unashamedly divisive, elitist and inegalitarian." His justifying of that requirement exemplifies Bernstein's view that arguments about the curriculum are arguments between different conceptions of the social order and are therefore profoundly moral. For in defending the authoritative transmission and testing of properly constituted knowledge, O'Hear placed a general value on the "hierarchies of worth" that "real distinctions" between people create and that education should recognize. It is from that perspective that the General Certificate of Secondary Education (GCSE) through which the attainments of almost all 16-year-olds are now examined and certified, and which subsumes what had been a separate examination for the "top 20%," is deplored as being rooted "in the egalitarian impulse" to conceal differences in achievement (Norcross, 1990; North, 1987). If the progressives in their 1960s heyday had indeed discovered that "a new hegemony can be created by . . . undervaluing structure and authority in favour of spontaneity and self-expression" (Cox, 1982, p. 24), then their present-day opponents pursue no less politically and socially transforming authoritarian objectives through their commitment to restoring "traditional standards of scholarship."

These conservative portrayals of classrooms abandoned to democratic license bear no resemblance, however, to what research shows most teaching to be like. If Her Majesty's Inspectors of Schools, routinely denounced by the Right as prime purveyors of progressive orthodoxies, really felt obliged to attack "teacher-dominated" lessons and "tear into any school whose pupils are not in continual conversation with their teachers and . . . not continually questioning everything they are taught" (O'Hear, 1991, p. 24), then the evidence indicates that they would be considerably overemployed. Far more commonly observable in classrooms, as HMI themselves note, are the very unequal rights of participation in pedagogic discourse that are created and sustained by the mutually acknowledged "fact" that the teacher knows and the pupils do not (Edwards & Westgate, 1994, pp. 42-50). Nor is a preoccupation with immediate relevance to pupils lives and interests a characteristic of most classrooms. On the contrary, classroom tasks are typically so detached from pupils' everyday lives that they "make sense" only as the kinds of thing that go on in school (Mercer, 1992) .

Bernstein's model of pedagogic discourse has been constructed, elaborated, and refined at an ever high level of abstraction. Its "integrating concept" is the "code" that regulates practice through the "principles of structuration" that it embodies (Bernstein, 1990, pp. 2-3). Although identifying the "surface manifestations" of those principles is undoubtedly "tricky" (Atkinson, 1985, p. 66), and although the "delicate" describing of classroom processes has been left largely to others, Bernstein presents a clear causal sequence that runs from the form of the pedagogic relationship through the consequent regulation of the participants' orientation to meaning, to selective and specific "textual productions." It should therefore be possible to work back from those productions, which are "the form of the social relationship made visible," to the nature of the relationship itself. Thus the "selection, creation, production and changing of texts are the means whereby the positioning of subjects is revealed (and reproduced or changed)" (Bernstein, 1990, p. 17).

Elsewhere in the book, Davies comments that classroom researchers have ignored, underused, or misused the power of that analysis. It has certainly been a source of particular irritation to Bernstein himself that some of his interpreters have questioned its core assumption that classrooms are "predicated on elaborated codes and their system of social relationships." Yet if codes are "culturally determined positioning devices in relation to an underlying semantic" (Bernstein, 1990, p. 13), then much of the evidence from analyzing classroom "texts" shows pupils being positioned in ways that confine their participation within the teacher's frame of reference. This was the basis for my own argument that "the underlying semantic" had characteristics of a restricted code where it is

> assumed by teacher and pupils alike that those being instructed are essentially ignorant of the matters in hand until they have been taught about them. This assumption brings severe functional constraints on the language pupils use because what they "can mean" has to be contained within the limits of what their teachers define as being relevant, appropriate, and correct. (Edwards, 1987, pp. 237-238)

It still seems to me that among the salient conditions for a restricted code is a nonreflexive relationship to knowledge that is to be received and displayed but not disturbed or challenged. In such conditions, pupils acquire the "ritual knowledge"—knowledge which Edwards and Mercer (1987, p. 165) described as being "procedural, routinized, expedient," , and which they contrasted with the "principled knowledge" that is available for reflection and for questioning because the grounds for accepting it have been made explicit. The knowledge being transmitted "ritually" can be seen, in Bernstein's terms, as combining reason and conclusion; its legitimacy then derives from the authority of the speaker rather than being "rationally" grounded, and so can be challenged only by challenging the pedagogic relationship. It is in similar terms that Young (1984) presented his view that most teaching constitutes "indoctrination."

In what ways is the structure of the pedagogic relation made visible in the exchanges of transmitter and acquirer? Part of Bernstein's defense against what he sees as a gross misunderstanding of his thesis is that those guilty of it try to answer that question by seeking evidence of code restriction in isolated surface features of teachers or pupils speech, in utterances abstracted from their context, or (at best) in single contexts detached from the set of related contexts in which the "underlying semantic" of the pedagogic relationship is "made visible" (Bernstein, 1990, p. 101). This defense misrepresents the evidence on which critics draw, although it also illustrates the perennial difficulty of drawing testable propositions from a theory of structuration which is located so deeply within pedagogic practice and which insists on being tested in its own terms. Thus Bernstein largely disregards work outside his theoretical frame even when that work is directly concerned with the structuring of school knowledge.

That a great deal of classroom research has lacked theory of any kind is noted by Davies as heightening the heuristic value of Bernstein's insistence that research should follow theory. Yet the criticism is palpably untrue of some recent investigations, in various theoretical traditions, although mainly sociolinguistic or constructionist, of how pedagogic relationships are created, confirmed, or challenged in the acts of speaking (for example, Cazden, 1988; Dillon, 1988; Edwards & Mercer, 1987; Heath, 1983; Mehan, 1984; Mercer, 1992; Newman, Griffith, & Coles, 1989; Wells, 1989; Young, 1992). Much of that work has focused on the "essential teaching exchange" through which pupils' responses to a teacher's question are not only evaluated for their relevance and correctness against the teacher's instructional agenda, but are liable to be reshaped by the teacher's formulations and reformulations of it into more usable material. Far from being isolated utterances or even isolated series of utterances, this sequence of (teacher) initiation—(pupil) response—(teacher) feedback represents the building block of classroom communication. In sociolinguistic terms, it is the unmarked pattern that demands deliberate action by the teacher if alternatives are to be achieved (Cazden, 1988, p. 53).

It is a pattern that embodies the intrinsically asymmetrical relationship of transmitter and acquirer because the third—feedback—move tends so strongly to be evaluative. Briefly, "the teacher provides a framework into which pupil talk is fitted, and that talk is assessed according to the closeness of fit" (Edwards & Furlong, 1978, p. 101). The assessment may be a direct confirmation or rejection of the appropriateness, correctness, and adequacy of the pupil's response. Or it may work less directly, though no less powerfully, through the teacher's reformulating or recontextualizing of what a pupil has said into something more convenient to the teacher's instructional agenda. Close study of such exchanges has helped to display teachers' extraordinary skill in achieving the answers they want and yet giving those answers the appearance of having been jointly produced. When such research focuses on the "underlying semantic" of pedagogic exchanges, they indicate how changes on the communicative surface may be only tactical shifts in the exercise of teacher control. They therefore raise questions, too complex methodologically to be considered here, about where a more symmetrical relation between teacher and pupils would be "evident in the text" (Edwards & Westgate, 1994, pp. 123-133).

In Bernstein's terms, any significant reduction in the essential asymmetry of the pedagogic relationship requires a blurring of the boundary between knowledge and ignorance. Thus, Singh's (1993) interesting account of apparently successful challenges to the teacher's "power to know" describes an area of the curriculum (computing) in which conspicuous expertise and a corresponding confidence may be acquired in the home. That particular and entirely male takeover was conceded by the teacher, despite working to the disadvantage of the girls. From a conservative position, however, any kind of renunciation by teachers of the authority bestowed by their superior knowledge is perceived as abdication and so as a betrayal of their pupils. Thus, the reference (cited earlier) to "easygoing discussion and opinionated vagueness" is intended as a rebuke to teachers who permit and may even encourage the "aimless chatter" which wastes time and is likely to represent a sharing (and reinforcing) of ignorance.

Yet those who advocate extensive opportunities for pupils to "talk their way into" knowledge as an indispensable part of their learning, a view comprehensively represented in the National Oracy Project (Norman, 1992), do so from a belief that it is precisely through discussion (rather than through those tightly controlled teacher interrogations which often pass for discussion) that pupils begin to take over not only the language but also the concepts and strategies of the teacher. And it is through the encouragement of reasoned argument, in which they have to formulate, defend, and reformulate their ideas, that children are enabled to see beyond the neat arranging of knowledge into packages which are to be taken but not disturbed (Maybin, 1991; Phillips, 1990). What is being proposed by the "progressives" is not an abandoning of transmission, but a much wider range of specialized learning contexts in which the teacher's role becomes sometimes and temporarily that of neutral chairperson, group member, or learning partner, according to highly contextualized rules of appropriate communication (Corden, 1992).

CLASSIFIED KNOWLEDGE

It is an obvious, although difficult, question whether such opening of pedagogic discourse is made easier when subject boundaries are blurred. In defending his thesis that classrooms are "predicated" on elaborated codes, Bernstein criticizes some of his (mis-) interpreters for confusing strong classification with strong framing. Classification refers to the strength of the boundaries between bodies of knowledge, most obviously to whether school knowledge is firmly organized into subjects (probably in some hierarchy of relative worth) or is marked off from everyday knowledge in topic, thematic, or other cross-curricular ways. Framing refers to the strength of the boundaries between knowledge (however defined) and ignorance and therefore to the extent of the teachers control (however authorized) over what can count as legitimate meanings and legitimate ways of expressing those meanings. That control may be no less pervasive when there is no recognized "subject" to transmit; indeed, Bernstein argues that strong classification reduces the teacher's power insofar as it provides ready made definitions of what is to be transmitted.

From a conservative perspective, the authority of the teacher is inseparable from the authority of a properly designated subject. Teachers lose pedagogic authority once subjects are replaced by "studies"—social, business, communication, environmental, peace, women's studies, and so on. Some studies are more obviously objectionable than others because of their political purposes (Scruton, Ellis-Jones, & O'Keeffe, 1985), but all represent regrettable departures from knowledge that is properly established or "disciplined." Subjects are a necessary part of the "knowledge, skills and culture upon which our society is founded" because they contribute to a strong sense of national identiy and so promote cultural cohesion (Hillgate Group, 1987, p. 3). Because they require a long initiation into their particular mysteries, they provide a defense against those who so dislike creating failure that they wish to reduce the content of schooling to what is accessible and relevant to all. Having their traditional content, rules of procedure, and authorized texts, they are also a defense against teachers who intrude tbeir personal beliefs or seek to transmit only what is politically correct. In the more everyday meaning of the word, they are seen as a safeguard against "indoctrination" (O'Hear, 1987).

The National Curriculum has been so strongly classified into (traditional) subjects that cross-curricular themes, officially sponsored only after strong boundaries were in place, have struggled to survive. Recent case studies within a large sample of secondary schools show some of those themes (notably "economic and industrial understanding") to have been so permeated that most pupils were unaware of having learned anything about them at all (Rowe & Whitty, 1993). The potential capacity of such themes to draw on pupils' common-sense knowledge and establish links with everyday life—advantages emphasized by Hirst (1993) in a formidable attack on the dominance of subjects over the "best available practices of living" as the foundation of the curriculum—may depend on conditions that acquire added irony when stated in Bernstein's terms. That is, the weak framing within the classroom and the weak boundaries in relation to the outside world that cross-curricular themes make possible may depend on strongly classified relationships with academic subjects because the permeation model causes them largely to disappear within subjects that are themselves strongly classified and strongly framed (Whitty, in press)

The dominance of subjects might have represented a conservative victory had the definitions of what should count as science, mathematics, and so on, not come from within the "educational establishment" which conservatives blame most for the erosion of academic standards. The consequence has been a series of rearguard actions, vividly illustrated in the attempts to Latinize English grammar and Anglicize English literature (Cox, 1993; Graham, 1993, pp. 44-52) But what should be the scope of a national curriculum has presented the Right with fundamental dilemmas. Neoliberals want a standard measuring rod against which consumers can compare the relative merits of schools, yet a belief in the free interplay of supply and demand leads them to reject extensive prescription as incompatible with a market. Neoconservatives seek state support for a strong social and moral order, want a curriculum which imparts the national culture and its linguistic, literary, and historical bulwarks, and so tend to doubt whether the defense of traditional subjects and traditional values can safely be left to a marketplace disposed to favor whatever is currently fashionable (Crowther, 1988; Hillgate Group, 1987). Yet they too extol parental choice, insofar as they assume that parents common-sense preference for authoritative teaching and proper subjects will curb the willfulness of schools. Both ideological strands favor inequality. Neoliberals see the market as a neutral mechanism for producing winners and losers. Neoconservatives believe that differences in achievement should be positively encouraged. In this respect, the National Curriculum serves several masters. The ostensibly egalitarian objective is to secure a high threshold of knowledge, skills, and understanding to which all should have access, regardless of where they live and go to school. Yet the structure of attainment targets and normal ranges of attainment identified at each key stage provides an unprecedented apparatus for creating and making public differences in attainment as these are measured against the traditional subjects which conservatives so zealously defend. The explicitness with which that framework is set out raises an intriguing question, framed in relation to Bernstein's concepts of "visible" and "invisible" pedagogy, about possible effects of the National Curriculum on the structuring of educational opportunity.

It has been Bernsteins misfortune that his work has often been absorbed into the "educability" domain (which is where I first encountered it and shaped my doctoral research around it) and treated distortingly as a theoretically elaborated contribution to explaining working-class underachievement in terms of the social structuring of language use (Danzig, 1992). Yet Bernstein is a rare exception to the general neglect of pedagogy in investigations of how educational opportunities are distributed. His most familiar explanation of working-class underachievement can be illustrated in the conclusion from recent research in Portugal conducted tightly within his theoretical framework—that "children from lower social levels have more difficulty in recognising the difference between [instructional] contexts," and so in producing the specialized texts appropriate to them (Morais, Fontinhas, & Neves, 1992, p. 264). The structure of normal pedagogic discourse acts as a powerfully discriminating filter because many children have not acquired, or are less willing to practice, those dispositions and skills which make a supposedly common curriculum truly accessible. Briefly, Bernstein describes middle-class children as being more likely to recognize instructional tasks, even when framing is potentially weak, as being a subcontext of the specialized context "school." They are then more likely, for example, to transform an apparently open question into one to which their answers will be evaluated. They are more likely to be verbally explicit and specific in their references to objects, persons, and events, even when they can reasonably assume that the teacher already knows, and, when abbreviated, implicit responses of a kind appropriate in other contexts when there is an expert listener would be unacceptable as demonstrations of what they themselves know.

It would follow from this account that a lack of explicitness about what is being demanded from "competent" pupils in specific instructional contexts is itself a powerful source of discrimination. The strangeness of classroom tasks can be exaggerated because they may be thoroughly disembedded from everyday experience and yet be firmly located in the specialized contexts of instruction (Mercer, 1992). Thus Daniels (1989), working within Bernstein's framework, demonstrated the highly developed sensitivity of "slow-learning" children to the rules regulating pedagogic discourse and defining specific instructional contexts. Nevertheless, many classroom tasks will be more and less familiar depending on the ways in which communication is typically organized in the home. This is evident from Heath's (1983) richly documented description of the difficulties which black working-class children experienced when asked typical classroom questions about what things are "called" or about discrete features of objects, persons, or events detached from any everyday context. The problem as defined by some teachers was that the children "don't seem to answer even the simplest questions"; to the children, the answers often appeared too obvious to be worth giving. Heath's account of the resulting discontinuity elaborates the explanation offered by a black parent for her own child's persistent silence in the classroom—namely, that "nobody plays by the rules he know." Nobody seems to have explained the rules of the new games either.

Uncertainty about what rules are in play also has powerful silencing effects. Bernstein's account of the greater accessibility of the "invisible pedagogy" of progressive practice to children from the "new" middle-class referred to their greater capacity and willingness to cope with ambiguity. Whereas the "visible pedagogy" associated with traditional teaching emphasizes the evaluation of pupils' spoken and written texts against external criteria so as to produce and announce differences, the "invisible pedagogy" associated with progressivism is apparently less directed to "matching the acquirers text against an external common standard" than to producing shared competences (Bernstein, 1990, pp. 20-21). If it is the latter, with its weak marking of time and activity and its discursive rules known only to the transmitter, which works most to the advantage of the "new" middle class, then some equalizing effects might be expected from the highly visible structure of targets and rules of progression which the National Curriculum embodies. If the testing of pupils' progress against those requirements produces a highly visible "stratification of acquirers," then the existence of the targets themselves have an equalizing potential. In Bernstein's formulation, the "sequential and pacing rules" are made unusually available in statements defining levels of attainment and in the programs of study that direct pupils toward them; the "progression of the transmission" is thereby made unusually clear, and the acquirer has some awareness of "his or her future state of expected legitimate consciousness and practice" (Bernstein, 1990, p. 37).

There is also an equalizing potential in the content of National Curriculum subjects. Among the main conclusions from the Portugese research cited earlier was that working-class pupils experienced greater difficulty in applying the scientific knowledge they had acquired to new problems, so that increasing the level of abstraction in classroom tasks increased social class differences in achievement. But they had also had much less classroom experience of tasks involving "understanding" rather than "acquisition." There was evidence that the level of conceptual demand made by the teachers was strongly related to how they characterized their school's intake, which prompted the conclusion that teachers need such "sociological knowledge" if they are to correct the depressing effect of sociocultural context on how what is ostensibly the same syllabus is transmitted (Domingos, 1989, p. 365; Morais et al., 1992). In England, the National Curriculum has been promoted by the government as raising the threshold of knowledge, skills, and understanding to which all children should have access wherever they live and go to school. Potentially then, it represents a far-reaching challenge to traditional definitions of how school knowledge should be distributed, provided that tasks involving understanding, investigation, and problem solving are not reserved for those higher levels in the attainment targets that many pupils will not reach. That the initial targets and programs of study in, for example, mathematics, science, and history gave prominence to investigation and problem solving from the early stages of their study partly accounts for the fervor with which critics from the Right have sought to restore hard facts and easily measurable skills to prominence in the main stages of schooling.

PRIVILEGED ORDERS OF MEANING AND RELEVANCE.

From the conservative perspective outlined earlier, true education is a necessarily prolonged induction into established bodies of knowledge. Learners must "submit to the habits of the discipline" before they can achieve "liberation through mastery" (O'Hear, 1991, p. 30). Before that liberation is achieved, it is useless to encourage "a spirit of criticism" because the uninitiated have no opinions worth eliciting. That pointedly undemocratic view of classroom processes resembles the authoritarian alternative in the two "native" strategies which Young described in his analogy of the student as "a traveller in a strange land" attempting to learn its language and customs. The natives may be tolerant of travellers' mistakes and provide good advice about the sites to be seen and the paths to be taken without rigidly prescribing them. Or they may hold the traveller accountable for any breaches of native custom, insist that there should be no wandering until the language is spoken well, and provide detailed itineraries which permit no diversions (Young, 1992, p. 90). This notion that the right to explore for themselves should be reserved for those whose successful initiation shows they deserve it raises questions about for whom and at what stage in their education that right is recognized. The answers to those questions may be closely connected. For if the right is only to be earned by prolonged socialization in the culture of the subject, then it may be witheld until the later stages of schooling and thereby confined to an academically and socially selected minority. Or it may be conceded earlier, but only to those whose extended schooling can reasonably be expected.

It was remarked earlier that research shaped by Bernstein's thesis has been unusual in exploring in relation to pedagogy the distribution of privileged orders of meaning. Thus, Pedro's investigations in Portguese primary schools, cited by Davies, indicated that it was more often the middle-class pupils who were expected to be "active" learners, who received more explanations of the facts they were acquiring, and whose relations with their teachers were more open to negotiation. Morais's (formerly Domingos) research indicated that science teachers were more likely to restrict working-class pupils to the acquisition of knowledge and to reserve for middle-class pupils the experience of applying their already acquired knowledge to new problems (Domingos, 1989, p. 365: Morais et al., 1992).

Studies of elite schooling, however, in which such encouragement of understanding might most be expected, are thin on pedagogical detail. In Anyon's (1980) rather rigid version of correspondence theory, for example, it was only in the "executive-elite" school that students were encouraged to develop "analytical intellectual powers," and only in the "affluent-professional" school that they engaged in "creative activity carried out independently." What was apparent elsewhere, including in the merely "middle-class" school, was a concern with right answers, an acceptance of what was in the textbooks, and an emphasis on following procedures. Despite a brief section on "the construction of teacher-pupil practices," pedagogy hardly appears among the contrasts between "ruling-class" and "working-class" schooling in Australian cities, and teacher-centered instruction was popular among parents in both "classes" (Connell, Ashenden, Kessler, & Dowsett, 1983). Walford's research in leading English independent schools, which he reports elsewhere in this book, failed to find in the formal curriculum that weak framing which might have been expected in the education of those likely in later life to be making decisions, solving problems, and coping with uncertainty.

Relatively weak framing might also be expected, for the same reason, in the elite postcompulsory stage of public education. In the English system, this is when the separation of future "leaders" from future "followers" has traditionally been marked by different institutions, curricula, modes of assessment, and qualification. In the "sixth form" (and I use deliberately the traditional term for those who stay on at school beyond the minimum leaving age of 16), the dominant form of curriculum has been three academic subjects studied in depth. It is a form perennially justified by assuming, to an extent long contradicted by the aspirations and destinations of a large minority of sixth formers, that this is essentially the preparatory stage for higher education. In the rhetoric surrounding it, it is the stage during which "pupils become students," "intellectual discipleship" becomes apparent, and "independent learning" is encouraged. Those distinguishing marks have retained their rhetorical force, even though they are taken from a 1959 report by the Ministry of Education's Central Advisory Council and even though the Council itself doubted whether they could be sustained amid rapidly rising student numbers. In fact, the continuing preoccupation of the Right with preserving traditional standards and boundaries has prompted strong resistance to any broadening (or "dilution") of the Advanced-level examinations that are now taken by about 25% of 18-year olds, some 40% of whom do not obtain the three passes that constitute the high-value credential. Resistance to reform has been powerfully reinforced by the vested interest of the private sector in preserving from "pollution" an examination in which the success rate of its leading schools adds greatly to their market appeal. But the objections of principle reflect a general objection to blurring the proper boundary between the academic elite and the rest, and particular objections to the fashionable but "anti-educational" nostrums in which an advocacy of core skills, cross-curricular study, and relevance to working life are seen to embody (O'Hear 1991; Pilkington 1991).

Notions of intellectual discipleship are readily translatable in terms of Bernstein's account of socialization into subject cultures, as is the defense of the purity of academic categories as being necessary to the general good ordering of society. It is therefore surprising that this peculiarly English institution should not have attracted his attention. Certainly, sixth formers are seen more easily than younger pupils as cultural apprentices to whom the mysteries of the academic trade are beginning to be revealed, and from whom are increasingly expected appropriate use of those special words and constructions which display "disciplined" thinking as this is defined within the terms of the subject (Sheeran & Barnes, 1991). If "the longer you've been doing a subject, the more you believe the story it tells you about itself" (Inglis, 1985, p. 77), then the more likely you are to start adopting its particular narrative style. Significant changes in the normal forms of pedagogic discourse might then be expected as both cause and effect

In pedagogic practice, however, there is little evidence that the learning of A-level students is heavily marked by that relative autonomy indicated by the myths. "The quality of work in sixth forms" is described by Her Majesty's Inspectors of Schools as being—at its best—scholarly, challenging, with students showing "an ability to engage in extended conversation and discussion" and to work independently; but rather more of the teaching observed had confined students very largely to being "passive recipients of information" who were given little opportunity for the "interchange of ideas" (Department of Education and Science, 1988, p. 29). "Most commonly," a later survey reported, "students were expected to listen to expositions by the teacher, to respond to questions, and to ask for clarification if they did not understand" (Department of Education and Science, 1991, p. 4). Conservatives might dismiss these strictures as ideologically motivated rebukes from the prophets of progressivism. As judgments grounded in observation, however, they suggest a notable continuity with previous stages of schooling and a notable contrast to the myths of a pedagogy characterized by a less asymmetrical relation between teacher and student. Indeed, it is interesting that although HMI seem not to differentiate in their expectations of good practice between the academic and vocational "curricular traditions" in postcompulsory educational provision, they also fail to find extensive departures from didactic teaching. In the classic tradition of the pedagogical "recitation," the most common teaching method they observed in 5,000 classes was "the presentation of information through a lecture, supported by a teacher-directed question and answer session" (Department of Education and Science, 1987, p. 22).

In relation both to A-level and to vocational courses leading to marketable qualifications, HMI recognized that high-stakes testing brings pressures to playing safe, and that playing safe is liable to focus learning too narrowly and produce an excess of exposition. But the entire post-16 stage displays conspicuously the well-developed capacity of the English education system to create educational failure. Indeed, the whole process of education 11-18 can be seen as an obstacle course constructed to weed out the majority; the effect has been low participation rates in education beyond the compulsory stage, which in turn produces an undereducated workforce at all levels below the well-qualified elite.

Viewed in that light, Bernstein's analysis of the curriculum in relation to the social division of labor appears superficially to produce a lack of fit. Strong classification and (contrary to the myth) strong framing seem to characterize the teaching of those moving toward professional and managerial occupations in which boundaries are likely to be weakly marked. In contrast, those whose positions in the labor market are likely to involve clear boundaries between tasks, between jobs, and between those who direct and those who are directed, are most likely to have experienced in the last years of schooling a replacement of subjects by studies and a deliberate blurring of the categories of "school" and "work." But the contrasts are more complex and more subtle than that. Although he did not elaborate on his brief comments, Bernstein observed a division between old and new ideologies—or what Ball (1990) called the "conservative restorationists" and modernized versions of the "industrial training" tradition. Both are elitist, but the first is based on "the hierarchy of knowledge and its class supports," although with a high-mindedly arrogant indifference to the stratification consequences of that hierarchy, and the other is based directly on the hierarchies of the labor market (Bernstein, 1990, pp. 63, 86-88). The first insists on the autonomy of properly classified academic knowledge studied for its own sake, whereas the other insists on useful learning so that knowledge is dehumanized and "regionalized" into distinct areas of application (Bernstein, 1990, p. 63). The clash of ideologies is vividly illustrated in O'Hear's (1987) defense of "humane sensibility" against the ravages inflicted on "true education" by a narrowly utilitarian pursuit of relevance and by his fear that city technology colleges—beacons of the new modernizing order—will turn their abler pupils into narrow technicists and their less able pupils into the "Bob Cratchits of the future . . .tied to their computer screens . . . without even the Victorian clerks pride in his handwriting" (quoted in Regan, 1990, p. 36).

In the past, prevocational education has tended to display strong framing because it is directed toward precisely defined "useful" knowledge and skills. It is this characteristic that figured prominently in neoconservative objections to the instrumentalism inherent in the pursuit of "relevance" and to the substitution of ill-defined skills for "real" academic knowledge. But as O'Keeffe (1990) argued, the "intellectual crisis rooted in the subversion of subjects" comes from various directions, which he called romantic (or progressive), egalitarian, and technicist. From that last direction has come the conclusion, in clear opposition to neoconservative assumptions, that a modern society has to educate its followers as well as its leaders. Thus, the variously termed *new vocationalism* or *vocational progressivism* appears superficially to be taking from progressive pedagogy an emphasis on practical, investigative, and collaborative styles of learning because these are now seen to be required by the culture of modern industry. It is not surprising then that the city technology colleges, with their promise of a "modern" high-technology alternative to traditional secondary education, see themselves as being especially equipped (and obliged) to break the mold of tradition in post-16 education by making it a "mass" third stage in which the academic-vocational divide has disappeared (Whitty, Edwards, & Gerwirtz, 1993, pp. 111-116). Other recent acts of category pollution, such as the Secretary of State's recent suggestion of vocational A-levels, reflect a movement to grant equivalent status (as though that could be done by fiat, across the grain of entrenched educational and social hierarchies) to qualifications distinctly different in the origins and destinations of the students (Further Education Unit, 1992). That raises empirical questions about the social distribution of forms of pedagogy at this stage of education for which Bernstein's work provides a powerful heuristic.

In relation to my own current research into modes of teaching and learning across the academic-vocational boundary, his brief but illuminating analysis indicates both co-existence and conflict between a tradition of segregated, autonomous subjects taught and examined authoritatively and leading to general qualifications, and a tradition of integrated or modular vocational courses taught "progressively" and leading to closely specified competences. It may be, then, that the weight supposedly given to understanding in the education of the academic elite is becoming more readily visible outside it. That seems an intriguing possibility.

REFERENCES

Anyon, J. (1980). Social class and the hidden curriculum of work. *Journal of Education*, 162, 67-92.

Atkinson, P. (1985). *Language, structure and reproduction.* London: Methuen.

Ball, S. (1990). *Politics and policy making in education: Explorations in policy sociology.* London: Routledge.

Bernstein, B. (1990). *The structuring of pedagogic discourse.* London: Routledge.

Cazden, C. (1988). *Classroom discourse.* Portsmouth, NH: Heinemann.

Connell, R., Ashenden, D., Kessler, S, & Dowsett, G. (1983). *Making the difference: Schools, families and social division.* Sydney: George Allen and Unwin.

Corden, R. (1992). The role of the teacher. In K. Norman (Ed.), *Thinking voices: The work of the National Oracy Project* (pp. 172-185).London: Hodder and Stoughton.

Cox, B. (1982). Progressive collapse: The counter revolution in English education. *Quadrant, 26*(3), 20-28.

Cox, B. (1993, March 1). The right is wrong on English teaching. *The Times,* p. 10.

Crowther, I. (1988). The politics of restoration. In R. Scruton (Ed.), *Conservative thoughts: Essays from the Salisbury Review* (pp. 115-130). London: Claridge Press.

Daniels, H. (1989). Visual displays as tacit relays of the structure of pedagogic practice. *British Journal of Sociology of Education, 10*(2), 123-140.

Danzig, A. (1992). Basil Bernstein's sociology of language applied to educational deficits, differences, and bewitchment. *Journal of Education Policy, 7*(3), 285-300.

Department of Education and Science. (1987). *Non-advanced further education in practice: An HMI Survey.* London: Her Majesty's Stationery Office.

Department of Education and Science. (1988). *Secondary schools: An appraisal by* HMI. London: Her Majesty's Stationery Office.

Department of Education and Science. (1991). *Programmes of students on GCE advanced-level courses.* London: Department of Education and Science.

Dillon, J.T.(1988). *Questioning and teaching.* London: Croom Helm.

Domingos, A.M. (1989). Influence of the social context of the school on the teacher's pedagogic practice. *British Journal of Sociology of Education, 10*(3), 351-366.

Edwards, A.D. (1987). Language codes and classroom practice. *Oxford Review of Education, 13*(3), 237-247.

Edwards, A.D., & Furlong, V.J. (1978). *The language of teaching.* London: Heinemann.

Edwards, A.D., & Westgate, D. (1994). *Investigating classroom talk* (2nd ed.). Lewes: Falmer Press.

Edwards, D., & Mercer, N. (1987). *Common knowledge.* London: Methuen.

Further Education Unit. (1992). A *basis for credit.* London: Author.

Graham, D. (1993). A lesson for us all: The making of the National Curriculum. London: Routledge.

Heath, S. (1983). Ways with words. Cambridge, UK: Cambridge University Press.

Hillgate Group. (1987). The reform of British education. London: Claridge Press.

Hirst, P. (1993). The foundations of the National Curriculum: Why subjects? In P. O'Hear & J. White (Eds.), Assessing the National Curriculum (pp. 31-37). London: Paul Chapman.

Inglis, F. (1985). The management of ignorance. Oxford: Blackwell.

Maybin, J. (1991). Children's informal talk and the construction of meaning. English in Education, 25(2), 34-49.

Mehan, H. (1984). Language and schooling. Sociology of Education, 57, 174-183.

Mercer, N. (1992). Culture, context and the construction of knowledge. In P. Light & G. Butterworth (Eds.), Context and cognition (pp. 28-46). London: Harvester/Wheatsehad.

Morais, A., Fontinhas, F., & Neves, I. (1992). Recognition and realisation rules in acquiring school science—the contribution of pedagogy and social background of students. British Journal of Sociology of Education, 13(2), 247-270.

Newman, D., Griffin, P, & Cole, M. (1989). The construction zone: Working for cognitive change in school. Cambridge: Cambridge University Press.

Norcross, L, (1990). The egalitarian fallacy. In Institute of Economic Affairs Education Unit (Ed.), GCSE (pp. 3-22). London: Institute of Economic Affairs.

Norman, K. (Ed.). (1992). Thinking voices: The work of the National Oracy Project (pp. 172-185). London: Hodder and Stoughton.

North, J. (Ed.). (1987). The GCSE: An examination. London: Claridge Press.

O'Hear, A. (1987). The importance of traditional learning. British Journal of Educational Studies, 35(2), 102-114.

O'Hear, A. (1991). Education and democracy: Against the educational establishment. London: Claridge Press.

O'Keeffe, D. (1990). Equality and childhood: Education and the myths of teacher training. In N. Graves (Ed.), Initial teacher education: Policies and progress (pp. 74-92). London: Kogan Page.

Phillips, T. (1990). Structuring context for exploratory talk. In D. Wray (Ed.), Talking and listening (pp. 59-72). London: Scholastic Publications.

Pilkington, P. (1991) End egalitarian delusion: Different education for different talents. London: Centre for Policy Studies.

Regan, D. (1990). City technology colleges: Potentialities and perils. London: Centre for Policy Studies.

Rowe. G., & Whitty, G. (1993, April 9). Five themes remain in the shad-
ows. *Times Educational Supplement*, p. 8.

Scruton, R., Ellis-Jones, A., & O'Keeffe, D. (1985). *Education and indoctrination*. London: Educational Research Centre.

Sheeran, Y., & Barnes, D. (1991). *Discovering the ground rules*. Milton
Keynes: Open University Press.

Singh, P. (1993). Institutional discourse and practice: A case study of
the social construction of technological competence in the primary classroom. *British Journal of Sociology of Education*, 14(1), 39-58.

Wells, G. (1989). Language in the classroom: Literacy and collaborative
talk. *Language in Education*, 3(4), 251-274.

Whitty, G. (in press). Subjects and themes in the school curriculum.
Research Papers in Education, 9(2).

Whitty, G., Edwards, T., & Gerwirtz, S. (1993). *Specialization and choice in
urban education*. London: Routledge.

Young, R. (1984). Teaching equals indoctrination: The dominant epistemic practices of our schools. *British Journal of Educational Studies*,
22(3), 220-238.

Young, R. (1992). *Critical theory and classroom talk*. Clevedon, UK:
Multilingual Matters.

6

Basil Bernstein and Aspects of the Sociology of the Curriculum

Ivor Goodson
University of Western Ontario

In this chapter, I sketch some personal comments about the significance of Basil Bernstein to my own notions of curriculum study, then move on to comment on the kind of programs of study that have developed, partly due to his influence. In short, I move from the personal to the programmatic. In doing so, I shall not try to cover all of Bernstein's influences on, or theories about, the school curriculum. I confine myself to issues of personal significance and to the terrain of curriculum studies with which I have been involved. In providing a personal introduction, the intention is to ground a discussion of academic discourses in some understanding, albiet limited, of social structure and lived experience.

SOME BIOGRAPHICAL BACKGROUND

I was born in 1943. My father was a gas fitter; my mother worked in a wartime munitions factory. My father was the youngest of 13 children (he was lucky enough to be preceded by 12 sisters); his father was an unskilled laborer, mostly unemployed, and his mother took in laundry. My mother was one of six children and had two sisters and three brothers. Her father and mother ran a workingman's cafe in Reading, UK. (It was while serving breakfast one morning in 1929 that she met my Dad.)

My parents married in 1932 and went to live in a working-class suburb of Reading, called Woodley. I was born during the war. My Dad was involved with the Gas Fitters Union, and in 1945 both parents voted for a Labour Government committed to bringing a better deal for working people and their children. This government was to substantially effect my schooling. In 1949, I went to a school attached to the Church of England; it was very ill-resourced having no textbooks, nor qualified teacher or separate classrooms (just one huge room with curtains across). I can still vividly recall the "earth closets" that passed as toilets. At the time I could not read or write. But the new Labour Government had initiated a vigorous campaign to build new "County Primary Schools." So in 1950, I left the earth closets behind to go to "Loddon County Primary School." At the time I still could not read but, given the ready supply of books and qualified teachers, I soon learned. Three years later I passed the "11-plus" examination.

The "Grammar School" to which I was directed was a long way away from my village, and I had to travel by bus and train or, in summer, undertake a long bicycle ride. This was only the beginning of a process that seemed calculated to take me away from my family and my culture. Within the school many features jarred with my cultural experiences. I was a 10-year-old child adrift in a very alien world. In retrospect, the major vehicle of alienation was the school curriculum—Latin, Greek, Ancient History, Grammar, English Literature, Physics, Chemistry, and so on. A classical curriculum utterly divorced from my experience of the world. Like so many of my class—as was well documented by Lacey (1970) and Hargreaves (1968)—I settled near the bottom of the class. In 1959, I took nine "O" level examinations and passed one subject (history). That summer, I went to work in a potato crisp factory with three of my mates from Woodley.

My history teacher must have been pleased with his singular success at teaching me something (compared with the other eight subject teachers), for he arrived at the crisp factory in September and announced that I should return to school. Shouting above the noise of the factory I said I might just do that. School had begun to look desirable.

So I worked hard, passed a few "O" levels that year, and joined the sixth form. In due course, I passed my "A"-level examinations and went off to London University. (London was in fact the only place I could go because, at that time, all other universities required Latin or Greek if you wanted to take history, at least that is what I was told at school.) I received an Economics Degree (specializing in Economic History) and did quite well in the final examinations, whereby I was offered a research studentship at the London School of Economics. For four years I fumbled away at a doctorate on Irish immigrants in Victorian England, and in my final year became a lecturer at what is now Kingston University.

But throughout this period, I spent increasing amounts of time back home in Woodley (which was an hour from London). This still felt like home. This was where my friends and family were. Moreover, the Grammar Schools were being replaced by comprehensive schools, and the word in the pubs and clubs of Woodley was that this would offer an education to my class of people that would be of more interest and relevance than Latin, Greek, and Ancient History. My friends spent a lot of time talking about all this as a political strategy of hope.

So I began to read more about education. In the summer of 1967, I came across an article called "Open Schools, Open Society" by Basil Bernstein, first published in *New Society*:

> We are moving from secondary schools where the teaching roles were insulated from each other, where the teacher had an assigned area of authority and autonomy, to secondary schools where the teaching role is less autonomous and where it is a shared or co-operative role. There has been a shift from a teaching role which is, so to speak, "given" (in the sense that one steps into assigned duties), to a role which has to be *achieved* in relation with other teachers. It is a role which is no longer made but *has to be made*. The teacher is no longer isolated from other teachers, as where the principle of integration is the relation of his subject to a public examination. The teacher is now in a complementary relation with other teachers at the level of his day-by-day teaching. (Bernstein, 1975, p. 71)

More or less, there and then I decided to stop wasting my time studying Victorian England and lecturing in higher education to the "sons and daughters of gentlefolk" and to get involved in teaching in comprehensive schools. I applied to the Institute of Education in London to train to be a teacher.

THE INSTITUTE OF EDUCATION, CIRCA 1969

In 1969, the Institute of Education was scattered throughout many buildings clustered around Senate House in Malet Street, WC1. On Taviton Street a number of terraced houses were grouped together to form the Sociology Department. It was here that my tutors, Brian Davies and Basil Bernstein, held their seminars and occasional personal tutorials.

I attended a range of "methods" courses, but some of my time was spent completing a term project on "working class students in the new comprehensive schools." As a result, I got a lot of papers pushed my way that Brian Davies, Michael Young, and Basil Bernstein were writing: I still have the papers and, of course, they were early drafts of work that later appeared in *Knowledge and Control* (Young, 1971) and *Class, Codes and Control* (Bernstein, 1975).

It is difficult to describe the liberating power of tutorials at the Institute at this time. After 15 years of schooling and being taught by people from another class about subjects utterly disconnected from anything I had experienced, suddenly everything changed. The tutors were mostly from a similar background, and the subject was essentially our experience of education and culture. The sociology department in 1969 was in a real sense like coming home (with all the tensions and ambivalences carried therein). And I was to know, for perhaps the first time, that learning did not have to be alienating, that connectedness was possible. I was also to likewise learn that disconnectedness was often socially constructed.

To experience what "could be" in terms of social science scholarship was also then to learn what was "not allowed to be." To learn what "could be" in terms of pedagogic discourse and relationships was to be shown with unforgettable clarity how curriculum, culture, and class were irrevocably enmeshed. For a few years (in the social democratic moment that followed 1968) in the sociology department a "contradictory gap" was opened up. During that time work on "knowledge and control" proceeded not only at the scholarly level but also at the level of the lived experience for those who clustered around the tables of Taviton Street and of the local pubs. Many conversations have stayed with me since. One I remember was between myself, Rob Walker (see Goodson & Walker, 1991) who was finishing a research degree with Bernstein and Bernstein himself. It started in Taviton Street with a long argument about styles of pedagogy and the comprehensive school. It then moved along the street to the Marlborough pub where it went on for hours. A good deal of the discussion turned on Bernstein's use of the term *transmission* in some of his work (see Bernstein, 1971, p. 47). This we argued was to use the language of dominant pedagogies while speaking of other visions. By the end of the evening we were, it has to be said, somewhat pissed.

In the cold light of day though I found myself nagging away at what had been said. Through the mists of the Marlborough a program of study began to tentatively emerge, and it was clear that the agent provocateur in all this was Bernstein himself.

TEACHING IN COMPREHENSIVE SCHOOLS

Bernstein's work in particular showed me that there were modes of academic study in which the everyday experiences of ordinary pupils and people might be investigated, in short, in which my experience of life and my intellectual questions about that experience might be finally reconnected. But, just as before, I had to abandon my intellectual interests to pass examinations; now, once again, I had to abandon an academic career as a university lecturer so that self and study might be reinvested with some degree of authenticity (Goodson, 1988b).

At the heart of the academic examinations and the academic career that had followed were the same alien and seemingly redundant bodies of knowledge. Was it merely a personal pathology that made me reject them? Some species of infantilism? Some battle with the "father figure"? Something worse? Was this a problem of *individual* response?

The decision to abandon a traditional academic career was essentially a positive redirection. Once I had identified the kind of work epitomized by Bernstein and his colleagues, I saw the newly organizing comprehensive schools as the place in which I wanted to work. Here, my own class background and experience might engage with that of my pupils in a "common language" of dialogue between teacher and students. For the new generation of pupils from working homes there might be something beyond the pervasive alienation I had experienced at school, an alienation intimately related to the form and content of the traditional grammar school curriculum. In the event, comprehensive schools often found themselves teaching many of these traditional grammar school subjects. As I have described elsewhere (Goodson, 1993), new subjects faced a bitterly contested battle for acceptance, and the traditional subjects normally maintained their supremacy. It became important to understand the problems of status, resources, and power that underlay and underpinned school subjects.

FROM THE PERSONAL TO THE PROGRAMMATIC

Let me now switch from the personal to the programmatic. In doing so, I switch voices, codes, and discourses. For the rest of this chapter, I adopt the disembodied voice of scholasticism. In this sense the chapter moves between the two "worlds" of my experience.

In his essay, "On the Classification and Framing of Educational Knowledge," Bernstein (1971) wrote:

> How a society selects, classifies, distributes, transmits and evaluates the educational knowledge it considers to be public, reflects both the distribution of power and the principles of social control. From this point of view, differences within and change in the organization, transmission and evaluation of educational knowledge should be a major area of sociological interest. (p. 47)

He extended this later in the chapter in a very suggestive paragraph:

> We can look at the question of the framing of knowledge in the peda-
> gogical relationship from another point of view. In a sense, educational
> knowledge is uncommonsense knowledge. It is knowledge freed from
> the particular, the local, through the various languages of the sciences
> or forms of reflexiveness of the arts which make possible either the cre-
> ation or the discovery of new realities. Now this immediately raises the
> question of the relationship between the uncommonsense knowledge
> of the school and the *commonsense* knowledge, everyday community
> knowledge, of the pupil, his family and his peer group. This formula-
> tion invites us to ask how strong are the frames of educational knowl-
> edge in relation to experiential, community-based non-school knowl-
> edge? I suggest that the frames of the collection code, very early in the
> child's life, socialize him into knowledge frames which discourage con-
> nections with everyday realities, or that there is a highly selective
> screening of the connection. Through such socialization, the pupil
> soon learns what of the outside may be brought into the pedagogical
> frame. Such framing also makes of educational knowledge something
> not ordinary or mundane, but something esoteric which gives a special
> significance to those who possess it. I suggest that when this frame is
> relaxed to include everyday realities, it is often and sometimes validly,
> not simply for the transmission of educational knowledge, but for pur-
> poses of social control of forms of deviancy. The weakening of this
> frame occurs usually with the less "able" children whom we have given
> up educating. (p. 58)

Bernstein's work on the school curriculum then exhorts us to
investigate how a society selects, classifies, distributes, and transmits its
educational knowledge and to relate this to issues of power and social
control. In Britain, the major vehicle for educational knowledge, certainly
at the secondary school level, has been the school subject. Moves
toward a different pattern of social relations and reproduction have often
focused on the attempts at "reforming" or "integrating" the subject-cen-
tered curriculum. A program of study focuses on school subjects thereby
offering some promise in furthering a project of social inquiry.

STUDYING SCHOOL SUBJECTS

The study of "modern" school subjects began as a part of university
scholarship in the early years of the century. The school subject became
the major focus of schooling for increasing numbers of pupils, especially in the upper years, with the growth of state systems of education. As
a result scholarship delved into the origins and development of school

subjects, and Watson (1909), a pioneer in this field, was clear that "owing to the rapid development of a system of County and Municipal Secondary Schools in England and Wales, at the present time, a special interest is centred on the place and function of the 'modern' subjects in the secondary schools" (p. vii). This statement anticipates in some manner the later exhortations of sociologists of knowledge, for he argued that is was time that "the historical facts with regard to the beginnings of the teaching of modern subjects in England were known, and known in connection with the history of the social forces which brought them into the educational curriculum" (p. viii). In the half century following 1909, few scholars followed Watson and sought to relate school subjects to the "social forces which brought them into the educational curriculum" in any general way.

By the 1960s, though, new initiatives to reformulate scholarship on school subjects came from sociologists such as Bernstein himself. Musgrove (1968), for instance, exhorted educational researchers to "examine subjects both within the school and the nation at large as social systems sustained by communication networks, material endowments, and ideologies" (p. 101). In the "communication networks," Esland (1971) later argued that research should focus, in part, on the subject perspective of the teacher. He, together with Dale, later developed this focus on teachers and subject communities:

> Teachers, as spokesmen for subject communities are involved in an elaborate organization of knowledge. The community has a history, and, through it, a body of respected knowledge. It has rules for recognizing "unwelcome" or "spurious" matter, and ways of avoiding cognitive contamination. It will have a philosophy and a set of authorities, all of which give strong legitimation to the activities which are acceptable to the community. Some members are accredited with the power to make "official statements"—for instance, editors of journals, presidents, chief examiners and inspectors. These are important as "significant others" who provide models to new or wavering members of appropriate belief and conduct. (Esland & Dale, 1973, pp. 70-71)

In particular, these sociologists were concerned that we developed scholarship that illuminated the role of professional groups in the social construction of school subjects. These groups can be seen as mediators of the "social forces" to which Watson (1909) had eluded:

> The subject associations of the teaching profession may be theoretically represented as segments and social movements involved in the negotiation of new alliances and rationales, as collectively-held reality constructions become transformed. Thus, applied to the professional

> identities of teachers within a school, it would be possible to reveal
> the conceptual regularities and changes which are generated through
> membership of particular subject communities, as they were manifest-
> ed in textbooks, syllabi, journals, conference reports, etc. (Esland,
> 1971, p. 107).

In the light of the importance of historical perspectives, Esland (1971)
added that "subjects can be shown to have 'careers' which are dependent on the social-structural and social-psychological correlates of
membership of epistemic communities" (p. 107).

The complex and dialectical relationship between "what counts
as education and issues of power and control" had been elucidated by
Williams (1975) in the *Long Revolution*. He noted:

> It is not only that the way in which education is organized can be seen
> to express consciously and unconsciously, the wider organization of a
> culture and a society so that what has been thought of a single distrib-
> ution is in fact an actual shaping to particular social ends. It is also
> that the content of education which is subject to great historical agna-
> tion, again expresses, again both consciously and unconsciously, cer-
> tain basic elements in the culture. What is thought of as "an education"
> being in fact a particular set of emphases and omissions. (p. 146)

It is necessary though to broaden Williams's notion of "the content of
education," for I have noted elsewhere that the battle over the *content* of
the curriculum, although often more visible, is in many senses less
important than the control over the underlying *forms* (Goodson, 1992)

In the important collection, *Knowledge and Control*, Young (1971)
sought to follow up the relationship between school knowledge and
social control and to do so in a manner that focused on content and
form. In this work he focused on the "organizing principles" that he dis-
cerned as underlying the academic curriculum:

> These are literacy, or an emphasis on written as opposed to oral pre-
> sentation, individualism (or avoidance of group work or cooperative-
> ness) which focused on how academic work is assessed and is a char-
> acteristic of both the "process" of learning and the way the "product" is
> presented; abstractness of the knowledge and its structuring and com-
> partmentalizing independently of the knowledge of the learner; finally
> and linked to the former is what I have called the unrelatedness of aca-
> demic curricula, which refers to the extent to which they are "at odds"
> with daily life and experience. (p. 38)

This emphasis on the form of school knowledge should not, however,
exclude concerns like those of Williams with the social construction of

particular contents. The crucial point to grasp is that it is the interrelated force of form *and* content that should be at the center of our study of school subjects. The study of subject form and content should moreover be placed in an historical perspective. When we are unable to situate the problems of contemporary education historically, we are again limited from understanding issues of politics and control. These limitations lead to the development of programs for studying school subject histories.

STUDYING THE SOCIAL HISTORY OF SCHOOL SUBJECTS

The important work by sociologists of knowledge such as Bernstein in defining research programs for studies of school knowledge led to an acknowledgment by some of them that historical study might complement and extend their project. In studying school subjects we have arrived at a new stage. Initial work in the early 20th century has provided some important precursors to our work; the sociologists of knowledge have subsequently played a vital role in rescuing and reasserting the validity of this intellectual project. In the process, however, some of the necessary focus on historical and empirical circumstances has been lost. The task now being undertaken is to reexamine the role of historical methods in the study of curriculum and to rearticulate a mode of study for carrying further our understanding of the social history of the school curriculum and, in this work, particularly school subjects.

In *School Subjects and Curriculum Change,* first published in 1983, I looked at the history of three subjects; geography, biology, and environmental studies (Goodson, 1993). Each of the subjects followed a similar evolutionary profile, and this initial work allowed a series of hypotheses to be developed about the way that status and resources, the structuration of school subjects, push school subject knowledge in particular directions: toward the embrace of what I call the "academic tradition." Following this work a new series, *Studies in Curriculum History,* was launched. In the first volume, *Social Histories of the Secondary Curriculum* (Goodson, 1985), work was collected on a wide range of subjects: classics (Stray, 1985, English) or science (Waring, 1985, who had written an earlier seminal study on Nuffield science), domestic subjects (Purvis, 1985), religious education (Bell, 1985), social studies (Franklin, 1985; Whitty, 1985), and modern languages (Radford, 1985). These studies reflect a growing interest in the history of curriculum and, besides elucidating symbolic drift of school knowledge toward the academic tradition, raise central questions about past and current explanations of school subjects, whether they be sociological or philosophical. Other work in the series, *Studies in Curriculum History,* has looked in detail at particular subjects: in 1985, McCulloch, Jenkins, and Layton (1985) produced *Technological Revolution*? This book examined the politics of school science and technology curriculum in England and Wales since World War II. Subsequent work by Woolnough (1988) looked at the history of physics teaching in schools in the period 1960 to 1985. Another area of emerging work is the history of school mathematics: Cooper's (1985) book, *Renegotiating Secondary School Mathematics*, looks at the fate of a number of traditions within mathematics and articulates a model for the redefinition of school subject knowledge; Moon's (1986) book, *The 'New Maths' Curriculum Controversy*, meanwhile looks at the relationship between math in England and America and has some very interesting work on the dissemination of textbooks.

Recent work in America has also begun to focus on the evolution of the school curriculum studied in an historical manner. Kliebard's (1986) seminal *The Struggle for the American Curriculum 1893-1958* discerns a number of the dominant traditions within the school curriculum. The book also comes to the intriguing conclusion that by the end of the period covered the traditional school subject remained "an impregnable fortress." But Kliebard's work does not take us into the detail of school life. In this respect, Franklin's (1986) book, *Building the American Community*, provides some valuable insights into a case study of Minneapolis. Here we see the vital negotiation from curriculum ideas, the terrain of Kliebard's work, toward implementation as school practice. In addition, a collection of papers put together by Popkewitz (1987) looks at the historical aspects of a range of subjects: early education (Bloch, 1987), art (Freedman, 1987), reading and writing (Monagha & Saul, 1987), biology (Rosenthal & Bybee, 1987), mathematics (Stanic, 1987), social studies (Lybarger, 1987), special education (Franklin, 1987; Sleeter, 1987), socialist curriculum (Teitelbaum, 1987), and a study of Ruggs's textbook by Kliebard and Wegner (1987).

Canadian curriculum history has been launched as a field most notably by Tomkins's (1986) pioneering work, *A Common Countenance*. This studies the patterns of curriculum stability and change in a range of school subjects over the past two centuries throughout Canada. The book has stimulated a wide range of important new work on curriculum history, for instance, Rowell and Gaskell's (1988) very generative study of the history of school physics. The Rowell and Gaskell piece provides one important case study in a new book, *International Perspectives in Curriculum History* (Goodson, 1988a) that seeks to bring together some of the more important work emerging in different countries on curriculum history. Besides some of the work already noted by Stanic, Moon, Franklin, McCulloch, Ball, and Rowell and Gaskell, there are important articles on Victorian School Science by Hodson (1988), on Science

Education by Smith (1988), on English on the Norwegian Common School by Gundem (1988), and on The Development of Senior School Geography in West Australia by Marsh (1988).

Importantly, new work has begun to look beyond traditional school subjects to broader topics. For example, Cunningham's (1988) book looks at the curriculum change in the primary school in Britain since 1945. Musgrave's (1988) book, *Whose Knowledge*, is a case study of the Victoria University Examinations Board 1964 to 1979. Here historical work begins to elucidate the change from curriculum content to examinable content that is such an important part of understanding the way that status and resources are apportioned within the school.

Recent work has begun to explore gender patterns in curriculum history. Bernard Powers's (1992) excellent study, *The Girl Question in Education*, is a pioneering work in this regard. Likewise, work is beginning on the modernist construction of curriculum as a world movement. The work of Meyer, Kamens, and Benavot with Cha and Wong (1992), *School Knowledge for the Masses*, provides a path-breaking study of national primary curricula categories in the 20th century throughout the world.

In many countries curriculum history is now being systematically analyzed and promoted. In the last couple of years educational journals in Brasil, Australia, Scandinavia, and Spain have provided special editions on curriculum history (Goodson, 1990a, 1990b, 1990c, 1991a, 1991b; Goodson & Dowbiggin, 1991), and new books are being planned in Germany, Portugal, Italy, and South Africa.

New directions for the study of school subjects and curriculum will require a broadened approach. In particular this work will have to move into examining the relationships between school subject content and form and issues of school practice and process. It is now vital in England and Wales to also redirect this work to an exploration and critique of the National Curriculum, for the resonances, certainly at the level of class, to previous patterns are overwhelming. The comparison between Bernstein's work on the curriculum and the current state of the art of curriculum analysis in the United Kingdom is a salutary reminder of the changes in political climate and responses within the academy. There could be no clearer indicator of the general climate of withdrawal and deference within the academy, for the National Curriculum cries out for the kind of social analysis epitomized by Bernstein and first called for by Watson (1909). To paraphrase, it is high time that the historical facts with regard to the National Curriculum were known, and known in connection with the social forces which brought them into the educational curriculum.

In terms of the Bernstein legacy and what I have called social constructionist study of the curriculum (Goodson, 1990d), this lacuna in studying the National Curriculum is little short of astounding. As I have detailed, work on the history of school subjects has been sustained, particularly in Britain, itself for over a decade of intensive scholarship. We now know a great deal about the class, gender, and racial biases of school subjects. Yet, in recent years, scholars close to these developments, with a few dignified exceptions, have virtually ignored this legacy in their work on the National Curriculum. The effect is to conspire with the Thatcherite view that the National Curriculum is a new and compelling revolution in educational provision. In fact, curriculum history indicates that nothing could be further from the truth. As I have argued elsewhere (Goodson, 1994), government policy and pronouncements have encouraged this amnesia (and a failure to present academic challenges has the same effect): "The obsessive presentism of many of the current government initiatives has successfully obscured this deeply-embedded connectedness which is of course relevant to the present and future of the UK as a class society" (Goodson, 1990e, p. 231).

Curriculum histories then should provide a systematic analysis of these ongoing social constructions and selections that form the school curriculum, pointing out continuities and discontinuities of social purpose over time. It is important to note that the prevailing paradigm, of curriculum study focusing on implementation, is devoid of such sociohistorical perspective, but more importantly so to is the more "radical" focus on curriculum that studies school-based "resistance" to new national directives. Not only is such work without sociohistorical range, but it focuses only on the reaction. To quote Jameson (personal communication, February 18, 1992; see also 1992), "The violence of the riposte says little about the terms of the engagement." And so it is with school resistance to the national curriculum. The social construction of the national curriculum sets the terms of the engagement and does so in ways that link to a history of social purposes.

Curriculum histories can elucidate and analyze this ongoing process of the social construction of curriculum. Such histories provide a new terrain of study in which the school subject might again be employed as an entry point for social analysis. It is an entry point though that can be clearly traced back to Basil Bernstein and his work at the Institute of Education in London.

REFERENCES

Bell, A. (1985). Agreed syllabuses of religious education since 1944. In I.F. Goodson (Ed.), *Social histories of the secondary curriculum* (pp. 177-

201). London and Philadelphia: Falmer.

Bernard Powers, J. (1992). *The girl question in education: Vocational education for young women in the progressive era*. London, New York, and Philadelphia: Falmer.

Bernstein, B. (1971). On the classification and framing of educational knowledge. In M.F.D. Young (Ed.), *Knowledge and control* (pp. 47-69). London: Collier-Macmillan.

Bernstein, B. (1975). *Class, codes and control, Vol. 3: Towards a theory of educational transmissions* (2nd ed.). London: Routledge and Kegan Paul.

Bloch, M.N. (1987). Becoming scientific and professional: An historical perspective on the aims and effects of early education. In T.S. Popkewitz (Ed.), *The formation of school subjects: The struggle for creating an American institution* (pp. 25-56). New York and Philadelphia: Falmer.

Cooper, B. (1985). *Renegotiating secondary school mathematics*. London and Philadelphia: Falmer.

Cunningham, P. (1988). *Curriculum change in the primary school since 1945*. London, New York and Philadelphia: Falmer.

Esland, G.M. (1971). Teaching and learning as the organization of knowledge. In M.F.D. Young (Ed.), *Knowledge and control: New directions for the sociology of education* (pp. 70-115). London: Collier-Macmillan.

Esland, G.M., & Dale, R. (Eds.). (1973). *School and society* (Course E282, Unit 2). Milton Keynes: Open University Press.

Franklin, B.M. (1985). The social efficiency movement and curriculum change 1939-1976. In I.F. Goodson (Ed.), *Social histories of the secondary curriculum* (pp. 239-268). London and Philadelphia: Falmer.

Franklin, B. (1986). *Building the American community*. London, New York and Philadelphia: Falmer.

Franklin, B. (1987). The first crusade for learning disabilities: The movement for the education of backward children. In T.S. Popkewitz (Ed.), *The formation of school subjects: The struggle for creating an American institution* (pp. 190-209). London, New York, and Philadelphia: Falmer.

Freedman, K. (1987). Art education as social production: Culture, society and politics in the formation of curriculum. In T.S. Popkewitz (Ed.), *The formation of school subjects: The struggle for creating an American institution* (pp. 63-84). London, New York, and Philadelphia: Falmer.

Goodson, I.F. (Ed.). (1985). *Social histories of the secondary curriculum*. London and Philadephia: Falmer.

Goodson, I.F. (Ed.). (1988a). *International perspectives in curriculum history* (2nd ed.). London and New York: Routledge.

Goodson, I.F. (1988b). *The making of curriculum: Collected essays*. London, New York, and Philadelphia: Falmer.

Goodson, I.F. (1990a). Laronplansforskning: Mot ett socialt konstruktivistiskt perspektiv. *Forskning om Utbildning*, 1, 4-18.

Goodson, I.F. (1990b). A social history of subjects. *Scandinavian Journal of Educational Research*, 34(2), 111-121.

Goodson, I.F. (1990c, December). Zur sozialgeschichte der schulfacher. *Bildung und Erziehung*, 379-389.

Goodson, I.F. (1990d). Studying curriculum: Towards a social constructionist perspective. *Journal of Curriculum Studies*, 22(4), 299-312.

Goodson, I.F. (1990e). 'Nations at risk' and 'national curriculum': Ideology and identity. *Politics of Education Association Yearbook 1990*, pp. 219-232.

Goodson, I.F. (1991a, August). La construccion del curriculum: Posibilidades y ambitos de investigacion de la historia del curriculum. *Revista de Educacion on Curriculum History I*, No. 295, 7-37.

Goodson, I.F. (1991b). Tornando-se una materia academica: Padroes de explicacao e evolucao. *Teoria and Educacao* (Brazil), No. 2, pp. 230-254.

Goodson, I.F. (1992). On curriculum form. *Sociology of Education*, 65(1), 66-75.

Goodson, I.F. (1993). *School subjects and curriculum change* (3rd ed.). London, New York, and Philadelphia: Falmer.

Goodson, I.F. (1994). *Studying curriculum: Cases and methods*. Milton Keynes, UK: Open University Press and New York: Teachers College Press.

Goodson, I.F., & Dowbiggin, I.R. (1991c). Vocational education and school reform: The case of the London (Canada) Technical School, 1990-1930. *History of Education Review*, 20(1), 39-60.

Goodson, I.F., & Walker, R. (1991). *Biography, identity and schooling*. London, New York, and Philadelphia: Falmer.

Gundem, B.B. (1988). The emergence and redefining of English for the Common School 1889-1984. In I.F. Goodson (Ed.), *International perspectives in curriculum history* (pp. 46-73). London and New York: Routledge.

Hargreaves, D. (1968). *Social relations in the secondary school*. London: Routledge and Kegan Paul.

Hodson, D. (1988). Science curriculum change in Victorian England: A case study of the science of common things. In I.F. Goodson (Ed.), *International perspectives in curriculum history* (pp. 139-178). London and New York: Routledge.

Jameson, F. (1992). *Postmodernism or, the cultural logic of late capitalism*. Durham, NC: Duke University Press.

Kliebard, H. (1986). *The struggle for the American curriculum 1893-1953*. London: Routledge and Kegan Paul.

Kliebard, H., & Wegner, G. (1987). Harold Rugg and the reconstruction of the social studies curriculum: The treatment of the Great War in his textbook series. In T.S. Popkewitz (Ed.), *The formation of school subjects: The struggle for creating an American institution* (pp. 268-287). London, New York, and Philadephia: Falmer.

Lybarger, M.B. (1987). Need as ideology: Social workers, social settlements, and the social studies. In T.S. Popkewitz (Ed.), *The formation of school subjects: The struggle for creating an American institution* (pp. 176-189). New York and Philadelphia: Falmer.

Lacey, C. (1970). *Hightown Grammar.* Manchester: Manchester University Press.

Marsh, C.J. (1988). The development of a senior school geography curriculum in Western Australia 1964-84. In I.F. Goodson (Ed.), *International perspectives in curriculum history* (pp. 179-208). London and New York: Routledge.

McCulloch, G., Jenkins, E., & Layton, D. (1985). *Technological Revolution?* London and Philadelphia: Falmer.

Meyer, J.W., Kamens, D.H., Benavot, A., with Cha, Y.K., & Wong, S.Y. (1992). *School knowledge for the masses.* London, New York. and Philadephia: Falmer.

Monagha, J., & Saul, W. (1987). The reader, the scribe, the thinker: A critical look at reading and writing instruction. In T.S. Popkewitz (Ed.), *The formation of school subjects: The struggle for creating an American institution* (pp. 85-122). London, New York, and Philadephia: Falmer.

Moon, B. (1986). *The 'new maths' curriculum controversy.* London, New York, and Philadelphia: Falmer.

Musgrave, P.W. (1988). *Whose Knowledge?* London, New York, and Philadelphia: Falmer.

Musgrove, F. (1968). The contribution of sociology to the study of the curriculum. In J.F. Kerr (Ed.), *Changing the curriculum* (pp. 96-109). London: University of London Press.

Popkewitz, T.S. (1987) *The formation of school subjects: The struggle for creating an American institution.* London, New York, and Philadelphia: Falmer.

Purvis, J. (1985). Domestic subjects since 1870. In I.F. Goodson (Ed.), *Social histories of the secondary curriculum* (pp. 203-237). London and Philadelphia: Falmer.

Radford, H. (1985). Domestic subjects since 1870. In I.F. Goodson (Ed.), *Social histories of the secondary curriculum* (pp. 203-287). London and Philadelphia: Falmer.

Rosenthal, D.B., & Bybee, R.W. (1987). Emergence of the biology curriculum: A science of life of a science of living? In T.S. Popkewitz (Ed.), *The formation of school subjects: The struggle for creating and American institute* (pp. 123-144). New York and Philadelphia: Falmer.

Rowell, P.M., & Gaskell, P.J. (1988). Tensions and realignments: School physics in British Columbia 1955-80. In I.F. Goodson (Ed.), *International perspectives in curriculum history* (pp. 74-106). London and New York: Routledge.

Sleeter, C.E. (1987). Why is there learning disabilities? A critical analysis of the birth of the field in its social context. In T.S. Popkewitz (Ed.), *The formation of school subjects: The struggle for creating an American institution* (pp. 210-237). London, New York, and Philadephia: Falmer.

Smith, L.M. (1988). Process of curriculum change: An historical sketch of science education in the Alte schools. In I.F. Goodson (Ed.), *International perspectives in curriculum history* (pp. 107-138). London and New York: Routledge.

Stanic, G.M.A. (1987). Mathematics education in the United States at the beginning of the twentieth century. In T.S. Popkewitz (Ed.), *The formation of school subjects: The struggle for creating an American institution* (pp. 145-175). London, New York, and Philadephia: Falmer.

Stray, C.A. (1985). From monopoly to marginality: Classics in English education since 1800. In I.F. Goodson (Ed.), *Social histories of the secondary curriculum* (pp. 19-51). London and Philadelphia: Falmer.

Teitelbaum, K. (1987). Outside the selective tradition: Socialist curriculum for children in the United States 1900-1920. In T.S. Popkewitz (Ed.), *The formation of school subjects: The struggle for creating an American institution* (pp. 238-267). London, New York, and Philadephia: Falmer.

Tomkins, G.S. (1986). *A common countenance: Stability and change in the Canadian curriculum.* Scarborough, Canada: Prentice-Hall.

Waring, M. (1985). To make the mind strong, rather than to make it full: Elementary school science teaching in London 1870-1904. In I.F. Goodson (Ed.), *Social histories of the secondary curriculum* (pp. 121-143). London and Philadelphia: Falmer.

Watson, F. (1909). *The beginning of the teaching of modern subjects in England.* London: Pitman.

Whitty, G. (1985). Social studies and political education in England since 1945. In I.F. Goodson (Ed.), *Social histories of the secondary curriculum* (pp. 269-288). London and Philadelphia: Falmer.

Williams, R. (1975). *The long revolution.* London: Penguin.

Woolnough, B.E. (1988). *Physics teaching in schools 1960-85: Of people, policy and power.* London, New York, and Philadelphia: Falmer.

Young, M.F.D. (Ed.). (1971). *Knowledge and control: New directions for the sociology of education.* London: Collier-Macmillan.

7

Bernstein on Classrooms

Brian Davies
University of Wales College at Cardiff

Somewhere around 1974, Basil Bernstein told me that the classroom was the graveyard of researcher intentions. I am sure that the warning was kindly meant, though it felt, at the time, like a reproach. It was delivered in a context of trying to think through a project protocol that would deliberately juxtapose the collection of extensive school system organizational and curricular data with school establishment and classroom observational work, which would require us to trace the everyday effects on teachers and pupils of macropolicy and mesofad. We were going to work together in a venture that would begin to put empirical flesh on the bones of the "Classification and Framing" paper (Bernstein, 1971a). In terms of his chronology, we were at that point at which the code theory, developed in the sociolinguistic and family contexts, was ready to go to school. I was convinced that the character of school experience not only depended on all those things that were not school, which his research, among others, had so marvellously illuminated, but that it was the organizational character of schooling—and particularly its "technological" or "work" aspects—that doomed teachers to a life of relatively unchanging practices and relations. The joint project never happened for reasons that I interpreted at the time as being roughly that Basil was not convinced of its intellectual quality. I would now redescribe that as his unwillingness to get involved with something that simply did not have a specification in sufficiently clear theoretical terms, although he was sufficiently kind and keen to help a young colleague to launch into a wing and a prayer pilot, but only from the tarmac. I have been left ever since with an abiding interest in what he

137

would do with classrooms when he got there. Now is as good a time as any to attempt a working evaluation. Happily, it amounts to more than an account of funerary rites.

The time is particularly apt because we have, at last, a generally available selection of empirical work on schooling, including work on classrooms, that has stemmed directly from his code theory (Cox-Danoso, 1986; Daniels, 1988, 1989; Diaz, 1984; Domingos, 1987, 1989; Jenkins, 1990; Morais (formerly Domingos) Fontinhas, & Neves, 1992; Pedro, 1981; Singh, 1993) or, more precisely, that has developed in interaction with it, in a way in which he described in detail for the first time in Bernstein (1992a). The empirical development of his ideas has not been confined to those directly working with him, though to date outside that direct line it has tended to be local and sporadic. In general, the ongoing Bernstein "rediscovery" among the heavies of contemporary sociology of education has not yet caught up with the existence of the school and classroom empirical work. Typically, Apple (1992), in homage conceding that his views depend on Bernstein, told us that his theoretical corpus, marred both by a rather mechanical, essentialist view of class and a lack of a theory of the state, is unaware of the danger of "asking what remains the same . . . in his suggestive investigation of the basically 'unchanging' nature of dominant pedagogic discourse, even when economic forms change markedly" (p. 144) now that the Right is resurgent.

Sadovnik (1991), in attempting to relate Bernstein's work on pedagogic practice to U.S. educational conflict and reform, also depicted it as "still, however, at a theoretical level": "Bernstein often refers to the potential of education to produce creative subjects and thus to create the possibility of change . . . perhaps the next major area of inquiry for Bernstein or for others who are working in his tradition" (1991, p. 61).

This simply shows unawareness of the fact that the whole thrust of his project and the empirical work to date is inexorably linked to precisely this question but has not come in a neat box labeled "policy analysis." Direct help is now at hand for those with such recognition problems, as Bernstein breaks the habit of a lifetime and begins to address in detail the postwar policy drama, taking the view that "reforms arise out of a struggle to construct and impose pedagogic identities considered to be crucial to the reproduction or production of the State's dominating principles as these are projected and institutionalised in education" (Bernstein, 1992b, p. 1).

In a recent state-of-the-art school-effects review, Kilgore and Pendleton (1993) made a rare reference outside of the canon to assert that "except for the seminal work of Bernstein |1975| on the social structural aspects of knowledge systems, the issue of accessibility has been relegated largely to the work of cognitive psychologists" (p. 66) in which accessibility "refers to the degree to which a learner is able to make sense of new information."

They did not develop this reference, but it is interesting that *Class Codes and Control, Volume 3* has lodged itself in the consciousness of a genre that does not easily recognize strangers. It may be that their analysis was ready to take on board variations in pedagogic practice of the sort that his later work now describes. This could begin a further advance in school-effects analysis as great as Bidwell and others achieved in their post-Coleman realization that a school was not one but many places to go to (Davies, 1992). It is now equally clear that beneath time, tracks, and schemes, the "opportunity to learn" (the current buzz word) badly needs some nontrivial "whos"and "whys" added.

The continuing need for intellectual penetration and grip is certainly evident in a field that slides all too easily from wish to false fulfillment or else loses its object in a welter of boxes whose loose theoretical coupling dooms it to triviality in the ineffective pursuit of effectiveness. The strength and weakness of the typical teacher effectiveness formulation is well displayed in Westerhof (1992), in which *effectiveness* in classroom terms was confined to teacher behavior that increased learning gain presented as a comparison of "direct" and "indirect" instruction in specific subject areas. Although interesting, the findings seem to be no more than yet another statistically sophisticated display of a Flanders-type (1970) analysis with all the nonsense about the benefits of indirectness extracted. It encounters the particularities of subjects, pedagogies, and pupil response as contextual contingencies that merely color in the conquering category system.

Bernstein is enjoying a more significant resurgence among that group within the broad church of classroom interactionists and ethnographers converging on the need for a rapprochement between those who have hitherto specialized in different aspects of classroom teaching/learning transactions. For example, researchers such as Pollard (1987) note the power of the convergence between constructionist psychological approaches and those of classroom social interactionists and see the possibility of synthesis in a Bernsteinian agenda.

Classroom studies must be a near perfect fit for illustrating the case of mainstream education discourse. It is dominated by the desire to do good by doing better and vice versa. It tends either not to ask questions about who decides what version of curriculum content and processes will be offered as a "good thing" to whom or else is so blocked by a priori answers that empirical work is redundant. It stands at the confluence of a number of conceptual and empirical "literatures" that concern both sociological and psychological pedagogical theories.

It has a history of dominant developmental/cognitive psychological influence, only lately acknowledging the awkward fact that life is not a continuous reportable quasi-experiment. The vogue, within this field, has shifted toward "constructivist" approaches, deemphasizing stage as limit or constraint, privileging the active, meaningful, and contextual. Not only do the preexisting contents of teacher and learner heads matter—their view of, their relation to, their knowledge scaffolding—but the centrality of teachers' decision making with respect to presentation, sequence, pace, and ownership and control of the learning process (and their learner counterparts) become pedagogical requirements of a latter-day rediscovery of ideas such as Vygotsky's (1987) view of the relation of learning and development. At least one of Simon's (1985) wishes is coming true—the neglect of pedagogy in educational studies, long guaranteed by dominant psychological paradigms that tactitly regarded classrooms as contingent messes, is being replaced by those which put it center stage. Fang (1992, pp. 39-40) referred to the "quiet revolution in developmental psychology" brought about by social constructivism's contribution "to the study of learning mainly through the elucidation of the basic processes of knowledge acquisition . . . through a social process with children participating in activities beyond their competence through the assistance of adults and more able peers."

The shift in focus is from teacher effectiveness, teaching styles, and the effect of social class on children, which neglected "socially meaningful analysis of the classroom situations in which teaching and learning are expected to take place" (Pollard, 1985, p. 5), toward "opportunity to learn" models that focus on "quality" of classroom tasks emphasizing "match" (Bennett, 1987; Bennett, Desforges, Cockburn, & Wilkinson, 1984). This task perspective draws deeply on a rich vein of work on pedagogical content knowledge and its correlates (Shulman, 1989, 1991) that focuses on "the transformation of subject matter knowledge . . . at the heart of teaching" (Fang, 1992, p. 54) and informs recent work in Britain such as the Leverhulme Primary Project (Wragg, Bennett, & Carre, 1989). It has become self-conscious of its essential product-process form, and its British progenitors have certainly become aware that the "implications of these studies for practice and policy are all too easily regarded as straightforward and have been notably privileged by press and politicians anxious to find extensive evidence of progressive rot in the system" (Fang, 1992, p. 59).

Although it still tends to ignore pupil perspectives, it is now ready to embrace interpretative studies, themselves at best full of meticulous stories that still tend to ignore curriculum content and continue to picture pedagogical or learning processes as "tangential to issues such as typification, group formation and the consequence of differentiation" (Pollard, 1990, p. 242). Pollard has been at the forefront urging for a redirection of sociologically dominant interactionism in classroom studies that, certainly in work like his own, has begun to move away from an exclusive celebration of differentiation and to refer to content and transmission modes as more than epiphenomena of class, gender, and ethnic labeling and reproduction.

However, just as clearly as there is convergence in this field, it becomes obvious that it is the case, at least in part, because there is relatively little worthwhile sociology with which to converge. We have largely decamped to the macro high ground and policy analysis sphere. Yet there has never been work of such quality and promise to engage with from other directions. To look at a study such as Cazden (1988) is to realize how expertly and tellingly fusion is possible among conceptual tightness, empirical appropriateness, and practitioner "feel." There is, at the moment, and as her contribution to this volume portrays, everything to be played for in terms of rewriting the grammar of the action that takes place within and between teachers and learners in classroom contents. The lights are going on in the "black box." What is the character of the Bernsteinian illumination?

The background glow goes back some time. The sociolinguistic thesis (Bernstein, 1971b, 1973) provided inspiration/goad for several decades of classroom talk analysis that I do not attempt to deal with here. Cazden, for example, not only refers to the importance of Bernstein's (1971b, p. 199) injunction that the culture of the teacher could not become part of the consciousness of the child until the reverse had happened, but also to his notion of boundary and "universalistic orders of meaning" as informing her thinking. There were indeed vital linkages between the misrecognized language/control thesis and an intercontinental industry on deficit/intervention, compensation/multiculturalism, much of it a good deal less than of the scholarly kind. The earliest educational applications in terms of pupil involvement and ritual evoked little empirical development. King's (1969) thesis, arising out of Bernstein (1966), tested values and involvement in a case study school but with no reference to pedagogical/classroom practices. The ritual paper has more recently been moved into a serious evaluation of Bernstein's contribution to the organizational analysis of school by Tyler (1988) to which I shall return. The Open/Closed Schools article (Bernstein, 1967) provided the preface to a generation of theses and essays produced by students who frequently believed that organic or mechanical solidarity were choice points for teachers, rather like caning, streaming, or compulsory games (or not).

The 1971 "Classification and Frame" paper provided a vocabulary for conceptualizing not only curriculum but educational transaction in general that has dominated much serious work since. It was at once massive, irritating, and unavoidable. It forced the obvious under our noses: The message systems content, pedagogy, and evaluation interpenetrated and "produced" educational and wider and cultural social relations in ways that depended on what and who were put together or held apart and who controlled the pace of their unfolding and their relation to others. The classroom microworld was where societal principles of power and control met what Bourdieu called "habitus" to (re)produce knowledge and social identity/destiny (Bourdieu & Passeron, 1977). We know in retrospect that the fundamental message of this work as to the indissolubility of Durkheimian form and content was buried under the naive overacceptance in much of the sociology of education of New Directions and its neo-Marxist aftermath and revisionism for much of the next decade. Bernstein (1977) successively elaborated his aperçu concerning the relation between the changing nature of the middle class and the emergence of invisible pedagogy and the wider thesis about the general relation between education and production. King alone among very many who would have loved to produce a definitive rebuttal of the Bernstein *oeuvre* at least did it the credit of believing that it needed to take empirical form. In a series of studies, he took on both the open-closed (1976, 1981) and then the visible-invisible formulations (1978, 1979), and failed both. Tyler (1988, pp. 160-163) argued that with respect to the former, King chose inappropriate simple correlational methods for the difficult task, arguing that his own work (Tyler, 1984), using more appropriate canonical correlational analysis, showed consistently high and significant relations between "structuring" (classification) and "control" (framing). King's not-quite-grounded action theory did little better in infant classrooms, leaving us no clearer on invisibility than before he entered them, though wiser about the fact that "testing" uncongenial ideas is more than a matter of mere method (in his case, always standing up, avoiding eye contact, and writing everything down).

How long is an educational gestation period? There was certainly a long leavening of the education-production thesis into the notions of the educational device and the forms of its realization that were the centerpiece of Bernstein's evolving analysis of pedagogic discourse after 1980 (Bernstein, 1985, 1990a; Bernstein & Diaz, 1984). Throughout this period, there were a series of empirical investigations conducted by his students/colleagues that, at each stage, interacted with the clarification and deepening of "the theory (which), however primitive has always come before the research" (1992a, p. 9). Indeed, he has described the whole 35 years of code theory development as "a journey (often rather bumpy) into the consciousness of the theoretical criteria as regulators of research endeavour" (1992a, p. 7). In Bernstein, it seems to me, nothing is lost over time; everything becomes more complete, more highly ramified around the study of symbolic systems that function as formal and informal pedagogic relays. In this respect, Atkinson (1985) cogently displayed the "oneness" of Bernstein's structuralism to which I have added a brief coda emphasizing its Durkheimian core (Davies, 1994). We have both been able to react to his own systematic reflections on his collected work as it has appeared in *Class, Codes and Control, Volumes* I-V.

In the sense that classrooms stand at the end of complex decisional and biographical (organizational and personal) chains, all his work, whether about family codes and control or about struggles for the control of the pedagogic device, have been germane. At the same time, in order to try to isolate what is directly available from the corpus to students of the classroom and is likely, if taken to the mainstream of classroom studies discourse, to enhance its trajectory, I confine my observations, in some cases very briefly, to the work of Pedro (1981), Domingos (1987, 1989), Tyler (1988), Daniels (1989), Morais, Fontinhas, and Neves (1992), and Singh (1993). They are, indicatively, mainly non-British, with a large number of them coming from places retaining high prestige for nontrivial yet researchable sociology, such as Latin America and Portugal, no doubt to whom some of the central substantive concepts, such as the shocking cross-cultural similarity of the pedagogical device and the lack of "own voice" in educational discourse, resonated with their lived perils of underdevelopment, repression, and revolution. In terms that, for the moment, stay outside of the specialist register that they share, it could be said that they explore the ways in which what differently "shaped" learners get is a question of who they are *qua* class, gender, and ethnicity; how the offering and its character is multiply shaped/determined by macro and meso relations of power and control conceived of as determining "rules" and "criteria"; how the process is one not of making new things but of rejigging things made elsewhere; how these ensure that the process is "run" by forces outside itself, though with its complicity; and how the central feature of that offering relates to access to the means to recognize what is more than or not now which become fully available only to those who are allowed to acquire the means of acquiring the content in ways that go further than, say, Lundgren's (1972) classroom pilots. The empirical "establishment" of these conditions and processes has mainly been through either recent historical "policy" analyses at national and institutional levels or quasi-experimental or observational school/classroom studies. The latter are of particular interest to our theme in the anatomization of pedagogical and pupil types.

Let us begin with Tyler's (1988) work which examined how far Bernstein's code theory can provide a basis for analyzing school organization. Bernstein's structuralism is pictured as a way of overcoming "the dualism between subjectivity and objectivity by locating the subject within a broader field of communicative structure and cultural practice focusing upon 'the forces which determine *performance* rather than *competence*" (pp. 149-150), in which codes are akin to deep structures or *langue* converging with Foucault's (1980) poststructuralism in the analysis of the pedagogic device:

> Both are concerned with the systems of control which produce *discourses*—those fields of practice constituted through the interpretation of knowledge and power. Both Bernstein's and Foucault's methods of analysis therefore deny that the intentions and meanings of the individual subject can be the beginnings of exploration, since the conditions of experience depend on the possibilities which the individual does not himself control (p. 164)

although Bernstein's theory allows "more room for human agents and their interaction to exploit the contradictions in dominant cultural modes . . . because the theory of codes is concerned ultimately with the operation and reproduction of power grounded in class relations and as such is a far more macro-level orientation" (p. 167).

In school structural terms, codes position individuals within a network of power and control, access to understanding which is not "just a matter of style or fashion but of a cognitive access to the possibilities for innovation and control provided within a social structure. . . . Privilege becomes not just inherited money or power but socialisation into access to distinctive kinds of communication" (pp. 150-151). The school comes to occupy a unique position in society in linking power, forms of consciousness, and knowledge "since it promotes the moral, cognitive and communicative principle which underpin its complex social structure" (p. 151).

In seeking a school organizational metaphor to transcend the "bittiness" of existing approaches, and that will answer questions of origins, formation, and change of school structural classificatory systems and relate them to the relevance, closure and sequencing of the generative patterns of interaction in the school, Tyler suggested a reprivileging of the neglected "discursive machinery of the school," including the "silent parameters of discourse" such as classroom shape, lesson length, and bodily arrangements which structure subjectivity and in which pupil interaction requires contexting. Surveillance and self-surveillance bear complex relation to organizational forms of power and control. The recontextualizing discourse of school is particularly vulnerable, having no direct link with distributive power principles. Over their relatively brief history, public educational organizations have moved from factory model/Panopticon to the "shopping mall," through what, in Tyler's view, may prove to have been a period of somewhat illusory teacher autonomy. It follows that issues in the elusive and fragile field of pedagogic discourse in public/state education are easily politicized and "resolved" by those outside the classroom "while the subtle reproductive effects of pedagogic discourse . . . continue to be exercised behind the disciplinary insulation of the fee-paying sector" (p. 193).

He contrasted avowedly rather caricatured pictures of a demoded collection-code school celebrating authority, punctuality and order with the "deritualized" secondary given to "a therapeutic control which depends on the successful management of the pupil's subjectivity" (p. 199), in order to highlight the dilemmas of reconstruction, recognizing that individual schools are fairly impotent to change the inherent problem of alienation. He asserted that most of the recent school-effectiveness work has pointed to "tight ship" individual school or local system "what research shows" strategies for "instructional effectiveness," tightening loose coupling, emphasizing the academic agenda, pitching the principal into curriculum controls, extending workflow integration, attempting participatory decision making and accountability, student and parent participation, and flexibilization of time and content. He saw their reliance on traditional outcomes and increasingly sophisticated, commercially prepared work schemes, no matter how openly displayed, as having the human-relations approach limitation of not reaching questions of deficiencies in underlying structures, positions, and practices. His strictures are well merited if aimed not so much at the pragmatic tinkerers of the school world but those who offer hi-tech solutions out of a bunch of empirical cut corners. It is not given to school improvers to get at the underlying structures, but it is ideological short-sell to define progress merely as a hearts and minds job.

Having outlined the corresponding strengths and limits of cultural pluralist, radical humanist, neoconservative, and new vocationalist strategies, Tyler suggested that loose coupling between school administrative and technical cores may be linked to institutional evolution, that breaking down school/community boundaries may further threaten the autonomy of pedagogic discourse, and that currently dominant market and vocationalist principles offer nihilistic and dangerous agendas. His positive pleas are for Litwakian "mechanisms which 'permit conflict' . . . the socio-technical model of schooling has yet to be developed in such a way that gives priority to the technical core" (p. 218).

Given the dominance of top-down development initiatives, the lack of development in the technologies themselves as well as in colle-

gial forms of control, and the continual pressure of discipline and the
wish to personalize

> the instructional practice will be determined by normative possibility
> rather than technological imperative . . . (whereas) the obvious need is
> for a more sophisticated resistance from the teachers in order to pro-
> tect the academic realm from more plausible judgements that are
> often removed from classroom realities. (pp. 218-219)

He also saw the need for a buffering between them and the
pastoral/counselling system and some sort of remaking of the insulation of teachers from cruder forms of self-interest weakened by the privileging of the vocational and market oriented.

Tyler is attempting here to juxtapose a version of a well-developed organizational line linking technical and organizational power of
the "power to solve a crisis" type in the tradition of Crozier (1964), with
a Bernsteinian definition of the crisis in which an understanding of how
their work is done threatens to see their voice engulfed unless a fragile
autonomy is buffered. I submit that it is proper rather than odd to
spend the space that I have on Tyler's sensitive and rich reading of
Bernstein as a source of organizational (meso)-level inspiration, as a
preface to a focus on more explicitly classroom (micro)-level work.
Understanding the specific form of the instructional apparatus requires
it to be seen in the organizational forms within which it takes place,
just as they must be set within the recontextualizing practice of the discursive field. Neither disembodied teachers nor pupils with "characteristics," nor pedagogical practices or classrooms, nor schools exist or
have meaning except in such relation.

A little-known paper (Bernstein, 1990b), focusing on the relations between democracy and education, reminds us that the distributive principles of the school concern the images they project and the
resources and knowledge made available. In practice, their unequal distribution "will affect the rights of participation, inclusion and individual
enhancement of groups of students" in a way in which "it is highly likely
that the students who do not receive these rights in the school come
from social groups who do not receive these rights in society" (p. 8). It
is a trick that requires more than Bourdieuian "neutrality" in the creation of a "mythical discourse" that generates "horizontal solidarities"
invoking national consciousness and integration and the interdependence of specialized functions, with the school having disconnected its
basic age stratifying principle from the outside and specializing failure
in "inborn," cultural deficit. Although preserving structural relations
between groups, education changes those relations between individuals enough to enhance aspiration, thereby displacing failure away from

class toward national consciousness. Children bring differing discursive rules to school with them (Holland, 1981); middle-class children at 7 already having "a hierarchy of discursive principles such that principles of classification embedded in a shared communal practice and context are *subordinate* to a dominant principle of classification which privileges an indirect relation to a specific, local, material base and is relatively free of such a context" (Bernstein, 1990b, p. 17; emphasis in original).

It is this principle with which school is concerned. Social class (as well as gender, ability, and ethnicity) also acts selectively on how the student is controlled in the classroom. Working with Bernstein, Pedro (1981) established through observation and recording in three primary school classes, chosen by social class composition, that in Portuguese language lessons the lower the social class of pupils "the more the children were subjected to imperative control (that is, commands), the more explicit the hierarchical relations, the less social relations were negotiated, and the more passive pupils were expected to be" (Bernstein, 1990b, p. 19).

In middle-class schools, there was less asymmetry, more explanation, individuality, and reference to context. Class not only acts selectively on control and teachers' decisions about pacing, sequencing, and progression, but, in general, as the pupil becomes older, and more markedly in some systems than others, the curriculum must be worked at outside of school as well as in it. Homes differ insofar as they provide satisfactory pedagogic contexts. There is a tendency in schools with "poor" catchments to abandon normal success expectations and to concentrate disproportionately on weakly paced local skills or for those with "mixed" intakes to "homogenize" teaching groups by estimated ability. Strong pacing rules emphasizing analysis rather than narrative privileges those who have suitable homework sites and whose families socialize them into pacing rules giving access to the analytic nonlinear and its social relations.

Domingos (subsequently Morais) worked with Bernstein, also in Portugal, on a sociological analysis of science underachievement (Domingos, 1987), distinguishing between A (acquisition of knowledge) and U (use of knowledge in new situations) competencies (both required in the official curriculum) and finding that "the greater the conceptual demand of a course and therefore of its level of abstraction, the greater the differential achievement between working class and middle class children" (Domingos, 1989, pp. 351-352). Against that background, a systematic exploration of teacher's pedagogic practice was attempted, recognizing it as a function both of training/background and context. Bernstein (1990b) described this as an opportunity to look at a system with very centrally controlled curriculum and pedagogic programs, enabling the following questions to be put forth: "Is it the case that if you centralise a curriculum you homogenise pedagogic practice? With a central curriculum and detailed plan, do you homogenise the transmission?" (p. 17).

The study design involved 1,300 secondary school pupils and 11 female teachers varied by age and experience in eight schools in big cities and country towns, all comprehensive and with either predominantly working-class or mixed-class populations. It required the establishment of how teachers distinguished A and U competencies in daily pedagogical practices, the weight they gave to them, and their level of U abstraction. Pupils were tested in each of three terms across a year with tests designed by the teachers themselves to maximize the fit between its content and what was actually taught. Over the year, the teachers converged with one another and the researcher's criteria in classifying test questions for A and U competencies, giving some reliability to pupil third-term marks. Nevertheless, the teachers varied in their third-term tests between setting, in effect, no U questions and those demanding a very high level of abstraction, as judged by teachers cross-classifying one another's questions. Teacher Z1, in a working-class country town school had, by this time, improved her ability to distinguish the A and U items of others, but not to produce any of the latter herself, illustrating in extreme fashion the great variation between teachers with respect to U competencies. Even with central control of a common curriculum, this young teacher's working-class pupils "were taught a different science where memory functions were privileged rather than analysis and problem solving" (Bernstein, 1992a, p. 18).

The teachers were also measured for marking consistency, differing greatly on U questions and less on A, with strictness associated with a higher level of conceptual demand in teaching which in its turn related, with notable exceptions, to the social class context of pupils. Whereas it was generally true that young teachers—those teaching in working-class or country schools—were "benevolent," one very strict teacher (having taught mainly in middle-class schools, worked in teacher training, and done research) produced relatively high working-class achievement and even greater relative gain among the pupils, leading Domingos to the view that "pedagogic practice is a crucial variable."

That practice was characterized and ranked in terms of the above and their competence in getting pupils to develop A and U competencies, to which further qualitative assessments were added. Teacher ranking was strongly related both to school context and "common competence" interaction with pupil-level expectations.

Domingos's (1989) plea for teacher awareness of "the sociological context of teaching [prerequisite to being] able to take steps to narrow the gap between . . . groups of children (and) to correct the depressing effect of that context upon the level of conceptual demand and principles of marking" (p. 365) is developed in her study, with others, reported in Morais et al. (1992). In Project ESSA, in ways that resonate with the work of Shayer and his colleagues (Shayer & Adey, 1981, 1991), they pursued improvement in science achievement, developing Bernstein's notion of recognition (C) rules and realization (F) rules, that is to say, the ability to identify A and U questions (for example, "what are renewable energies?" and "why does perspiration give us a feeling of coldness?" respectively).

Eighty students over four classes (age 10 to 12) in one fundamentally working-class school in Lisbon were taught by the same female teacher, who used three pedagogic practices (P1, P2, P3) "carefully defined in terms of spaces, discourses and agents in both the regulative and instructional contexts": P1 was characterized, in general, by weaker classifications and framings; P3, stronger on both; with P2 (which two classes received) like P3 in its strong, explicit framing of evaluation criteria (Morais, Fontinhas, & Neves, 1992, p. 249). The classes were made as similar as possible in terms of gender, ability, and ethnic mix. In practice, analysis of instructional and regulative practices showed them to be more similar than planned, when characterized by two observers in term three, after two previous terms' monitoring. Two tests a term gave measures out of 100 of A and U competencies, divided 60-40. Cognitive development was characterized using Shayer's Piagetian tasks, and social background was classified by parental occupation and educational level. In relation to their established ability, pupils were expected to gain most from P3 and least from P1 experiences in the recognition and production of U texts. A subsample of 30 pupils across the classes was chosen for detailed study.

The findings on achievement show that class is correlated with relatively low recognition and realization scores, and that black children (mainly from the lowest social group) scored worst. P1 seemed to favor most of its girls (4 out of 5) on both recognition and realization. That apart, given that P3 appeared to have "converged" in essential respects with P2, the latter's mix of relatively strong framing in the explication of A and U contexts coupled with weak framing of conduct and group relations within class was generally effective and more effective for disadvantaged groups. The researchers emphasized that virtually all students were incapable of producing a free correct U answer "having only passive rather than active realisation competence" (Morais et al., p. 267), with mean U achievements being very low. They were aware that the disadvantaged might be further disadvantaged by measures of how they can (or cannot) transact academic-nonacademic boundaries in a system that strongly classifies the two. However, they were equally aware that effective change requires clarity about differential acquisition and work on its conditions and possibilities if school knowledge is to be distributed more equitably, particularly among those whose home pedagogical practices did not provide them with "an elaborated orientation, and sensitivity to the pedagogic code of the school," as was the case with relatively high-scoring, low-class Z36 (Morais et al., 1992, p. 264).

Daniels (1989) also studied pupils' recognition and realization rules in relation to discursive, organizational, and interactional practices in British Special Educational Provision for children with Moderate Learning Difficulties whose "population . . . contains many children who have peers in mainstream school with very similar academic profiles" (p. 124). He compared two schools (CH and TC) with very different classification and framing values; the first highly structured with little choice over learning, the other tending to have a broad, integrated thematic approach, roughly approximating Bernsteinian "collection" and "integration" respectively, subjecting his detailed accounts to both classroom teacher and head teacher triangulation in both schools. The teaching of art was used to illustrate the rules children were expected to acquire, roughly corresponding to reproductive and productive aesthetic codes, respectively. In CH, art was about results— good productions—rather than experiencing materials. In TC, children were encouraged to experiment with a variety of materials. He used teacher displays of visual materials—the arranged artwork of the children—to infer and illustrate coding practices that, in terms of theories of curriculum sequencing, celebrated Gagné (1985) and Bruner (1986), respectively. In interviews, three groups of three children (aged 9-12) from both schools were asked to group photographs of the artwork, which they were told came from two schools:

> This they all did correctly, that is they grouped the photographs on the basis of the school of origin. The groups were then shown photographs in groups of three and asked to say what was the same about the two photographs from the one school and different about the photographs from the other school. (p. 133)

Their responses were presented and analyzed in terms of construct theory, "corrupted" so as "only to provide general indicators of group perceptions" (p. 133).

Constructs related to items such as how they were made, what was in them, what they were about, and so on. Daniels suggested that "In summary, all the children appear to be able to read many signs from these displays. Children in a structured school (CH) were concerned with individual identity in relation to performance whereas in the other school (TC) the children emphasised principles of social relation" (p. 137). Teachers were surprised both at the extent to which their displays emitted such non-neutral signs and the extent to which children could read them. Although conceding possible methodological limitations, Daniels claimed that his measures of discursive, organizational, and interactional practices revealed connection "between the rules the children used to make sense of their pedagogic world and the modality of that world" (p. 139).

Specifically, in CH, "the dominating discourse appears to be that of instruction, whereas instructional discourse in TC is so deeply embedded in regulative discourse that aspects of this discourse appear to predominate in children's views of school practice" (p. 139). He saw this finding as relevant not only for children in special schools, but for pedagogic practice in general.

Singh (1993) reported a further study of pedagogic communication, set in four affluent socioeconomic Australian schools, officially judged "as exemplary in the area of computer pedagogics" (p 40). Six classes were studied over six months; students were interviewed and their interactions in relation to computers were recorded. A year-5 classroom in Murwin Primary was reported with particular respect to the relation between gender and the construction of technical competence. Its teacher was experienced, well qualified, and committed to gender equity. The four girls focused on regarded themselves as computer competent, and all of them, like most of the seven boys, had learned it at home. The boys monopolized computer use; two in particular achieving "a position in the pedagogic practice of classroom computing to exercise power/control over knowledge relations," withholding software information, challenging "the teacher's authority and power to know," in effect, becoming an interest group struggling to control the pedagogic device that structured "the production and reproduction of 'legitimate' or 'thinkable' school knowledge," as experts on software that the teacher distributed to them with "little knowledge of the internal structure of the texts" (p. 42). By extra practice, cheating, and hacking, they became, in effect, "teachers" from whom their teacher learned. The seven boys were far from homogeneous in relation to computer skills or knowledge and their definitions as a group of "experts;" each one was positioned by the regulative discourse collectively produced and sustained or naturalized by the teacher who could "do nothing" about their physically tinged monopoly. The pedagogic relay of the key package through which they exercised their hegemony reinforced patriarchy. The package "voice" was male, further contributing to "the silencing of girls and the fictionalised construction of inherent male superiority in computing |supported| through institutional time which recorded the past and present pacing of males through the game programme" (p. 46).

By not only giving three of the boys "knowledge producer" status, but sanctifying it as "gee whiz" natural, the teacher "recontextualised the girls' computer competence and positioned them within the visible pedagogic code of domestics denied . . . opportunities of solving computer-based problems" (p. 54). This did not mean that the girls were silenced; some, at least, saw the fiction, were able to deconstruct the relations that pinioned them, although they were unable to alter them. Indeed, Singh concluded "alternative narratives of the feminine," a "discourse of empowerment will need to incorporate an analysis of the inner voice," which "penetrates the unconscious" (p. 56).

Without such an analysis of the power relations of schooling that includes "the production, fixing and canalisation of desire, . . . a girl . . . must negotiate positions within discourses of the other" (pp. 56-57). Singh specifically juxtaposed Bernstein's ideas with those of Walkerdine (1990), whose fit betokens complex mutual sharing of subtextual influences from Lacan (1977) and Foucault.

Although I have concentrated on a selection of those in "direct line" to Bernstein—all people who have worked with him directly as students or extensively as colleagues—there have also been those outside who have picked up the oeuvre and run. To trace them adequately would be the task of another chapter. I offer one example, which is full of interest as an analysis of the curricular/pedagogic discourse level, if not classroom level, from Physical Education (PE). It is hardly surprising that aspects of Bernstein's theory have been attractive to PE specialists. The notion of "ritual" has been applied to public school sport in Britain by Mangan (1981) and U.S. high schools by Rees (1992). Rather, more interestingly, the notion of pedagogic discourse has been applied to Physical Education in Australia by Kirk and Colquhoun (1989), particularly exploring the notion of the embeddedness of instruction within regulative discourse, and Evans (1990), who analyzed the development of changes in games and moves to Health Related Fitness in School PE curricula in Britain, subsequently developed into a gripping account of the struggle for control of the pedagogic device enacted around the development of the National Curriculum in PE (Evans, 1990; Evans & Penny, in press). None of these are "classroom studies," although empirical work at this level is in progress and is to be more than usually eagerly anticipated in a field in which measurement has for too long been substituted for relevance.

What then, in brief, can one expect for the moment from Bernstein on classrooms? At the very least, it must be the wisdom to abjure quick-fix perspectives and to draw into a multilevel theoretical corpus the promising although partial. From the latter point of view, for example, consider the possibilities of Alton-Lee, Nuthall, and Patrick (1993) and what the marvelous detail of their work on children's actual classroom experiences and meanings would amount to, tied to a more substantial view of the pedagogic device. It might also restore some balance to the perennial U.S. debate (and although we all have classrooms, it certainly dominates the trade in talk about them) that oscillates between turning the whole world into a set of achievable, measurable competencies and the "good teacherism" exemplified by Labaree (1992), in which any technical gain becomes a rationalization of classroom instruction and is to be feared as a democratic threat, "professional barriers to public influence over classroom instruction" (p. 149).

There is a huge agenda to be pursued in terms of delineating the nature and limits of pedagogic practice across cultures and organizations. In doing this, Bernstein is offering a theoretical corpus within which we can locate instructional learning and interactive practices tied to sociopolitical, organizational, cultural, and everyday levels of determination and influence. He and his students have also shown how to begin to go about it. This is an extraordinary achievement in a field in which, across diverse disciplines, theory and description have too often failed to meet. Most of us, not least Bernstein, are in the improvement, if not transformation, "biz." It is a complex scene. There is plenty of scope for the impression managers, epic directors, method actors, fantasists, horror producers, radical companies, mime artists, and scene shifters. My favorite passages in the plot relate to the social, cultural, political, moral, and practical importances of the local/universal distinction, one of the most fundamental aspects of the vision, and the struggle to relate it to modifiable pedagogical practices that can make a difference to one who inhabits whatever side of this divide. That is the story of my life—determinations that may be changed. Whatever your bag—and there are lots more—what helps most is a good intellectual agent who pays you in deepened understanding of how to go on every time you ring up. Such is the character of the opportunities offered by the long-established, still-evolving, Bernstein service.

REFERENCES

Alton-Lee, A., Nuthall, G., & Patrick, J. (1993). Reframing classroom research: A lesson from the private world of children. *Harvard Educational Review*, 63(1), 51-84.

Apple, M.W. (1992). Education, culture and class power: Basil Bernstein and the neo-Marxist sociology of education. *Educational Theory*, 42(2), 127-146.

Atkinson, P. (1985). *Language, structure and reproduction*. London: Methuen.

Bennett, N. (1987). Changing perspectives on teaching-learning processes in the post-Plowden Era. *Oxford Review of Education*, 13(1), 67-79.

Bennett, N., Desforges, C., Cockburn, A., & Wilkinson, B. (1984). *The quality of pupil learning experiences*. London: Erlbaum.

Bernstein, B. (1966). Sources of consensus and disaffection in education. *Journal of Assistant Mistresses*, 17(1), 4-11.

Bernstein, B. (1967, September 14). Open schools, open society? *New Society*, pp. 351-353.

Bernstein, B. (1971a). On the classification and framing of educational knowledge. In M.F.D. Young (Ed.), *Knowledge and control* (pp. 47-69). London: Collier Macmillan.

Bernstein, B. (1971b). *Class, codes and control* (Vol. 1). London: Routledge & Kegan Paul.

Bernstein, B. (Ed.). (1973). *Class, codes and control* (Vol. 2). London: Routledge & Kegan Paul.

Bernstein, B. (1975). *Class, codes and control* (Vol. 3). London: Routledge & Kegan Paul.

Bernstein, B. (1977). *Class, codes and control* (Vol. 3, rev. ed.). London: Routledge & Kegan Paul.

Bernstein, B. (1985). On pedagogic discourse. In J. Richardson (Ed.), *Handbook of theory and research in the sociology of education* (pp. 206-240). Westport, CT: Greenwood Press.

Bernstein, B. (1990a). *Class, codes and control* (Vol. 4). London: Routledge & Kegan Paul.

Bernstein, B. (1990b). *Democracy, cultures and education* |Mimeo|. Paper to UNESCO. (Also published as "Educacion y Democracia: Algunos commentarios. In *Poder Educacion y conciencia: Sociologia de la transmission cultural*. Barcelona, Spain: El Roure Editorial SA.)

Bernstein, B. (1992a). *Code theory and research* (Vol. 5) |Mimeo| (Published in 1993 as *Code Theory and Research for the Sociology of Education*. Barcelona, Spain: El Roure.)

Bernstein, B. (1992b). *Educational reforms and pedagogic identities*. Unpublished paper to Ministry of Education, Santiago Conference.

Bernstein, B., Elvin, H.L., & Peters, R.S. (1966). Ritual in education. *Philosophical Transactions of the Royal Society of London*, Series B, 251, 772.

Bernstein, B., & Diaz, M. (1984). Towards a theory of pedagogic discourse. *Collected Original Reports in Education*, 8(3).

Bourdieu, P., & Passeron, J.P. (1977). *Reproduction in education, society and culture*. Beverly Hills: CA Sage.

Bruner, J.S. (1986). *Actual minds, possible worlds.* Cambridge, MA: Harvard University Press.

Cazden, C. (1988). *Classroom discourse. The language of teaching and learning.* Portsmouth, NH: Heinemann.

Cox-Danoso, C. (1986). Continuity, conflict and change in state education in Chile. *Collected Original Reports in Education,* 10, 2.

Crozier, M. (1964). *The bureaucratic phenomenon.* London: Tavistock.

Daniels, H. (1988). An enquiry into different forms of special school organisation. Pedagogic practice and pupil discrimination. CORE, 12, 2.

Daniels, H. (1989). Visual displays as tacit relays of the structure of pedagogic practice. *British Journal of Sociology of Education,* 10(2), 123-140.

Davies, B. (1992). Social class, school effectiveness and school diversity. In J. Lynch, C. Mogdil, & S. Mogdil (Eds.), *Cultural diversity and the schools* (Vol 3, pp. 131-147). London: Falmer Press.

Davies, B. (1994). Durkheim and the sociology of education in Britain. *British Journal of Sociology of Education,* 15(1), 3-25.

Diaz, M. (1984). *A model of pedagogic discourse with special application to Columbia: Primary level.* Unpublished doctoral thesis. Universtiy of London.

Domingos, A.M. (1987). *Social class, pedagogic practice and achievement in science: A study of secondary schools in Portugal.* (Collected original resources in education.) *Collected Original Reports in Education,* 11, 2.

Domingos, A.M. (1989). Influence of the social context of the school on the teacher's pedagogic practice. *British Journal of Sociology of Education,* 10(3), 351-366.

Evans, J. (1990). Defining a subject: The rise and rise of the new PE. *British Journal of Sociology of Education,* 11(2), 155-169.

Evans, J., & Penny, D. (in press). The politics of pedagogy: Making a national curriculum in PE. *Journal of Educational Policy.*

Fang, D.-L. (1992). *A study of pedagogical processes and interaction in the primary classroom.* Unpublished doctoral thesis, University of Wales, Cardiff.

Flanders, N.A. (1970). *Analyzing teacher behaviour.* Reading, MA: Addison-Wesley.

Foucault, M. (1980). *Power/knowledge: Selected interviews and other writings, 1972-1977* (C. Gordon, ed.). New York: Pantheon/Brighton, Harvester.

Gagnè, R.M. (1985). *The conditions of learning and theory of instruction.* Newport, RI: Holt, Rinehart & Winston.

Holland, J. (1981). Social class and changes in the orientation of meanings. *Sociology,* 15(1), 1-18.

Jenkins, C. (1990). The professional middle class and the origins of progressivism. *Collected Original Reports in Education,* 14, 1.

Kilgore, S.B., & Pendleton, W.W. (1993). The organisational context of learning: Framework for understanding the acquisition of knowledge. *Sociology of Education, 66*, 63-87.

King, R.A. (1969). *Values and involvement in a grammar school.* London: Routledge & Kegan Paul.

King, R.A. (1976). Bernstein's sociology of the school: Some propositions tested. *British Journal of Sociology, 27*, 430-443.

King, R.A. (1978). *All things bright and beautiful? A sociological study of infants' classrooms.* London: Wiley.

King, R.A. (1979). The search for the "invisible" pedagogy. *Sociology, 13*, 445-458.

King, R.A. (1981). Bernstein's sociology of the school—a further testing. *British Journal of Sociology, 32*, 259-265.

Kirk, D., & Colquhoun, D. (1990). Healthism and Physical Education. *British Journal of Sociology of Education, 10*(4), 417-435.

Labaree, D. (1992), Power, knowledge and the rationalisation of teaching: A genealogy of the movement to professionalise teaching. *Harvard Educational Review, 62*(2), 123-154.

Lacan, J. (1977). *Écrits: a selection.* London: Tavistock.

Lundgren, U.P. (1972). *Frame factors and the teaching process: A contribution to curriculum theory and the theory of teaching.* Stockholm: Almqvist and Wiksell.

Mangan, J.A. (1981). *Athleticism in the Victorian and Edwardian public school.* Cambridge, UK: Cambridge University Press.

Morais, A., Fontinhas, F., & Neves, I. (1992). Recognition and realisation rules in acquiring school science—the contribution of pedagogy and social background of students. *British Journal of Sociology of Education, 13*(2), 247-270.

Pedro, E.R. (1981). *Social stratification and classroom discourse: A sociolinguistic analysis of classroom practice.* Lund: Liber Laromedal.

Pollard, A. (1985). *The social world of the primary school.* London: Holt, Rinehart & Winston

Pollard, A. (1987). Introduction: New perspectives on children. In A Pollard (Ed.), *Children and their primary schools* (pp. 1-11). London: Falmer Press.

Pollard, A. (1990). Toward a sociology of learning in primary schools. *British Journal of Sociology of Education, 11*(2), 241-256.

Rees, C.R. (1992). What price victory? Myths, rituals, athletics and the dilemma of schooling. In T. Williams, L. Almond, & A. Sparkes (Eds.), *Sport and physical activity: Moving towards excellence* (pp. 74-84). London: E & F N Spong.

Sadovnik, A.R. (1991). Basil Bernstein's theory of pedagogic practice: A structuralist approach. *Sociology of Education, 64*, 48-63.

Shayer, M., & Adey, P. (1981). *Towards a science of science teaching—Cognitive development and curriculum demand.* London: Heinemann.

Shayer, M., & Adey, P. (1991). Accelerating the development of formal thinking in middle and high schools students II: Post project effects. *Journal Research in Science Teaching,* 28.

Shulman, L.S. (1989). Knowledge and teaching foundations of the new reform. *Harvard Educational Review,* 57(1), 1-22.

Shulman, L.S. (1991). Introduction: Ways of seeing, ways of knowing; ways of teaching, ways of learning about teaching. *Journal of Curriculum Studies,* 23(5), 393-395.

Simon, B. (1985). Why no pedagogy in England. In B. Simon (Ed.), *Does education matter?* (pp. 77-105). London: Lawrence & Wishart.

Singh, P.L. (1993). Institutional discourse and practice: A case study of the social construction of technological competence in the primary classroom. *British Journal of Sociology of Education,* 14(1), 39-58.

Tyler, W. (1984). *Organisations, factors and codes: A methodological enquiry into Bernstein's theory of educational transmissions.* Unpublished doctoral thesis, University of Kent at Canterbury.

Tyler, W. (1988). *School organisation: A sociological perspective.* London: Croom Helm.

Vygotsky, L.S. (1987). *The collected works of S. Vygotsky, Vol. 1: Problems of general psychology,* (R.W. Richer & A.S. Carton, eds.). New York: Plenum Press.

Walkerdine, V. (1990). *Schoolgirl fictions.* London: Verso.

Westerhof, K.J. (1992). On the effectiveness of teaching: Direct versus indirect instruction. *School Effectiveness and school Improvement,* 3(3) 204-215.

Wragg, E., Bennett, N., & Carre, C. (1989). Primary teachers and the National Curriculum. *Research Papers in Education,* 4(3), 17-45.

8

Visible and Invisible Pedagogies in Literacy Education*

Courtney B. Cazden
Harvard University

Prominent educational discourse in the United States argues that changes in the economy demand deeper understanding of knowledge, greater flexibility of skills, and more interpersonal competencies for all students than even many of the elite achieved in the past. When we remember Bernstein's (1975) statement that "the weak classification and frames of the invisible pedagogy emphasize the importance of *ways* of knowing, of constructing problems" (p. 134; emphasis in the original), it is not surprising that contemporary statements of educational reform goals often echo tenets of progressive education of an earlier era.

The following are two examples: one from policy makers, the other from a school principal. First, from a report commissioned by the Carnegie Forum on Education and the Economy (1986), A *Nation Prepared: Teachers for the 21st Century.* The introduction to this report, titled "A time for ferment," describes the "ferment":

> Much of our system of elementary and secondary education evolved in the context of an economy based on mass production. It emphasized development of the routinized skills necessary for routinized work.

*Support from the Spencer Foundation for travel and research is gratefully acknowledged.

These are skills that are now called "basic," [such as] the fundamentals of composition and the reading of straightforward texts.

The skills needed now are not routine. Our economy will be increasingly dependent on people who have a good intuitive grasp of the ways in which all kinds of physical and social systems work. The must possess a feeling for mathematical concepts and the ways in which they can be applied to difficult problems, an ability to see patterns of meaning where others see only confusions, a cultivated creativity that leads them to new problems and new services.

Such people will have the need and the ability to learn all the time, as the knowledge required to do their work twists and turns with new challenges and the progress of science and technology. They will, of course, have to have facts and how-how to carry out basic procedures, but it will be essential for them to understand how those facts are derived and why those procedures work. They will spend a lifetime deciding which facts are relevant and which procedures will work for a constantly changing array of problems.

We are describing people who have the tools they need to think for themselves, people who can act independently, and with others, who can render critical judgment and contribute constructively to many enterprises, whose knowledge is wide-ranging and whose understanding runs deep. (shortened from pp. 15, 20)

The second statement is by Deborah Meier, a secondary school principal and director of a coalition of small, innovative public secondary schools in inner-city New York, winner of one of the prestigious MacArthur Foundation "genius" awards and, since then, arguably the most visible school principal in the United States:

It is not hyperbole to say that today's school reform debate is critical to our national destiny. The challenge is a thrilling one: to make every child the possessor of a kind of intellectual competence once available to only a small minority. This inspiring—and new—task means granting all young citizens the conviction that they can have wonderful ideas, invent theories, analyze evidence and make their personal mark on this most complex world. Such a transformation of the idea of why children go to school would in turn transform the American workplace, as well as the very nature of American life. (Meier, 1992, p. 271)

Both of these statements come from the United States, but they express one view of the challenge facing many industrialized countries because of new relationships between the economy and education. Whether the economic analysis on which this view is based is valid or not, I agree with Meier that the vision of education is worth working for. Even if the analysis turns out to be wrong and the promised jobs are not available, students so educated should be better prepared as citizens for critique and collective action.[1]

At the same time as neoprogressive educational environments are being advocated, a few voices in the United States are raising questions about the power of such environments, with their invisible pedagogies, to achieve the promised goals with all students. In discussions of the English/Language Arts curriculum, one influential critic is Lisa Delpit, an African-American educator (and also a MacArthur fellow). In two widely cited articles in the *Harvard Educational Review* in 1986 and 1988, Delpit calls for more explicit teaching, more "visible pedagogy" in Bernstein's terms, of the "discourses of power."

In the final chapter of a new book on teaching in multicultural classrooms, Delpit further explains her concerns. Here she takes issue with what she considers "a dangerous kind of determinism" in recent writings of James Gee (1989, 1990), a sociolinguist whose writings she (and I) otherwise admire. Delpit (1993) writes:

> There are two aspects of Gee's arguments which I find problemaic. First is Gee's notion that people who have not been born into dominant Discourses will find it exceedingly difficult, if not impossible, to acquire such a Discourse. He argues strongly that Discourses cannot be "overtly" taught, particularly in a classroom, but can only be acquired by enculturation in the home or by "apprenticeship" into social practices.

> The second aspect of Gee's work that I find troubling suggests that an individual who is born into one Discourse with one set of values may experience major conflicts when attempting to acquire another Discourse with another set of values . . .

> Despite the difficulty entailed in the process, almost any African American or other disenfranchised individual who has become "successful" has done so by acquiring a Discourse other than the one into

---

[1]Bernstein (1990) contrasts two forms of visible pedagogy: "visible pedagogies justified by intrinsic possibilities of knowledge itself and visible pedagogies justified by their market relevance" (p. 86). From the statements quoted here as well as from other information about Meier's schools and the Carnegie Forum's recommendations (see especially the latter's imaginary scenario of what "schools for the twenty-first century might be like" [pp. 45-46, reprinted in Cazden, 1992, pp. 163-164]), Meier and Carnegie can be contrasted as more autonomous versus more market-oriented pedagogies, whatever their visible/invisible mix.

In a historical analysis of reform in the state educational system in Chile done under Bernstein's guidance, Cox (1984) describes the changes introduced by the Christian Democrats in 1964-1970 (pre-Allende) as reducing the separation between transmission of facts and transmission of principles and suggests that this was seen as "producing more flexible workers under conditions of rapid technological change" (pp. 236-237).

which he or she was born. And almost all can attribute that acquisition
to what happened as a result of the work of one or more committed
teachers. (pp. 286, 290)

If we believe both Meier and Delpit, then teaching that enables such
acquisition entails resolving the dilemma about how to achieve flexible
competencies from explicit teaching.

This dilemma can be set forth in the terms of Bernstein's analysis of visible and invisible pedagogies (1975, Chap. 6; 1990, Chap. 2).
Such recasting both generalizes the problem beyond its United States
particulars and may help to explain why resolution, although worth
struggling for, seems so hard to achieve.

According to Bernstein (1975), invisible pedagogy, characterized by weak classification and framing, was institutionalized in the
British infant schools by, and for, the "new middle class." This is the
class whose members "are filling the ever-expanding major and minor
professional class, concerned with the servicing of persons" (p. 136).
For members of this class, socialization at home and in such schools

> leads to ambiguous personal identity and flexible role performances. . . .
> [T]hey stand for variety against inflexibility, expression against repres-
> sion, the inter-personal against the inter-positional. . . . [A]lthough prop-
> erty in the physical sense remains crucial, it has been partly psycholo-
> gized and appears in the form of ownership of valued skills made avail-
> able in educational institutions. (pp. 122-123).

In Tuman's (1988) rephrasing of Bernstein's analysis,

> [I]t is even possible to define professional class socialization as motivat-
> ed by the parents' desire to reproduce in the child, not their specific
> practices, but the same flexibility and openness in tackling new tasks
> that so often lie at the basis on their economic success. 1988, (pp. 48-49)

I believe that achieving such "flexibility and openness" by students not already socialized at home with the cultural capital that
enables them to infer the required underlying principles and strategies
will only happen in environments with some yet-to-be theorized mix of
invisible and visible pedagogy. In this chapter I describe aspects of four
very different programs that constitute in each case what I call a mixture of invisible and visible pedagogy: two individual schools—
Cambridge Friends School and one I call Bay Area Middle School—and
two multisite programs—Reading Recovery and Puente. All four began
with a concern for low-achieving students, including (or, in Bay Area
Middle School and Puente, especially) students from ethnic minorities;

all four are considered "successful" innovations for those students. At the end, I connect these descriptions back to Bernstein.

FOUR PROGRAMS

My knowledge is not equal in the four cases. Cambridge Friends School I have known by local reputation over the years, but I have not yet seen its classrooms in action, and my description comes only from the writings of members of its faculty. Bay Area Middle School I first learned of from a national study of relationships between school restructuring and changes in modes of teaching and learning. I spent two days in the school visiting classes and talking with teachers, especially about the teaching of writing. Reading Recovery I have seen both in action and on videotapes, and I have talked with Reading Recovery teachers in all four countries where it is now operating. There is also an extensive published literature about the program's ways of teaching and its achievement outcomes. Puente I have not visited, and publicly available documentation is only about its outcomes, not its processes. My description comes from conference presentations by Puente teachers, one videotape, and several conversations with its leadership.

Cambridge Friends School

Cambridge Friends School (CFS) is an independent primary school established some 30 years ago "under the care of" (in Quaker discourse) the local Friends Meeting. In many publicly acknowledged ways, its curriculum and teaching embody features of invisible pedagogy. The uniqueness of each child is affirmed as an expression of Quaker belief in "that of God in every person." Children are grouped into combined grades (1-2, 3-4, etc.), so that age expectations are lessened. Multidisciplinary themes are common in the curriculum—for example, one group studies wool and weaving in different parts of the world (Mizell, Bennett, Bowman, & Morin, 1993). A weak boundary between home and school is evidenced by the experiment a few years ago to allow four teachers all pregnant at the same time to bring their infants into their classrooms for the first four motnhs. After subsequent reflection and evaluation, the practice of welcoming babies at school was not continued, but the fact that it could be seriously tried says much about the family "feel" of the school.

One-quarter of the students are "children of color," and African-American staff and parents became increasingly aware that although the school was a fine school, "it was not as fine for some students as for others" (Greeley & Mizell, 1993, p. 221). The head of the school (white) and the admissions director (African American) describe the school's ongoing struggle to "achieve our goal of a multicultural, anti-racist, anti-homophobic community" (Mission Statement, 8/91):

> From its inception 30 years ago, CFS has always considered itself a non-racist, multicultural community. After all, peaceful conflict resolution, respect for individual differences, and concern for social and racial justice are fundamental to Quakerism. What was different in 1988, following the workshop experience [a series of intensive three-day racism awareness workshops], was a new-found commitment to becoming an anti-racist school, to not only confront overt racism within the CFS community, but to also begin changing the structures which make racism silent, invisible, and inevitable. (Johnson & Mizell, 1992, p. 3)

The focus of these efforts has been on changing structures in the school, not on changing the children. "As Enid Lee [an Afro-Caribbean consultant] has said so clearly, we must stop asking what we can do to build the self-esteem of children of color, and instead ask ourselves what we do that erodes their self-esteem" (Mizell et al., 1993, p. 42).

Many of the changes have brought previously unheard voices into the curriculum and encouraged children's questioning of standard materials: "'Look Laraine,' they say, with a mix of indignation and anger, 'there are 12 pages of maps devoted to the United States, and 4 to tiny little Australia, but only 2 to Africa. Only 2 maps for that whole big giant continent! Why?'" (Mizell et al., 1993, p. 43).

Other changes have introduced more visible pedagogy. For example, the learning specialist in the school introduced explicit teaching of graphic organizers (such as webbing) into the writing program (Mizell et al., 1993). And less directly related to literacy, a kindergarten teacher reports a number of changes in her classroom that were all in the direction of what she called "more structure":

- a new physical layout in the classroom [with] five "private desks" as alternative work spaces to the former group/table setting
- a new approach to choice time, with a different activity each week that each child was expected to do at least once
- clearer expectations for listening during meeting times, including calling on children who had not volunteered

The teacher herself expressed the hybrid quality of her changed classroom:

It is interesting that as we move toward a classroom that truly values
diversity among the students, we also move toward a classroom that is
more structured and offers less freedom of choice in some ways than our
classroom has before. Paradoxically, in becoming more teacher-directed,
we are also becoming more child-centered. (Fiveash, 1992, pp. 13-14)

Bay Area Middle School

Bay Area Middle School is a public school for grades 6-8 with an ethnically diverse study body and teaching staff. Two events in its history
have influenced much of the school's present character: first (both
chronologically and in importance), a court-ordered plan for resolving
the complaints (upheld by the U.S. Supreme Court) that students in the
school district who came to school not speaking English were denied
equal educational opportunities: and second, a more recent restructuring of the school's governance and its internal organization.

Several all-school structures apparent in my 2-day visit are
examples of weak classifications that one would expect to co-exist with
other features of invisible pedagogy:

- Members of the teaching staff carry out many functions usually reserved for the school principal, such as presiding at
  meetings of the faculty governing council (on a rotating
  basis) and preparing and presenting a spreadsheet of the
  school budget complete with options for faculty decision. (In
  fact, another first-time visitor at the same council meeting
  told me later than he did not even know who the principal
  was until almost the end of the meeting.)
- Curriculum planning is done by each team of four teachers
  (social studies, English, math, and science) who together
  have responsibility for 100 students—teachers and students
  together are called a "family." The teachers work had at three
  kinds of coordination across subject areas—in themes such
  as the ocean in science and social studies, in skills such as
  writing problem-solution compositions about both personal
  issues in English and public matters in social studies and science; and in resources needed for individually chosen interdisciplinary "challenge" projects.
- The school schedule is composed of 50-minute periods. But
  no bell rings, and each team can arrange its weekly schedule
  in fewer longer or more shorter class times, as it sees fit, subject only to coordinating the use of schoolwide facilities such

as the computer lab with other teams.

- In all three grades, students are grouped heterogeneously by ability as well as ethnicity to avoid streaming and ensure greater equity in curriculum and teaching.

But there are also striking features of visible pedagogy, especially with respect to criteria for students' expected work. For example, all the students in each class are often working on the same writing assignment—a problem-solution letter the day I was visiting. Therefore, the teacher's guidelines written out on the board for peer-response groups—in this case, pairs, could be specific to this genre:

> "Did the writer remind the person what the problem is, and about the history of the problem?
>
> Is it clear why the problem exists?
>
> Are 2-3 possible solutions presented in the letter? . . ."

These explicit guidelines contrast markedly with the more all-purpose guidelines that are often advocated in professional books on the teaching of writing—

> "Tell the author what you liked best about the piece, and where you'd like to know more . . ."—

and that fit a classroom where at any one time students are working on different individually chosen genres on individually chosen topics.

Bay Area Middle School has an outstanding reputation, both locally and among national research groups studying successful schools. But its combination of a single curriculum for a very heterogeneous student body must produce a need for what Bernstein calls "a repair system (1990, p. 74) to help some students catch up. I do not know what form such repair efforts take at Bay Area Middle School. But that is exactly what the next two programs are designed to do.

Reading Recovery

Reading Recovery is a multisite program for initial literacy now operating in four countries. It was designed in New Zealand, where primary education throughout the country's single educational system has been consistently "progressive" for some decades.[2] Because of its demon-

---

[2]Jenkins's (1989) analysis of the class origins of leaders of the progressive education movement lists in Appendix 1 the members of the New Educational Fellowship

strated success, it has been imported into Australia, the United States, and England in that order. It is a carefully designed and implemented intervention for 6-year-old children who have not caught on to reading and writing after a year in school. Although "remedial" in Bernstein's sense, it is called an "accelerated" program by its leaders because "catching up" requires faster than normal progress.

Daily individual half-hour lessons are given to children in the lowest achieving 10%-20% in any one school. Selection of children for this help always starts from the lowest achievers, with the final percentage receiving Reading Recovery help depending on the availability of trained teachers. Any one child remains in the program only until a carefully specified criterion of independent reading is achieved, usually 15-20 weeks. Reading Recovery is thus a temporary repair system for those who need it.

Careful records and statistical analyses in all four countries show that, with such help, all but 1% or 2% of the entire age cohort is then able to keep up with the average reading and writing work of their grade without further special assistance, at least for the three years for which longitudinal records have been kept (see Office for Standards in Education, 1993, for one policy report).

Despite its demonstrated success, however, Reading Recovery continues to be controversial. In part, under tight budget conditions in all four countries, its very success creates unhappy competitors who advocate alternatives but have a harder time receiving funding for them. More relevant here, some of the controversy is conceptual.

Part of the controversy is about purpose. The designer, New Zealander developmental psychologist Marie Clay, acknowledged the expectation built into even New Zealand's progressive school curriculum that children should learn to read and write by the end of their first year of school and set out to prevent children who could not keep up with that pace from falling further and further behind. Teaching in Reading Recovery is individualized to build on the particular strengths of each child and personalized in that the writing segment of each daily lesson consists of teachers and child together transcribing a sentence that the child has composed. But there are clear standards that the children must meet before they will be "discontinued." Purer progressive educators are unhappy that children are not left in their classrooms to progress at what they consider the children's own pace, and

---

from 1920-1950. Professional identifications are given for almost the entire list. One listed but not identified is "C.E. Beeby." He was Director General of Education in New Zealand for 20 years in the 1940-1950s and is generally credited with changing primary education in New Zealand from a traditional British to a more Deweyian model. In his introductory essay in Renwick (1986), Beeby describes a New Educational Fellowship Conference held in New Zealand in 1937.

they also find the pace of teaching within the Reading Recovery lessons too fast and intense.

Part of the controversy is about teaching methods. Reading Recovery cannot be easily classified as either progressive education or basic skills ("whole language" or "phonics" in current U.S. terms). Clay and Cazden (1990) explain why:

> It differs from most whole language programs in recognizing the need for temporary instructional detours in which the child's attention is called to particular cues available in speech or print. It differs from phonics in conceptualizing phonological awareness as an outcome of reading and writing rather than as their prerequisite, and in developing children's awareness of sounds in oral language rather than teaching letter-sound relationships. It differs from both in the frequent observation and recording of the reading and writing repertoire of the individual child as the basis of teacher initiative (as in choosing the next book) and response (in moment-to-moment decisions about when, and how, to help). (1990, pp. 129-130)

Basic skills advocates want to prescribe a more standardized sequence of component skills.

Puente

Like Reading Recovery, Puente is a temporary structure for repair that its designers call an "accelerated" program because it too was established to help students "catch up." The students are Mexican-American high school graduates attending 2-year California community colleges who need help if they are to transfer successfully to 4-year colleges and receive a degree. Although such transfer is what community colleges are supposed to make possible, the transfer rate for Mexican-American students was extremely low. Puente—Spanish for "bridge"—was designed for them, and has been dramatically successful in raising the transfer rate at 27 community colleges from 2% to over 40%.

Puente is a two-semester course in college English. In the daily classes, students receive intensive academic reading and writing, counseling and mentoring. It is co-taught by an English teacher of any ethnicity and a Hispanic counselor. Both work to "bridge the gulf between the predominantly Anglo culture of the community college and the Mexican American/Latino culture of much of the surrounding community" (Healy, 1990, p. 40). The teacher creates a textual bridge with literature—fiction, poetry, and essays—by Hispanic authors; the counselor creates a human bridge by connecting each student with a community mentor. Together, teacher and counselor construct the classroom as a supportive "family."

Academically, the two semesters are spent on writing. In the first semester, students write about their own lives, the literature they read, and their mentors; in the second semester they learn to write the kind of research papers expected in college. Thus the program helps the students expand their discourse repertoire beyond narrative into analysis. A major purpose of teacher, counselor, and mentors alike is continuously validating the students' cultural identity and pride, and both teachers and counselors believe that the intensive writing curriculum is critical for developing not only skills, but also the sense of personal power.

Teacher and counselor together also give explicit guidance about how to use the college as a resource for learning without being defeated by its bureaucracy.

DISCUSSION

Bernstein's two chapters (1975, 1990) on visible/invisible pedagogy, written 15 years apart, are both usually read as strong theoretical rationales for the benefits of visible pedagogy for working-class and other educationally disadvantaged students. But in both chapters, and more strongly in the 1990 version that was written during the Thatcher government's enactment of the National Curriculum, these benefits are qualified:

> Inasmuch as the pacing of knowledge to be transmitted is relaxed [in invisible pedagogy] and the emphasis upon early attainment of specific competencies is reduced, the progression is less marked by middle-class assumptions. . . . It would appear that the invisible pedagogy carries a beneficial potential for working-class children. (1975, p. 127)

> With strong pacing [in visible pedagogy], time is at a premium, and this regulates examples, illustrations, narratives which facilitate acquisition. . . . The dominant modality of human communication is not that of analysis but that of narrative. . . . In this structure children of the disadvantaged class are doubly disadvantaged. There is no second site of acquisition [the family] and their orientation to language, narrative, is not privileged by the pedagogic communication of the school, either in form or in content. . . . Currently the visible pedagogy of the school is cheap to transmit because it is subsidized by the middle-class family and paid for by the alienation and failure of children of the disadvantaged classes and groups. (1990, p. 78)

It is certainly possible to create a visible pedagogy which would weaken the relation between social class and educational achievement. This may well require a supportive pre-school structure, a relaxation of the framing on pacing and sequencing rules, and a weakening of the framing regulating the flow of communication between the school classroom and the community(ies) the school draws upon. (1990, p. 79)

The four programs described earlier were all designed to "weaken the relation between social class and educational achievement." Reading Recovery can be considered a functional equivalent of a "pre-school structure," providing young children with a "second site" for initial literacy learning in addition to their regular classrooms (whose pedagogical structure varies both among and within the four countries). In effect, the children are learning how to be acquirers: of the strategies of independent learning from text and from classroom patterns of teacher-child communication. The other three programs all reduce the boundary "regulating the flow of communication between the school classroom and the community(ies) the school draws on." Puente also validates narratives, especially during the first of its two semesters, for just the reason given by Bernstein.[3]

I have emphasized the experiences of the students in these four programs, but there are also special aspects of the experiences of the teachers. As Atkinson's (1985) discussion of Bernstein's ideas makes especially clear, "Just as there is a change in the way pupil identities are constructed, so too are teacher identities based on contrasting principles. . . . The development of the integrated code requires shared adherence to the principle of curriculum and pedagogy which inform [sic] the code and its realization" (pp. 151-152). In all four programs, mechanisms for building not just "shared ambience" but shared pride in a significant mission are firmly in place: meetings within the school in Cambridge Friends School and Bay Area Middle school, and in-service workshops and conferences that bring teachers together across a state for Puente and across an entire nation for Reading Recovery.

As Bernstein would predict, these modifications are expensive,

---

[3]One program not included here is "genre teaching" in Australia. In the words of Jim Martin, the linguist founder of the movement, "Basil Bernstein has been the most important influence on our work" (lecture, Vancouver, July 5, 1993). It is, again in Martin's words, "another version of visible pedagogy." I have not included it as a fifth example because it is still being developed and because there are pedagogical conflicts within the movement—conflicts that will in the end be productive, but that make it harder to summarize accurately. Cope and Kalantzis (1993) provide excellent discussions of the complex scene. Terms used by advocates of one or another version of genre pedagogy to refer to their mission—"postprogressive" and (more specific to writing) "going on beyond process"—could also be used to refer to all four programs included here.

and so the three programs that are part of the state educational system (all, that is, except Cambridge Friends School) are vulnerable to cuts in public funds for education during a recession. But they stand as examples of the possible.

REFERENCES

Atkinson, P. (1985). *Language, structure and reproduction: An introduction to the sociology of Basil Bernstein.* London: Methuen.

Bernstein, B. (1975). *Class, codes and control, Vol. 3: Towards a theory of educational transmissions.* London: Routledge & Kegan Paul.

Bernstein, B. (1990). *Class, codes and control, Vol. 4: The structuring of pedagogic discourse.* London and New York: Routledge.

Carnegie Forum on Education and the Economy. (1986). *A nation prepared: Teachers for the 21st century.* New York: Carnegie Corporation.

Cazden, C.B. (1992). *Whole language plus: Essays on literacy in the United States and New Zealand.* New York: Teachers College Press.

Clay, M., & Cazden, C.B. (1990). A Vygotskian interpretation of Reading Recovery. In L. Moll (Ed.), *Vygotsky and education* (pp. 114-135). New York: Cambridge University Press. (Reprinted in Cazden, 1992.)

Cope, B., & Kalantzis, M. (Eds.). (1993). *The powers of literacy: A genre approach to teaching writing.* London & Philadephia: Falmer.

Cox, C.D. (1984). *Continuity, conflict and change in state education in Chile: A study of the pedagogic projects of the Christian Democratic and Popular Unity Governments.* Unpublished doctoral thesis, University of London.

Delpit, L. (1986). Skills and other dilemmas of a progressive black educator. *Harvard Educational Review, 56,* 379-385.

Delpit, L. (1988). The silenced dialogue: Power and pedagogy in educating other people's children. *Harvard Educational Review, 58,* 280-298.

Delpit, L. (1993). The politics of teaching literate discourse. In T. Perry & J.W. Fraser (Eds.), *Freedom's plow: Teaching in the multicultural classroom* (pp. 285-295). New York & London: Routledge.

Fiveash, K. (1992, November). *The Cadbury Courier,* pp. 13-14.

Gee, J. (1989). Literacy, discourse and linguistics: Essays by James Paul Gee. *Journal of Education, 171*(1, Whole issue). (Also in Gee, 1990.)

Gee. J.P. (1990). *Social linguistics and literacies: Ideology in discourses.* London & Philadelphia: Falmer.

Greeley, K., & Mizell, L. (1993). One step among many: Affirming identity in anti-racist schools. In T. Perry & J.W. Fraser (Eds.), *Freedom's plow: Teaching in the multicultural classroom* (pp. 215-229). New York & London: Routledge.

Healy, M.K. (1990, August). *Effecting change in schools: A personal account.*

Proceedings of the International Conference on the Teaching of English, pp. 37-45. Auckland.

Jenkins, C. (1989). *The professional middle class and the origins of progressivism: A case study of the New Education Fellowship, 1920-1950.* Unpublished doctoral thesis, University of London.

Johnson, M., & Mizell, L. (1992, September). Diversity at Cambridge Friends School. *Peacework* (Cambridge: American Friends Service Committee), pp. 3-4.

Meier, D. (1992, September 21). Myths, lies and public schools. *The Nation*, pp. 271-272.

Mizell, L., Benett, S., Bowman, B., & Morin, L. (1993). Different ways of seeing: Teaching in an anti-racist school. In T. Perry & J.W. Fraser (Eds.), *Freedom's plow: Teaching in the multicultural classroom* (pp. 27-46). New York & London: Routledge.

Office for Standards in Education. (1993). *Reading Recovery in New Zealand: A report from the office of Her Majesty's Chief Inspector of Schools.* London: Her Majesty's Stationery Office.

Renwick, W.L. (1986). *Moving targets: Six essays on educational policy.* Wellington: New Zealand Council for Educational Research.

Tuman, M. (1988). Class, codes, and composition: Basil Bernstein and the critique of pedagogy. *College Composition and Communication, 39,* 42-51.

9

Decoding Childhood

Chris Jenks
Goldsmiths' College
University of London

Children . . . have no use for psychology. They detest sociology. They
still believe in God, the family, angels, devils, witches, goblins, logic,
clarity, punctuation and other such obsolete stuff. . . . When a book is
boring, they yawn openly. They don't expect their writer to redeem
humanity, but leave to adults such childish illusions.(Singer, 1978, p. 7)

Over the last two decades, and with an accelerative intensity, sociology
has, in the manner of Levi-Strauss's primitive cosmologist, sought to
transform the natural into the cultural. Its practice has been dedicated
to the desecration of images and realities previously enshrined in the
sacred realm of utter naturalness. In modern parlance it has therefore
rendered the mundane and taken-for-granted problematic. Now in one
sense this is nothing new; it always has been sociology's project.
Durkheim was adamant that the social should always be explained in
terms of the social, and each of his theses, from suicide to religion, is
polemical in its sustained assaults on all other attempts to explain and
thus appropriate his chosen phenomenon through extrasocial forms of
discourse. Durkheim would also have approved of what might appear
as an epistemological imperialism that engulfs all phenomena within
its territory and leaves no natural state of affairs free to explain itself,
without social structures. In this one sense, such modern initiatives
complete Comte's law of three stages by ensuring that sociology should
transcend all other forms of explanation; but this is only one sense,
albeit an important one.

To a greater extent these modern sociological developments have been motivated by a different politic. The contemporary debunkings of the kind of reasoning that runs "its only human nature" have been part of an emergent attitude toward the revelation of more and yet more covert forms of social stratification within an advanced, capitalist division of labor; a compulsive redemocratization of the grounds of all existing social relations.

Sociology was grounded on the canon that the natural divisions between people (though primarily men) should be properly understood as issues of social class, and although this is an auspice for theorizing most closely identified with Marx, it is clearly central to the ideas of Durkheim and Weber as well. The discourse of stratification thus, for a considerable period, became enshrined in the language of social class. Modern sociology has opened up the parameters of such discourse and taken it beyond social class, quite often at the expense of social class. Modern sociology has enculturated, primarily, the natural realms of sex, which we now know to be an issue of gender, and race, which is thus to be understood in terms of ethnicity; more recent frontiers are those of age, sexuality, and disability.

In 1971, I postgraduated from Basil Bernstein's department at London University and went off to teach the sociology of education. I had adopted a radical phenomenological perspective, and I now understood the secret contained within all phenomena—they were socially constructed! I still believed that education was a vehicle for social change, a belief deriving from personal experience rather than from structural evidence, and I set about revealing the constraints placed on this process by patterns inherent in forms of the curriculum. I carried this through with a zeal peculiar to the young pedagogue. Gradually I confronted the irony of a phenomenologically constituted view of the curriculum populated by nonintentional actors. Who were these silent recipients of the curriculum complex? Were they essentially different to the social roles, peer group orientations, deferred gratifications, contest mobilities, and general socialization-theory fodder that I had so vehemently rejected in the past? I had a need for real, active, children, but actually, this was a naturalistic reduction. I had a need to articulate childhood, the state of being within culture, the way that different societies and different epochs represented this ontology, acted in relation to such imagery, and thus variously enabled the emergent qualities of its newness. I was struck by O'Neill's (1973) dictum, "Any theory of child socialization is implicitly a theory of the construction of social reality, if not a particular historical social order" (p. 65).

So I assembled and integrated a series of readings that seemed to express this important theme, published as The Sociology of Childhood

(1982). I had denaturalized the child; I had discovered the sociology of childhood; well, I had given it a name, and its development would prove to be far more influential and significant than its christening.

I came to see that our collective images of childhood and our subsequent relations with children could be regarded as indices of the contemporary state of the social structure; this formulation was familiar: not Husserl, Heidegger, or Merleau-Ponty, no, it was the "naughty functionalist" Emile Durkheim speaking. I had arrived at the interminable problem of attempting to explain the relationship between the symbolic order and the social structure; this was the problem most clearly established by Durkheim in *The Division of Labour in Society* (1893) and refined, though not exhausted, in *Primitive Classification* (1903) and *The Elementary Forms of the Religious Life* (1912). This was the problem adopted by Durkheim's living heir, Basil Bernstein, who would go on to write Durkheim's previously nascent theory of socialization and develop his implicit theory of social consciousness. Bernstein's work, in generating an excitingly original sociolinguistic framework for the explanation of cultural reproduction and through his constructive thesis on the social organization of the educational dimensions of curriculum, pedagogy, and evaluation was, in many senses, to complete Durkheim's project. It was through this medium, and mentor, that the word had come to inhabit my topic.

Bernstein's method proceeds from appearance and works toward actual form through a peeling away of layers. As Douglas (1972) explained:

> Whatever he does, whether analysing how a mother controls her child, how a teacher teaches, how a patient confronts a psychoanalyst, how the curriculum is worked out in a school or college, he looks at four elements in the social process. First, the system of control; second, the boundaries it sets up; third, the justification or ideology which sanctifies the boundaries; and fourth, the power itself which is hidden by the rest. The analysis always ends by revealing the distribution of power. This is the trick of demystification. (p. 312)

Bernstein had been talking about children all the time; not real, embodied children as the clients of the educational system, but metaphors for the different forms of consciousness within different realizations of solidarity. Mediated through the "codes" Bernstein had produced two models of fresh, but not natural, enculturated childhood consciousness—they were both the intentional and structural constituents of the social bond. The history, imagery, and contextualization of these models became my substantive interest, as I show here.

Although it is clearly the case that children are omnipresent in human society both across space and through time, it is nevertheless true to say that childhood is a relatively recent phenomenon in the social sciences. As Mead and Wolfenstein (1954) stated, "Although each historical period of which we have any record has had its own version of childhood . . . childhood was still something that one took for granted, a figure of speech, a mythological subject rather than a subject of artic- ulate scrutiny" (p.3).

It would appear that the idea of childhood only emerged at a comparatively late stage in the historical process. This is an idea pro- pounded by many theorists including Hoyles (1979) who plainly stated: "Both childhood and our present day nuclear family are comparatively recent inventions" (p. 16).

This contemporary topicality is itself an instance of the thesis that this chapter seeks to unravel. That a state of being, such as child- hood, should be formulated through the "analytic gaze" within a partic- ular epoch must tell us as much about the condition of our society as it does about our children.

Today children are thought of everywhere as normal. As such, common sense is redolent with images and understandings that con- trive to produce the child not just as normal, but also as utterly natural. Yet as Hoyles (1979) asserted: "Childhood is a social convention and not just a natural state" (p. 27).

Seemingly, the absolute necessity of children as real presences throughout history, as opposed to the temporary and fragile character of other phenomena such as capitalism, the HIV virus, and the European Community—however serious their impact on human being—has rendered childhood completely mundane; we simply take it for granted. Unlike the poor, in reality it is children that are always with us. As an event childhood is not even different enough to specify a mode of experience that is peculiar to certain groups of people; it is what everyone does or has done at a stage in their lives. Beyond this childhood is a transitory phenomenon, we "grow out of it;" it is routine- ly disregarded on our way to achieving our proper destiny, adult ratio- nal life. This normative assumption is reflected in our chastisement of people for "acting childishly." Being grownup must surely be the pur- pose of being (Jenks, 1989).

Now such an elaboration of what everyone knows about child- hood is not particularly informative. My intention in rehearsing such ideas is to indicate the embeddedness of our "knowing" about children in conceptions of the "normal" and the "natural." We must shift our per- spective to another site. Childhood is not a brief physical inhabitation of a lilliputian world owned and ruled by others, but is rather an histor- ical and cultural experience and its meaning, interpretations, and inter-

ests reside within such contexts. These contexts, these social structures, become our topic. It is here that normative expectations arise,
and it is to an analysis of such structures that we proceed.

What I cannot aspire to, in a work of this scale, is a chronology of
the changing images of the child and patterns of child care through history; this is a major task and has been attempted in a number of sources.
The leading figure in producing an archaeology of such images is Aries
(1962) whose ideas are influential in all subsequent theorizing about the
child. To this extent they are worthy of review for their implications are
quite radical in relation to the common sense view of the child.

Primarily Aries informed us that there was a time before which
children were invisible. Up to and including the Middle Ages it would
seem that there was no collective perception of children as being
essentially different than anyone else. People populated the world, but
their status was not established in terms of their age nor their physical
maturity. At first hearing this is a difficult proposition to accept; we
have already conceded that children are a fact, that they have always
been with us. However, what Aries pointed out is that the manner of
their recognition by adults and thus the forms of their relationships
with adults has altered through the passage of time. This is not such a
taxing idea to grasp once we think of the more contemporary case of
the invention of the "adolescent" or "teenager" over, say, the last 50
years. Here we have a quite clearly distinguishable group of people
within our society (albeit only within the Western world) who occupy a
now firmly established twilight zone of the quasi-child or crypto-adult.

To return from this example to Aries, he argued that children
have not always existed in the way that we now know them; they have
not always been the same thing. In the Middle Ages, he stated, there
was no concept of childhood, and it is from this absence that our current view of the child has evolved. Ancient society, we are told, may
well have understood the difference of childhood and grasped the
necessity of their development, whereas medieval civilization seems to
have either abandoned or mislaid such a recognition. The reason for
this loss is unexplained, but the evidence of its impact Aries derived
from a study of painting and iconography: "Medieval art until about the
twelfth century did not know childhood or did not attempt to portray it.
It is hard to believe that this neglect was due to incompetence or inca-
pacity; it seems more probable that there was no place for childhood in
the medieval world" (p. 97).

The art of the Middle Ages does exhibit an extraordinary dearth
of depictions of children; they were apparently considered of such little
importance that they did not warrant representation in this form. When
such images do occur, as by necessity in the Madonna and child, the

baby Jesus appears uniformly, from example to example, as a small man, a wizened homonculus without the rounded appeal and vulnerability of the latterday infant. This then is our baseline; we have to imagine a world of people differentiated only by whether they are being weaned or they are working. Aries now takes us on a journey to the present.

Following in the wake of the Middle Ages children in history emerged initially as playthings. They were not separate from the adult world, but provided it with delight or entertainment. Thus although through the 16th and into the 17th century people took pleasure in pampering or "coddling" their children, they were only gradually beginning to realize their presence as a different way of being in the world. Neither was this a universal response to the condition of infancy. Only particular privileged groups or classes could afford the luxury of childhood with its demands on time and emotion and its paraphernalia of toys and special clothing. For most people children were potential sources of contribution to the economy of the family, and large families were both an investment and a hedge against infant mortality.

Aries located the genesis of the modern conception of the child in the 18th century, and this is a view that is shared throughout the body of the literature on this topic. Robertson (1976), for example, stated:

> If the philosophy of the Enlightenment brought to eighteenth century Europe a new confidence in the possibility of human happiness, special credit must go to Rousseau for calling attention to the needs of children. For the first time in history, he made a large group of people believe that childhood was worth the attention of intelligent adults, encouraging an interest in the process of growing up rather than just the product. Education of children was part of the interest in progress which was so predominant in the intellectual trends of the time. (p. 407)

Children, through this period, had, it would seem, escaped into difference. We witness the arrival of a new category of being, one that is fresh and frail and consequently a target for correction and training by the growing standards of rationality that came to pervade the time. Once a concern with the child's physical health and well-being had been institutionalized along with an attention to their moral welfare, then our model for modernity is almost complete. The child has moved through time from obscurity to the center stage. The child is forever assured the spotlight of public policy and attention and also a primary place in the family. Indeed one might argue that the family has come to be defined in terms of the child's presence.

We should note that the thesis provided by Aries is both persuasive and formative, and although alternative and critical accounts have been presented, and well gathered by Pollock (1983), they rarely succeed in achieving more than a modification of his central ideas. For Aries the history of childhood is a transition from darkness into light, and he set not just a pattern for future analysis, but also an optimism and a justification of modern-day childrearing that we might properly treat with caution.

DeMause (1976), in similar vein, was most expressive of the dark side and thus overenthusiastic concerning the illuminating potential of today's parenting. DeMause described the history of childhood as "a nightmare from which we have only recently begun to awake," and continued "the further back in history one goes, the lower the level of child care, and the more likely children are to be killed, abandoned, beaten, terrorised and sexually abused" (p. 1).

He put forward what he calls a "psychogenic theory of history" that revolves around the notion that history consists in the evolution of the human personality brought about through successive and positive developments in the relationship between parents and children. The stages in this process that he put forward begin with the routine infanticide of antiquity and conclude with the partially realized "Helping Mode" of the late 20th century; the latter being a kind of systematic facilitation of the child's unique intent through maturation.

Last in my inventory of child evolutionists, though there are many more, is Shorter (1976). He appears extremely congratulatory of the humane achievements in childrearing that have come to be crystallized in the form of today's nuclear family. Our changing attitudes have apparently transformed children from the status of object, worthy only of disregard, into the status of subject, and subject of our central attention and self-sacrifice. "Good mothering," we are informed, "is an invention of modernisation" (p. 26).

The point, I trust, is clear. The child in history has metamorphosed into an ontology, a subject in its own right, a source of identity and, more than this, a promise of the future good. The child has come to symbolize all that is decent and caring about a society; it is the very index of a civilization—witness the outrage and general moral disapproval at the revelations concerning Romanian orphanages, an obvious signifier of the corruption of Communist social structures!

In the examination of childhood that follows I concur with the thesis so far stated, but only so far. It is a theory not without tropes and a process laden with ironies. The modern image of the child is one that is clear, visible, and in need of containment. The historical liberation of the child from adulthood has led, in turn, to the necessity of its constraint by collective practices. The obvious high profile of children in our contemporary patterns of relationship has rendered them subject to new forms of control. As Rose stated:

> Childhood is the most intensively governed sector of personal exis-
> tence. In different ways, at different times, and by many different routes
> varying from one section of society to another, the health, welfare, and
> rearing of children have been linked in thought and practice to the des-
> tiny of the nation and the responsibilities of the state. The modern
> child has become the focus of innumerable projects that purport to
> safeguard it from physical, sexual, and moral danger, to ensure its "nor-
> mal" development, to actively promote certain capacities of attributes
> such as intelligence, educability and emotional stability. (1989, p. 121).

Similarly, just as the delineation of the child's particularity has
given rise to specially fashioned forms of control, so also has the
diminution of public ignorance and disdain toward the child privatized
new and intrusive forms of violence extending from neurotic families to
parental sexual abuse.

What I produce is a framework for an analysis of the shifting
patterns of normality that have been applied to the child through the
massive turbulence, upheaval, and transformations that occurred in
Europe with the advent of the Modern Age. This is the period that
brought sociology itself into being and was marked by the acceleration
of a number of significant structural processes such as the division of
labor, industrialization, urbanization, the market economy, and the secularization of belief systems away from consensual obedience to the
deity toward an allegiance to the necessities of science, technology,
and progress through growth.

The analysis depends on the assumption that its subject—in
this case childhood—emerges from a particular structuring of social
relationships and that its various meanings derive from the forms of
discourse that accompany those relationships. Childhood appears in
different forms in different cultures in relation to structural variables
such as rates of mortality and life expectancy, organizations of family
life and structure, kinship patterns, and different ideologies of care and
philosophies of need and dependency. A discourse providing for childhood in modern Western society might be that of a pediatrician, a parent, a teacher, or an educational psychologist, or equally well those of a
television producer and an advertising executive (Jenks, 1989).

These different forms of discourse clearly do not have an equivalence. They move in and out of focus according to the different aspects
of the subject that is being considered. Sometimes this occurs in parallel but sometimes in competition, and often such discourses are
arranged hierarchically, for example, the child discourse of social workers or juvenile magistrates have a power and efficacy in excess of those
of the sibling or parent. But all such discourses contribute to and, in
turn, derive from the dominant cultural image of the "normal" child.

This, of necessity, implies that the child is part of a social structure and thus functional within a network of relations, a matrix of partial interests and a complex of forms of professional knowledge that are beyond the physical experience of being a child.

Hillman (1975), writing in relation to analytical psychology, stated that "whatever we say about children and childhood is not altogether really about children and childhood" (p. 8).

He is, in the original context, referring to childhood as a causal repository for the explanation of self and the progress of the psyche, but he may equally be read as suggesting that theories of the child are always pointers toward the social construction of reality. Just as I have argued that the child is neither simply "natural" nor merely "normal," we may claim to have established, in addition, that the child is not neutral but rather always moral and political. Thus the way that we treat our children is indicative of the state of our social structure, a measure of the achievement of our civilization, or even an index of the degree to which humanism has outstripped the economic motive in everyday life. Similarly, the way that we control our children reflects, perhaps as a continuous microcosm, the strategies through which we exercise power and constraint in the wider society. For Durkheim (1961), quite clearly, the purpose of pedagogic theory and practice, as the formal mode of socialization, is to ensure the quality and achievement of a society through the necessary process of cultural reproduction. For others, such as Bourdieu and Passeron (1977), socialization is the mechanism through which we continue to confer power and privilege through the investment of "cultural capital" by virtue of the unnecessary process of social stratification.

Throughout the historical and cross-cultural literature on childhood, what seems to emerge are two dominant ways of talking and thinking about children (which we might refer to as *codes*); two traditions of conceptualizing the child that although, at different times, practically supported and was reinforced by various religious beliefs, political ideologies, and scientific doctrines, are too old and pervasive to be explained in terms of such cultural regimes. For this reason I formulate them as images arising from mythology—myths being the devices that people have always employed to account for anomalies or the seemingly inexplicable in their cosmologies. These two images I refer to as the *Dionysian* and the *Apollonian* views of childhood. To add to the complexity of these configurations I suggest that although they are competitive to the point of absolute incompatibility, within cultures they are used to understand childhood primarily through history but also synchronically, that is, in parallel at the same time.

What I am calling the *Dionysian* image rests on the assumption of an initial evil or corruption within the child—Dionysus being the prince of wine, revelry, and nature. A major buttress to such imagery can be found in the doctrine of Adamic original sin. Children, it is supposed, enter the world as a willful material force; they are impish and harbor a potential evil. This primal force will be mobilized if, in any part, the adult world should allow them to stray away from the appropriate path that the blueprint of human culture has provided for them. Such children must not fall into bad company, establish bad habits, or develop idle hands—all of these contexts will enable outlets for the demonic force within which is, of course, potentially destructive, not just of the child but of the adult collectivity as well. The child is Dionysian in as much as it loves pleasure, it celebrates self-gratification, and it is wholly demanding in relation to any object, or indeed subject, that prevents its satiation. The intrusive noise that is childhood is expressive of a single-minded solipsistic array of demands in relation to which all other interests become peripheral and all other presences become satellites to enable this goal.

Christianity has provided a significant contribution to this way of regarding the child, even though, as Shipman (1972) pointed out, the fall in infant mortality through modernity has reduced our urgency and anxiety about their state of grace at an early age. Aries directed us to the 16th century view of the child as weak, which was accompanied by the practice of "coddling"; but this was not a weakness in the sense of vulnerability so much as a weakness in the form of susceptibility to corruption and being "easily led." Parenting consequently consisted of distant and strict moral guidance, through physical direction. Stemming from this period, in the tradition of this image, a severe view of the child sustained, one that saw socialization as almost a battle but certainly a form of combat in which the headstrong and stubborn subject had to be "broken," but all for its own good. This harsh campaign of childrearing persisted throughout the Puritanism of the 17th century, with rods not being spared in order to spoil children, and even on into the 19th century, with an evangelical zeal that sought out and waged war on the depravity of drunkenness, idleness, or childhood wherever it was found. Dickens is a great source of such tales of our institutionalized violence toward the young, and Coveney (1957) provided a fine collection and analysis of this image of the child throughout literature. In practical terms the Dionysian child was being deafened, blinded, and exploited through factory labor and still being sent up chimneys with brushes as late as 1850—in Britain alone.

It would be convenient to regard what I am calling the Dionysian child as an image of a former time, a set of ideas belonging to a simpler, more primitive people than our own, and to some degree this is so. However, we must not disregard the systematic secular exploration of the soul that has been practiced and recommended by psychoanalysis throughout the last century. It was Freud who most recently and forcefully formulated this image of the child through his concept of the Id and in relation to his theory of infantile sexuality. Of the triumvirate that comprise the self for Freud, the Superego is the possession of the collectivity, the Ego the realm of the adult, and the Id (together with its immature adult counterpart "neurosis") the special province of the child. The Id, as we know, is that libidinal repository of insatiable desire. It is the dark driving force that acts as the source of all creativity, yet that is required to be quelled or "repressed" so that people can live in relation to one another and have some regard for the mutual incompatibility of their systems of desire. The social bond resides in this repression; the story of and its implications for childrearing are familiar, if more subtle.

What now of the Apollonian child, the heir to the sunshine and light, the espouser of poetry and beauty? This does appear to be, much more, the modern, Western, but only "public," way of regarding the child. Such infants are angelic, innocent, and untainted by the world that they have recently entered. They have a natural goodness and a clarity of vision that we might "idolize" or even "worship" as the source of all that is best in human nature (note the character of these two metaphors *idolize* and *worship* so often used to denote the love relation between parent and child). Such children play and chuckle, smile and laugh, both spontaneously but also with our sustained encouragement. We cannot abide their tears and tantrums; we want only the illumination from their halo. This is humankind before either Eve or the apple. It is within this model that we honor and celebrate the child and dedicate ourselves to reveal its newness and uniqueness. Gone are the strictures of uniformity, here, with romantic vision; we explore the particularity of the person. Such thinking has been instructive of all child-centered learning and special-needs education from Montessori, the Plowden Report, A.S. Neill, and the Warnock Report, and indeed much of primary teaching in the last three decades. This Apollonian image lies at the heart of attempts to protect the unborn through legislation concerning voluntary termination of pregnancies and endeavors in the United States to criminalize certain "unfit" states of motherhood such as drug addiction or HIV infection.

Children in this image are not curbed nor beaten into submission; they are encouraged, enabled, and facilitated. The formalization of the Apollonian child occurs with Rousseau, the author of their manifesto *Emile* (1762). It is in this work that Rousseau reveals the child's innate and immanent capacity for reason, and he instructed us that they have natural virtues and dispositions that only require coaxing out into the open. Rousseau provided a rationale for the idea that children are born good, and beyond showing us that each child has a unique potential, he stated something completely new for its time and formative for the future—'namely, that children are different from adults; they are an ontology in its own right and as such deserve special treatment and care.

Let us be clear: These two images of the child that I have designated as the Dionysian and the Apollonian are not literal descriptions of the ways that children intrinsically differ; they are no more than images. Yet these images are immensely powerful; they live on and give force to the different discourses that we have about children; they constitute summaries of the way we have, over time, come to treat and process children "normally." What I point to here is that these images are informative of the shifting strategies that Western society has exercised in its increasing need to control, socialize, and constrain people in the transition toward modernity. As contexts of control they bear a striking resemblance to the "positional" and the "personal."

For this part of the analysis I draw on the work of Foucault (1977) in his genealogy of discipline and punishment in modern society which, although not specifically about children, has profound implications for our changing ways of thinking about the child.

Foucault offered us a breakdown of the changes in what he called the "anatomy of power" in Western culture, and a pivotal change occurs, he suggested, in the mid-18th century—parallel with Rousseau's announcement of the modern child. What we are offered is a description of two images of discipline that reflect two modes of control, that are, in turn, aspects of two forms of social integration shifting from an old European order to the new order of modern industrial society. These two images resonate strongly with my depictions of the Dionysian and the Apollonian child. Foucault set out from the mode of imprisonment characteristic of the *ancien regime* in France, one rooted in the barbarities of medieval times, and he proceeded to unravel the new penology of the postrevolutionary state—a style of punishment that is premised on very different ideas concerning the appropriate nature of correction. The year 1789 did not provide an immediate and dramatic break in continuity; there was what might be described as a preparadigmatic stage of penology when the more advanced thinkers of the age set out to defame and undermine the old system of punishment and establish in its place a new system theorized much more in terms of dissuasion. The newly emergent methods of discipline show similarities with and influences from other areas of social life such as, for example, the armed forces and the school system. So as Sheridan (1980) pointed out, in relation to Foucault's thesis, "there is an astonishing coincidence between the new prison and other contemporary institutions: hospital, factory, school and barracks" (p. 52) and, for our purposes, regimes of child care.

Foucault's essay begins with an account of the appalling violence and degradation publicly inflicted on a man found guilty of attempting to murder King Louis XVth of France. It consists of plucking of the flesh, burning with oil and sulphur, dismembering, and drawing and quartering. From this hyperbole of retributive punishment, Foucault informs us that such awe-full spectacles diminish as we move into the 19th century. Through this historical period, it would seem, attention moves away from the execution of punishment to the mechanism of trial and sentence. In essence, the display of excessive symbolism is replaced by rational process. This transition in punishment is taken to reflect an overall change of collective attitudes into the form of society in which there seems to be more kindness and, at least, an appearance of public humanism. This is matched by a diminution in brutality and a recognition of the impropriety of pain. In terms of judicial regimes this brings a transition from retribution to restitution. Violence against the physical body is gradually transformed into a more subtle and intrusive correction and training of the very soul. The government of the individual in modernity has moved from the outside to the inside. It will be recalled that Durkheim turned to an examination of judicial systems as indicators of the real but intangible forms of solidarity.

Clearly the implementation of discipline at the societal level cannot be random and spontaneous; it requires a number of concerted strategies to ensure a uniform application and result. Primary among these is the exercise and manipulation of space. People are controlled in relation to the different spaces they inhabit; discipline works through the division and subdivision of action into spatial units. Think of children having a particular seat at the dinner table or in the car, being sent to their room, playing outside, going to school, attending assemblies, working in classes or gymnasia and, of course, being seated at desks, in rows, in groups, or whatever. The "reading corner" takes on a new significance. Foucault tells us that the original model for spatial control was the monastery cell or indeed the dungeon—this cellular metaphor extends out into other social institutions. The logistics of modernity turn masses of soldiers into lines of tents or barracks; factories become production lines with workers isolated by task within the division of labor; and hospitals become the classification of sickness on a ward system.

The other major strategy of control is temporal. The whole being of a child is delineated and paced according to a timetable. This too, Foucault tells us, is of monastic origin. The child's rising and sleeping, eating and entertainment, are all prescribed in time. The very idea of a school curriculum is an organization of activities around a political economy of form in relation to content. What people learn is scheduled in relation to decisions about relevance and compulsion. The practice of being a child is marked out in stages, solidified and institutionalized by Piaget and conceptualized as "development." The implications of an individual's response to such an organization of time is critical to his or her placement on hierarchies of merit and achievement, which ultimately relate to the existing system of social stratification and the distribution of life chances in the wider society. Even the child's body is organized temporally in terms of its ablution, nutrician, excretion, exercise, and so on, and all of this is homologous to the drilling that occurs in the armed forces and the specialization and division of labor on the factory floor. These are the modern ergonomics of fitting people to functions.

Power is organized through the combination of strategies, barrages of controlling mechanisms are arranged in tactics; subjects become objects to be gathered, transported, and located through collective action. Foucault agrees, implicitly, with Durkheim before him, that the individual emerges from patterns of constraint. Indeed, the character of social structures provides for the possibility of personal expression. The individual, whether adult or child, when rendered object itself becomes instrumental in the exercise of power—such is the force of ideology, the impersonal impact of partial ideas on action. As Deleuze and Guattari (1983) told us, the modern nuclear family structure is one of the foremost devices for shaping the individual and restricting desire in capitalist societies, and it is psychoanalysis in adulthood that helps to reinforce that restraint.

Modern power does not exercise itself with the omnipotent symbolism of the scaffold; no longer are we witness to the excessive and triumphant zeal that was directed toward the Dionysian child. Modern power is calculating; it is suspicious, and it always appears modest in its application. It operates through scopic regimes, through observation that is organized hierarchically, through judgments rendered normative within social structures and through scrutiny and examination. Observation has become a primary metaphor in the social sciences as it reflects the dominant form of the relations between people and certainly the relations between adults and the new, visible, Apollonian child. The crudity of the old regime of control in social relations gives way to the modern disciplinary apparatus, the post-Rousseauian way of looking to and monitoring the child in mind and body. Surveillance, in the form of child care, proliferates in its intensity and penetration through the agencies of midwives and health visitors, nurses and doctors, postnatal clinics, schools and teachers, psychometric testing, examinations, educational psychology, counseling, social workers, and so on and on through the layers of scrutiny and isolation, all constituted for the child's own good. The Apollonian child is truly visible; it is most certainly seen and not heard.

Such a "seeing" social structure Foucault epitomizes through the symbol of the "ideal prison"—namely, Jeremy Bentham's sinister invention, the *panopticon*. The panopticon, unlike the more familiar "star" prison, was circular with cells arranged in layers of rings around a central observation tower. Each cell would contain one isolated inmate, illuminated by natural lighting from behind and at the front, wholly exposed, through the complete cage, to the constant gaze of the observation tower. The surveillance from the observation tower takes place through slots that are not illuminated from behind; thus the inmates of the cells did not know when, or indeed if, they were being watched. Effectively, then, it was as if they were being watched all of the time. One might properly suggest that the constant surveillance became a feature of the prisoners' consciousness, a motive in their demeanor and self-presentation; they grew to watch themselves. The *panopticon* presents itself at a variety of levels: It was a reality, such institutions were built; symbolically it is the embodiment of an ideal for maximizing scrutiny and control, thereby minimizing the response and intervention of those being controlled; and finally it stands as an apt metaphor for the exercise of power in modern society—in terms of our interests in this chapter—socialization, education, child care, and provision. There is a delicacy and a rapidity in the management of persons through panopticism.

In summary, we might suggest that the Dionysian child is an instance of a social structure in which the rules and beliefs are external and consensual: a society in which people are less different, and it is the affirmation of their similarities that is at the basis of their views on childrearing. The offending, or evil, child has to be beaten into submission, an external and public act that celebrates and reaffirms the shared values of their historical period. Any transgression in the form of childish behavior threatens the very core of the collectivity. To be socialized is to become one with the normative social structure, and so the idea of evil that is projected into the image of the Dionysian child is, in fact, providing a vehicle for expunging all sentiments that threaten the sacred cohesion of the adult world. To this end real children in such a society sacrifice their childhood to the cause of the collective adult good. Through such control the growing individual learns a respect for society through the experience of shame.

The Apollonian child, on the other hand, may be seen to occupy a social structure permeated by panopticism. The rules and beliefs are more diffuse; people are more different and isolated, and it is consequently more difficult for them to operate within a sense of shared values. Within such a world people manifest their uniqueness, and children must be reared to express what is peculiarly special about their personalities. All of this difference is, of course, both volatile and subversive and must be policed if collective life is to sustain at all. The control moves subtly in response to such a potentially fragmented social structure; as few symbols are shared, externality is an improper arena in which to uphold the sacred. Consequently the control moves inside, from the public to the private, and so we monitor and examine and watch the Apollonian child; he or she in turn learns to watch over him- or herself, and shame is replaced by guilt. The panopticon dream is now complete through the internalization of surveillance in the formation of children's psyches. The Apollonian projection into childhood now appears as a way of resolving the loss of freedom and creativity in adult life.

Bernstein (1967), drawing on Durkheim's (1964) analysis of simple and complex forms of social organization, provided an earlier model for an examination of different kinds of relationship between adults and children in the form of different ways of organizing schooling. This, like the ideas of Foucault already discussed, is also instructive of different visions of society. Bernstein's work is most important in this context because he precisely addresses the transition that has occurred in our image of the learner (the child) and treats it as indicative of changing standards of normality within modern society. In line with my conception of the Dionysian child and Foucault's conception of the *ancien regime* of punishment, Bernstein had already described the "closed" curriculum, and for the Apollonian child and panopticism, the "open" curriculum. In the transition toward modernity from one form of schooling into another, Bernstein tells us that there is a weakening of the symbolic significance and ritualization of punishment. Controls in schools become more personalized; children are confronted more as individuals, and there is a reduced appeal to shared loyalties. A child's activities are less likely to be prescribed by formal categories such as gender, IQ, and age, but rather by the individual's needs and special qualities. There is a complementary alteration in the authority structure between adult and child; the teacher becomes a problem poser, and the authority resides within the learning material. Thus the act of learning through self-discovery celebrates choice and difference. Overall, the learning child has greater autonomy, higher levels of personal aspiration, and more available choice. Bernstein (1967) concludes his analysis by saying that "none of this should be taken in the spirit that yesterday there was order today only flux. Neither should it be taken as a long sigh over the weakening of authority and its social basis. Rather we should be eager to explore changes in the forms of social integration in order to re-examine the basis of social control" (p. 353).

This is a significant imperative for any sociological understanding of childhood: that the child is always revealing of the grounds of social control. Thus in one sense we get the children we deserve or, to put it more formally, our historical perspectives on normality in childhood reflect the changes in the organization of our social structure.

Therefore, when Donzelot (1986) tells us that the child has become the interface between politics and psychology, he is developing a wider argument about the functioning of control in modern life. The contemporary state no longer addresses the polity as a whole, but rather treats the family as its basic unit of control. All ideas and practices concerning the care of, justice for, and protection of the child can be seen to be instrumental in the ideological network that preserves the status quo. The "tutelary complex" that Donzelot describes, is one that has become established through the practices of social workers and professional carers, and this complex intrudes into "difficult" families but treads a careful line between repression and dependency such that the family is preserved as the unit of attention and the house of the child.

REFERENCES

Aries, P. (1962). *Centuries of Childhood*. London: Cape.

Bernstein, B. (1967, September 14). Open schools—Open society? *New Society*, pp. 351-353.

Bourdieu, P., & Passeron, J.-C. (1977). *Reproduction: In education, society and culture*. London: Sage.

Coveney, P. (1957). *Poor monkey*. London: Rockcliff.

Deleuze, G., & Guattari, F. (1983). *Anti-Oedipus*. New York: Viking.

DeMause, L. (1976). *The history of childhood*. London: Souvenir.

Donzelot, J. (1986). *The policing of families*. London: Hutchinson.

Douglas, M. (1972, March 9). Speech, class and Basil Bernstein. *The Listener*, pp. 312.

Durkheim, E. (1961). *Moral education*. New York: Free Press.

Durkheim, E. (1964a). *The division of labour in society*. New York: Free Press. (Originally published 1893)

Durkheim, E. (1964b). *The elementary forms of the religious life*. London: Allen & Unwin. (Originally published 1912)

Durkheim, E., & Mauss, M. (1963). *Primitive classification*. London: Cohen & West. (Originally published 1903)

Foucault, M. (1977). *Discipline and punish*. London: Allen Lane.

Hillman, J. (1975). *Loose ends*. New York: Spring Publications.

Hoyles, M. (Ed.). (1979). *Changing childhood*. London: Writers and Readers Publishing Cooperative.

Jenks, C. (Ed.). (1982). *The sociology of childhood—Essential readings*. London: Batsford. (Reprinted in 1992 by Aldershot: Gregg).

Jenks, C. (1989). Social theorizing and the child . . . Constraints and possibilities. In S. Doxiadis (Ed.), *Early influences shaping the individual* (NATO Advanced Studies Workshop, pp. 93-102). London: Plenum.

Mead, M., & Wolfenstein, M. (1954). *Childhood in contemporary cultures*. Chicago: University of Chicago Press.

O'Neill, J. (1973). Embodiment and child development: A phenomenological approach. In H.P. Dreitzel (Ed.), *Recent sociology* (No. 5, pp. 65-81) New York: Macmillan.

Pollock, L.(1983). *Forgotten children*. Cambridge: Cambridge University Press.

Robertson, P. (1976). Home as a nest: Middle class childhood in nineteenth century Europe. In L. DeMause (Ed.), *The history of childhood* (pp. 115-129). London: Souvenir.

Rose, N. (1989). *Governing the soul: The shaping of the private self.* London: Routledge.

Rousseau, J.-J. (1973). *Emile*. Paris: Bordas. (Originally published 1762)

Sheridan, A. (1980). *Michel Foucault: The will to truth*. London: Tavistock.

Shipman, M. (1972). *Childhood: A sociological perspective*. Slough, UK: National Foundation for Educational Research.

Shorter, E. (1976). *The making of the modern family*. London: Collins.

Singer, I.B. (1978, December 17). Speech on receiving the Nobel Prize for literature. *The Observer*, p. 7.

10

Classification and Framing in English Public Boarding Schools*

Geoffrey Walford
Aston Business School

In 1990, John Major campaigned for the leadership of the British Conservative Party and the position of Prime Minister on the platform of a classless society. He spoke of his hope of building a society of opportunity in which individual success would depend on talent and application and not on luck or good fortune. John Major's own rise to power might be seen as a reflection of his desire for this classless society, for his family was lower working class and he left school at age 16 with few qualifications to his name. Yet Major's choice of members for his first Cabinet showed that the classless society had not yet arrived.

Of the 22 members of Major's first Cabinet, 19 had attended private schools—mostly of the status that usually confers on the school the somewhat confusing title of "public" school. Included within the Cabinet group were former pupils of Marlborough College, Shrewsbury, Loretto, Dulwich, Sedbergh, George Heriot's, Charterhouse, and St. Paul's. Two schools—Rugby and Eton—had two members each. Most of these men, selected by John Major for the highest political positions in the country, spent their early years as boarders at one of a select group of highly prestigious and elite schools.

---

*This chapter updates and extends an earlier article: Walford, G. (1986). Ruling-class classification and framing. British Educational Research Journal, 12(2), 183-195. We are grateful to Carfax Publications for permission to use that earlier article.

Moreover, only one of the members of the Cabinet had entrusted the education of his own children entirely to the state-maintained sector. Sixteen of them used the private sector alone for their children, whereas the rest used a judicious mixture of state-maintained and private schools. Clearly the government as a whole was not uniformly supportive of the idea of a classless society, for these leading members were prepared to pay high fees in the belief that private schooling would ensure a better than fair chance of success for their own children.

But it is possible that they were wasting their money? That certain private schools have been the traditional nurseries of statesmen and of those with high power, wealth and prestige, does not mean that they still retain that role. This chapter discusses the relationships among school, higher education, and work for pupils at these elite English public boarding schools. It uses the concepts of classification and framing developed by Basil Bernstein to illuminate the continuities and contradictions in experience of these pupils as they pass from school to university and into their careers.

The aspect of Bernstein's work that is considered here is that relating to the curriculum and pedagogy, drawing particularly on his concepts of classification and framing. These concepts were first introduced in a much quoted article (Bernstein, 1971) in which two educational knowledge codes were discussed, differing according to the underlying principles that shape curriculum, pedagogy, and evaluation. A curriculum of a *collection* type is characterized by strongly bounded knowledge areas with little linkage between them. The learner is required to collect a group of favored contents in order to satisfy some criteria of evaluation. On the other hand, an *integrated* curriculum emphasizes the interdependence of various areas of knowledge and attempts to transcend traditional boundaries. Bernstein argued that any structure for the transmission of knowledge will symbolically reproduce the distribution of power in society and introduced the concept of *classification* to clarify this relationship:

> Where classification is strong, contents are well insulated from each other by strong boundaries. Where classification is weak, there is reduced insulation between contents, for the boundaries between contents are weak or blurred. *Classification thus refers to the degree of boundary maintenance between contents.* (Bernstein, 1971, p. 49; emphasis in original)

The concept of *frame* is also introduced to refer to the strength of the boundary between what may be transmitted and what may not be transmitted in the pedagogic relationship. It indicates "the degree of control teacher and pupil possess over the section, organization, pacing, and timing of knowledge transmitted and received in the pedagogical relationship" (p. 50).

The strength of framing thus refers to the range of options available to teacher and taught in the control of what is transmitted and received. Thus, "from the perspective of this analysis, the basic structure of the message system, curriculum is given by variations in the strength of classification, and the basic structure of the message system, pedagogy is given by variations in the strengths of frames" (Bernstein, 1971p. 50).

Since that first paper, Bernstein has developed these ideas considerably (Bernstein, 1990a), but unfortunately his exposition of these developments is virtually unreadable, and the complexity is such that the original illuminative nature of the concepts has been obscured. The opacity of Bernstein's writing is also partly responsible for the continued criticism to which it has been subjected. In fact, since the original formulation, criticisms appear to have been more plentiful than examples of use. One prominent critic is King (1976, 1981) who argued against the concepts on empirical and theoretical grounds. Another is Pring (1975) who questioned the theoretical structure of Bernstein's dichotomous categories. Gibson (1977, 1984) extended this critique and claimed that it is "an exercise in mystification" and that the original "paper actually distorts, and directs attention away from the sociological thesis it sets out to demonstrate" (p. 118). The attack thus focused particularly on the lack of clarity and the ambiguity of concepts employed, both at the theoretical and operational levels. In spite of Bernstein's (1990b) attempts to deal with this criticism, much of it is undoubtedly justified. However, it must be recognized that Bernstein (1975) himself originally saw this part of his work as "a search for the basic concepts themselves" (p. 15).

In spite of this extensive criticism, several authors have found the general framework useful in attempting to clarify a range of educational problems. Walker (1983), for example, has used Bernstein's concepts of classification and framing within an historical analysis of different social regimes in colleges of education over a century, and Aggleton and Whitty (1985) have applied them to a study of the subcultural practices of a group of new middle-class students in an English college of further education. Examples of broader and more flexible usage include Rodger's (1985) study of a large public inquiry and Walford's (1981) account of problems within postgraduate research.

The usefulness of the concepts, however, can perhaps best be seen in Bernstein's own early articles. In "Class and Pedagogies: Visible and Invisible" (Bernstein, 1973), they are used to uncover the relationship between social class and educational advantage in progressive preschool and infant school classrooms. He showed that the invisible pedagogy which is at the base of progressive methods is inherently advantageous to pupils from new middle-class families, whereas children from working-class homes are at a disadvantage. A more important article in the context of the present discussion is "Aspects of the Relations Between Education and Production" (1977), which looks at the continuities and discontinuities between education and work. Here, the earlier definitions of classification and framing are broadened; they "have become more abstract and the link between power and classification and framing and control has become more explicit" (p. 84). Bernstein argued against a simple correspondence theory of education that assumes that dispositions valued in the school are identical to dispositions required by the workplace and used these developed concepts to argue that classification and framing in schools does not always mesh with the classification and framing required in the workplace.

Bernstein's main example is that of less able working-class pupils, rather like those discussed by Willis (1977) and Corrigan (1979), who (if they are to be employed at all) are likely to occupy unskilled or lowly skilled manual jobs. The most clear example might be production-line assembly work. These jobs are ones where the ability to follow instructions within an organized hierarchy of command is valued and in which initiative, individuality, creativity, and criticism are discouraged. In short, they are usually jobs in which both classification and framing are high. There is high insulation between those who control the production process and those who execute production and between the various tasks and grades of production personnel. Tasks are simple, repetitive, and tightly defined. The pacing, organization, and timing of the production process is strictly controlled by people other than those actually doing the work.

If there was continuity between the educational system and the world of work, then it would be expected that the classification and framing experienced by these pupils in schools would be similarly high. Yet, in practice, this is exactly the group of secondary school pupils for whom the curriculum is most likely to be weakly classified and framed. although more able students are tackling the collection code of public examinations, this group is most likely to be involved in the integrated code of combined sciences, integrated humanities, project work, social and life skills, and so on.

At the time Bernstein was writing, the grip of the examination system had yet to become all pervasive, and weak levels of classification and framing were still occurring where pupils were expected to take few, if any, external examinations. Schools had developed more integrated course structures for this group of pupils in an attempt to maintain interest or just some semblance of control. But the consequence of this was that far from the schools acting smoothly as agents of reproduction of the workforce, they acted here as interrupters and produced a clear discontinuity in the system.

It is worth noting that this discontinuity in classification and framing, which, at least to some extent, must be seen as the result of resistance and fighting back on the part of liberal teachers and working-class pupils themselves, is currently undergoing rapid change. The introduction of the National Curriculum with its associated testing and the extension of examinations to pupils of practically all abilities is leading to much strengthened classification and framing for these pupils. For those lucky enough to find work, movement is toward greater continuity of experience between school and employment. Ironically, of course, such tight classification and framing is totally inadequate for the lengthy periods of unemployment that many such young people now have to suffer.

CLASSIFICATION AND FRAMING IN PUBLIC SCHOOLS—A FIRST LOOK

Although some discontinuities in the social reproduction process have been located in the relationship between working-class schooling and jobs, it would seem likely that the ruling class would ensure that there was a much firmer continuity between the two for its own offspring. It is thus of interest to examine the classification and framing experienced by pupils in the separate public school sector and to determine the extent of continuity or discontinuity between schooling and the type of occupations in which those from public school are likely to spend their later years.

The data and argument presented in this section are based on a wide range of documentary data and an ethnographic study conducted in two of the major public boarding schools in England. About a month was spent in one school and a whole term in the second. Interviews were conducted with teaching, administrative, and domestic staff as well as pupils, and time was spent observing lessons, meetings, sports, and both formal and informal social occasions. A full report is published elsewhere (Walford, 1984, 1986).

Although the private school sector in England is small, serving only about 8% of the relevant age range, it is highly diverse. The highly prestigious and well-known boarding schools such as Rugby, Eton, and Charterhouse are only a small part of a very wide range of schools which, at the lower end, offer anything but advantage to the children who happen to be confined in them by their parents or guardians (Walford, 1991). It is important to emphasize that the elite schools with which this chapter is concerned are only a small part of the private sector and that these schools have traditionally been schools for boys only.

Terminology is difficult and open to dispute in this area. Some would claim that the 233 schools with headmasters who are members of the Headmasters Conference are entitled to use the term "public school" in referring to themselves, but in the context of the reproduction of the ruling class, a much smaller group is central. There are, perhaps, some 40 to 50, mainly boarding schools, that have had, in the past, a significant part to play in ruling-class education. This is not to say that all pupils at these schools are necessarily from ruling-class backgrounds. The incidence of scholarships of various kinds, including the government's Assisted Places Scheme, as well as children from families with "new" money, mean that these schools do not serve pupils with homogeneous class backgrounds. On the other hand, these public boarding schools have been the traditional place at which ruling-class parents educate their sons.

Although there has been a shift toward day provision and away from boarding, it is clear that many ruling-class parents still prefer to have their children educated in these public schools rather than trust the state comprehensive system. They expect that these schools will educate their children in such a way that the hierarchical class structure of society can be maintained and that they will be able to pass on to their own children their high and advantageous positions, legitimatized through the academic and personal success of their children (Fox, 1985). In short, they expect there to be considerable continuity between schooling and the leading occupations that they hope their children will eventually occupy.

In terms of classification and framing, however, a parent might have cause for concern about the usefulness of his or her investment. Over the last two decades the leading public schools have become fiercely and openly academic (Rae, 1981; Walford, 1986). The increased competition from pupils at state-maintained schools and colleges for entry to universities and professions has meant that examination success has become the central preoccupation toward which the public schools orientate. Two fistfuls of GCSEs (General Certificate of Secondary Education) and one fistful of Advanced levels have become the mark of a successful "product" of these schools. The formal curriculum of the schools is thus an almost pure collection code. Classification and framing are uniformly high with the pressures of the examination syllabus being felt throughout the school. On entry at age 13, boys start a 3-, or sometimes 2-year course toward a GCSE. They will usually be taking between 8 and 12 separate GCSE academic subjects. The teaching throughout will be rigidly time-tabled, with each different subject being taught by specialist academic staff. There may be no integration whatsoever between subjects. On achieving GCSEs, the expectation is that pupils will then stay two years longer and take at least three A-level subjects. The vast majority do so and have a high rate of success. In 1991, nearly 90% of the leavers who had taken A-level examinations or similar in the Headmasters Conference schools went on to higher education. The rather smaller group of highly prestigious public boarding schools has an even higher rate of entry to higher education.

Yet, although strong classification and framing in public schools does give a high chance of entry to higher education, there is considerable discontinuity between the strength of classification and framing in schooling and the strength required in the higher education institutions and the high-status and ruling-class occupations for which these pupils hope they are destined. The archetypal professional occupation is weakly classified and framed. The professional is expected to be creative and forward-looking, to initiate and control rather than be controlled. The nature and extent of occupational responsibilities are not firmly bounded, but expand as new initiatives are taken. The division between work and play is porous, as professional commitments overlap with family responsibilities, professional colleagues merge with personal friends, and work from the office overflows into the home study. The professional does not work set hours, but works until the particular projects with which he or she is concerned are completed to satisfaction. Organization, pacing, and timing of the work are set by the professional rather than any superior. It would be difficult to conceive of anything more different from the strongly classified and framed formal curriculum of public schools.

The immediate move to higher education would also appear to mark a distinct discontinuity, for there is rarely a strong system demanding that work be regularly and conscientiously completed. In most universities students could do little work for an entire term without any lecturers noticing. Incidentally, the traditional tutorial system at Oxbridge is better designed to meet the problems that ex-public school pupils may face than the majority of other universities, for undergraduates there have weekly tutorials at which work must be produced. The recent pressures on all universities to increase student numbers will mean that, even at Oxbridge, large group teaching will probably become the norm, and classification and framing will weaken. At one of the research schools, I attended a meeting of staff at which the "poor tutorial arrangements" at universities were discussed. Without exception the staff saw the fault as being with the universities for not pushing students as hard as was done in schools. None saw the necessity to allow students to take responsibility for their own work. Their concern, however, was justified in that it sprang from reports of past "good" students failing, or doing badly, at the end of the first year at university.

THE FORMAL EXTRACURRICULUM AND FORMAL SOCIAL LIFE

The preceding analysis would seem to indicate that the discontinuities between schooling and work are as dramatic with ruling-class pupils as they are with pupils from working-class families. In practice, such a claim is not straightforward for, so far, only the strength of the classification and framing of the formal curriculum have been considered. In public boarding schools the term *curriculum* has to be widened to include a much broader range of pupil activities, for much that would elsewhere be regarded as outside the province of the school is a necessary part of public school life.

In day schools, extracurricular activities are, by definition, ultimately optional, but in boarding schools these very same activities traditionally become part of the formal expectations. Perhaps the clearest example is sports. Boys are not only expected to take part in the main sport according to the season, but must usually take on other sporting activities on some of the days when the main sport is not played. Thus, rugby or soccer in the winter and cricket or rowing in the summer may occupy three or four afternoons each week and, apart from practice sessions, there are interhouse matches for each age group. Only very few are able to escape playing for their house at some level. The expectations of the school do not stop there, however, for many of the schools set aside a further afternoon each week for so-called "minor games" that can include those more individual sports such as golf, squash, or swimming, or team games such as basketball, hockey, or water polo. Again, competitions are organized at both the house and school level, and the pressures of small numbers in each house are so great that even boys who are not particularly keen or able still find themselves involved at a competitive level.

The formal extracurriculum extends further than sport. Cultural and artistic activities are often far from truly optional so that although no boy would be actually forced to play an instrument, the encouragement to do so is high. Major concerts, in which outside musicians are hired by the school, are occasions at which much of the audience actually might well prefer to be elsewhere. Drama has a tendency to engulf many more pupils than might be expected and, where house plays are the order of the day, each house extends its powers of persuasion so that most of the members are either acting or working in front or backstage.

Societies and activities in themselves are usually viewed as desirable. Many of the schools have set times when pupils must be engaged in some officially recognized "activity." The list of possibilities is usually wide from chess and cycling, to mahjong and mountaineering and to stamps and scuba. The choice may be wide and open to negotiation, but the important point to recognize is that each pupil has to choose at least one of these pursuits and become active in it.

Most of the public schools were established to further a particular religious viewpoint. Those with medieval parentage still cluster around cathedrals, whereas the Victorian foundations usually have the chapel as the geographical focus of the group of rambling buildings. Undoubtedly chapel now plays a much smaller part in the lives of the schools than formerly, but it is still a clear area in which public boarding schools extend the formal extracurriculum into areas almost untouched in day schools. Chapel services may now be only two or three mornings each week rather than six, and these services are mercifully short, but many schools still retain compulsory chapel on one occasion each Sunday.

In boarding schools the school curriculum must be thought of as far wider than merely time-tabled lessons and even these formal extracurricular activities, for the influence of the school extends deep into areas that elsewhere would be in the private domain and not the business of the school. Day pupils live only part of their lives in schools, and, for many, school-based judgments play only a small part in their own self-conceptions or in the evaluations made of them by others. The influence of parents in the home and, perhaps, friends drawn from a range of extraschool interests will probably have a far greater impact than that of the school. For the boarding school pupil, however, life is lived completely within the school's influence for the whole of the term. Official regulations thus extend to cover all activities of pupils from the time a pupil must be out of bed and into breakfast until the time that lights must be extinguished in the dormitories. There are regulations as to where pupils may or may not be at all times of the day, what they may wear, and how they should behave. But, although the rules may be many, this part of the total school curriculum is essentially *weakly* classified and framed. Individual rules and restrictions are open to negotiation between masters and pupils and as it is simply not possible to lay down rules for every eventuality, schools rely on a general overarching rule such as "You are expected to show common sense, good discipline and good manners at all times" with all its possible ambiguity and space for different interpretations.

Within the houses pupils have considerable autonomy of action for, as long as they do the required time-table activities, they are free to spend the rest of the time much as they wish. Masters will generally only interfere in social activities if they are perceived to go beyond the general rule of "common sense, good discipline, and good manners" that can never be explicitly defined. Yet, although these expectations are poorly defined and diffuse, pupils recognize that they are of major importance and know that masters expect an "appropriate" level of keenness, enthusiasm, responsibility, behavior, and so on from them throughout the entire time they are at school. As with child-centered progressivism in the infant classroom, a far wider range of the pupils' attributes and activities are seen as legitimate objects of evaluation and scrutiny. Judgments of success or failure are based on a multiplicity of dimensions.

CLASSIFICATION AND FRAMING IN PUBLIC SCHOOLS—A SECOND LOOK

The universities and other institutions of higher education force both private and state-maintained schools to adopt a highly classified and framed curriculum for academically able pupils. They demand the acquisition of numerous A-level and GCSE passes in a variety of set subjects and pressure the schools toward collection codes and the visible pedagogy for pupils who wish to enter higher education and hence the professional occupations. Although public schoolboys may still have a slight unfair advantage in terms of Oxbridge admissions (Halsey, Heath, & Ridge, 1984), the differences are now small, and university entry cannot be gained without the necessary clutch of high grade A-level passes.

Although the strong classification and framing within the formal curriculum may be seen as a direct result of the increasingly meritocratic pressures on all schools, the public schools, through the formal extracurriculum and the formalization of social life, have been able to offer a total school curriculum that has elements of far weaker classification and framing. It has been possible for the public schools to offer a curriculum based on the invisible pedagogy and the integrated code alongside the visible pedagogy and the collection code. The key to understanding this is that, in public boarding schools, work and play become intertwined, whereas for day pupils work and play are essentially separate domains. There may be, of course, some overlap of geographical location of what is regarded as work for all school pupils—homework is taken home—but the day pupil can clearly differentiate what is "homework" (the work of the school carried into another geographical location) from "play." For the boarding school pupil the work and responsibilities of school are ever present. The day pupil interacts with teachers who for all practical purposes only exist between 9 and 4 for five days a week, but the boarding school pupil has to take account of school authority continuously. Lives are lived in the expectation that all aspects of work and play, be these academic, cultural, behavioral, or attitudinal, are open to being evaluated at any time.

Pupils in public boarding schools essentially live under the invisible pedagogy, in which criteria for evaluation are multiple and diffuse. Their activities are constantly open to evaluation (in the formal curriculum of subject teaching, the extracurriculum of sport and cultural activities, and in the social activities in houses), and that evaluation is conducted by the very same schoolmasters. The master who teaches English may coach cricket and act as an assistant housemaster. Thus he may pervade all aspects of a pupil's life. The expectation is that the best pupils will not only be successful academically, but they will also flourish at sport, art, and other cultural pursuits as well. Just as important, pupils are expected to acquire a whole set of behavior patterns, morals, tastes, and attitudes that are the essence of appropriate character training for their anticipated future positions in society. Here the emphasis is on the whole person who is taught and evaluated through the invisible pedagogy, in which there is much reduced emphasis on the mere transmission and acquisition of specific skills as in the visible pedagogy.

To summarize, boarding school pupils experience a total curriculum in which work and play are intertwined. Within classroom subject work the classification and framing may well be as strong as found anywhere and, indeed, the organized "prep" periods, for younger pupils at least, ensures that the direct extension of subject work into "homework" is far more strongly classified and framed than most day pupils would experience. But, although day pupils live essentially in two separate domains, the unified world of the public boarding school with its much extended curriculum allows there to be a flourishing additional invisible pedagogy in operation. In a similar way to the infant school pupils discussed by Bernstein (1973), pupils here know that they are expected to be constructively "busy" throughout their time at the school. They know that the quality of their "busyness" will be evaluated on multiple and diffuse criteria by the same people who evaluate daily their academic work.

Having recognized the several elements of the curriculum available in public boarding schools, it is necessary to reevaluate the degree of continuity that there is between school and work for these pupils. It was shown that, at the surface level, there appeared to be a distinct discontinuity between the strong classification and framing found in the formal curriculum and that required in desirable occupations for this group. The ruling-class and professional-level occupations that are sought by parents and pupils at public schools may be characterized by their weak classification and framing, for success in the business world, for example, requires a broad range of abilities, interests, and attitudes. The golf and yachting club provide not only a forum at which business people may meet, but also an informal social setting at which others may be evaluated as being worthy of doing business with. Individuals will be evaluated on a whole range of diffuse criteria, and judgments will be made about whether or not he or she is the "right sort" of person. Professionals are always "on call"; work spills over from time-tabled limitations into personal life; the boundaries between work and play are low; the pacing, organization, and timing of activities in both spheres are largely controlled by the professional. In terms of the formal curriculum of public boarding schools, there is a clear discontinuity here between school and work but, as has just been shown, the extension of the school's evaluation and scrutiny into the "formal extracurriculum" and "formal" social life is such that pupils are well prepared for the needs of professional and ruling-class occupations.

The public schools have managed to find a way of organizing the entire curriculum such that strong classification and framing are imposed in subject teaching to facilitate high qualifications and entry into higher education. Yet, at the same time, pupils experience elements of weaker classification and framing and the invisible pedagogy that enable them to experience the correct code for their future preferred occupations. A balance seems to have been achieved that will enable public school pupils to acquire certification and legitimation of their position and also the necessary personal skills to become successful within their chosen occupations.

SPECULATIONS

Although most schools or parents would not express it in Bernstein's terms, both are clearly aware that public boarding schools attempt to offer a balanced mixture of both weak and strong classification and framing. Schools make elaborate claims to be educating the "whole person" and to not just be concerned with narrow academic success. The prospectuses of schools make it clear that a whole range of what Lambert (1975) has catalogued as "expressive goals" are to be seen as an essential part of the school process. With regard to parents, Fox (1984, 1985) has shown that the reasons they choose public schools for their boys center on two general features that the public schools are perceived to be able to offer—the ability to produce better academic results and to develop the character by instilling discipline. The second of these may be seen to be related to educating the "whole person" and thus to the invisible pedagogy of the wider curriculum of these schools.

However, the balanced mixture of both weak and strong classification and framing is difficult to maintain, and there are signs that it
is beginning to tip too far toward strong classification and framing. This
section of the chapter is necessarily speculative for it attempts to
assess potential future possibilities as a result of past and present
trends. The direction of change, however, points toward interesting
future problems for the schools.

The last two decades or so have seen considerable changes in
many aspects of life in public schools. John Rae (1981), then
Headmaster of Westminster School, went as far as calling it a revolution, whereas the research on which this chapter is based acknowledges
both change and continuity (Walford, 1986). A very significant change
has been the move toward co-education. HMC schools have traditionally been for boys only and have been designed to equip these boys for
elite positions within an almost totally male-dominated society. For a
variety of reasons (Walford, 1983), more than two-thirds of these HMC
schools now accept girls as well as boys—either for all ages or for girls
taking A-level only. In itself, this change need not modify classification
and framing within the schools, yet, in practice, on average the girls
selected have usually been of higher academic ability than the boys,
which has reinforced the emphasis on examinations.

Even when the schools have declined to become co-educational, the increased competition from state-maintained schools has led to
a shift toward the preeminence of academic work, with its strong classification and framing. The schools have employed a greater number of
specialist, highly academic, subject staff and invested heavily in science, technology, computing, and other expensive teaching facilities.
However, although there has been an increase in the importance of academic certification, there has been a corresponding decrease in other
activities. Sporting activities no longer hold a great power over most
pupils, and the "bloods" have seen their power wither. The Combined
Cadet Force has faded greatly in importance, as has chapel and religious commitment. Older pupils now seem less inclined to play major
parts in the organization of the younger boys in the houses, and the
claims of work are more frequently heard to be in conflict with prefec-
tural duties or playing sport for the house or the school.

Many would undoubtedly argue that such changes were very
necessary and that the present balance is far preferable to the old.
However, there are indications that the balance may have tipped too far.
Several of the schoolmasters interviewed in the two research boarding
schools, for example, expressed concern that their schools had become
too much like "exam mills"—certainly producing a high-quality product
on that criterion but, they thought, at cost to other, perhaps more valu-

able, criteria. The evidence is mixed, of course—some of the new highly academic staff are well pleased by the emphasis given to their examination work. Others, however, felt increasingly that they were being evaluated in terms of the examination marks that their pupils obtained and, correspondingly, that pupils were being evaluated increasingly on this one dimension rather than on the diffuse and varied aspects that combine to form the "whole person." Not untypically one said:

> I think that we are too examination ridden—it's difficult to get away from it, but we're now an examination mill. And parents' expectations when a boy gets accepted by the school are often quite unrealistic. . . . But, I think it's quite understandable when parents are paying out high fees. If the father's a businessman, he regards it as an investment and he wants the dividend in success for his son.

Another claimed:

> The pressures on staff from parents have increased tremendously. They want their sons to get to university, and see it as our job to push so hard that they get there.

Fox (1985) has shown that this pressure from parents is widespread, but the demands for greater academic success come from pupils as well as parents as another schoolmaster interviewed indicated:

> I suppose that one of the greatest changes is that the boys generate their own pressure. They now work very hard, right from [a young age]. . . . The boys are also interested in a career from very early on.

One housemaster stated:

> I've found recently that boys are more wary of taking up extra commitments. They're less keen to captain the cricket or even be Head of House—although I haven't had one refuse yet! They know that it could eat into their time for work.

This information from schoolmasters was supported by the pupils. In a survey of about 200 of the younger boys at one of the schools, over 70% said on an open-ended question that the main reason for their being at the school was to obtain better qualifications, or similar statements.

Overall, the indications are that the integrated curriculum and invisible pedagogy that are made possible by a much broader total curriculum, and that give a degree of correspondence between the strengths of classification and framing at school and at university and work, would seem to be declining in importance. As success and failure have increasingly been seen in terms of examination results, so the broader and more wide-ranging criteria on which evaluation of the person could take place have decreased in importance. Tapper and Salter (1984) have argued that there is a growing convergence of experiences of pupils in public boarding schools and those of the majority of academically able pupils elsewhere.

This trend toward neglecting or deemphasizing those distinctive aspects of the wider curriculum that are more weakly classified and framed is exaggerated by the drift away from boarding itself in the public school sector. In 1974, when the Independent Schools Information Service first surveyed its membership, there were 207 Headmasters Conference schools with 46,208 of the 109,503 boys (42%) as boarders. In addition, 33% of the 3,525 girls in these schools were boarders. By 1992, there were 233 HMC schools, but only 28% of the 126,886 boys were boarders. The percentage of girls who boarded had also decreased to 28% of the 29,068 girls. Thus therehas been some increase in the number of boarding girls at these schools as more have become co-educational, but this has been at the expense of the girls' private schools in which boarding places have dropped dramatically. Overall, boarding has become far less popular than it was, and there are now hardly any HMC schools that only cater to boarding pupils. The vast majority have expanded their total rolls by taking in high numbers of day pupils. This presents a further threat to the school's ability to be able to offer both the visible and invisible pedagogy, for as the proportion of day pupils increase, so too does the "ethos" of the school change and the formal curriculum dominate.

Changes brought about by the 1988 Education Reform Act and more recent Education Acts have led to strong competition between schools. Private schools are now in direct competition for pupils with grant-maintained schools, city technology colleges and other state-maintained schools, and many parents who might use the private sector now look carefully at what certain state-maintained schools have to offer. All schools, including private schools, are now required by law to publish a wide range of information for prospective parents that includes their examination results. Being easily, if misleadingly, comparable from one school to another, from 1992, private schools have found themselves on "league tables" of examination results alongside state-maintained schools. Some have found themselves near the bottom rather than the top and are under great pressure to improve their scores.

The result of all these changes is an ever-increasing predominance of stronger classification and framing of the formal curriculum at the expense of the weaker classification and framing of the wider cur-

riculum. This may have considerable effect. It seems likely that the elite
public schools will still be able to ensure that a good proportion of
their pupils enter higher education, but after that stage, upon entry into
work, ex-public school pupils will no longer have an advantage in having prior experience of the invisible pedagogy. There will be a resulting
contradiction between the experiences of school and work in terms of
the strengths of classification and framing. If this is so, and if
Bernstein's theory has any predictive validity, we should expect that, in
the future, once university entry has been gained, the advantages of a
public school education will have a smaller part to play in ensuring
success in professional ruling-class occupations. The public schools
may have helped the members of John Major's Cabinet to their positions of eminence, but they may be wasting their money in paying for
private education for their children.

REFERENCES.

Aggleton, P., & Whitty, G. (1985). Rebels without a cause? Socialization
    and subcultural style among the children of the new middle class.
    Sociology of Education, 58, 60-72.
Bernstein, B. (1971). On the classification and framing of educational
    knowledge. In M.F.D. Young (Ed.), *Knowledge and control* (pp. 47-69).
    London: Collier-Macmillan.
Bernstein, B. (1973). *Class and pedagogies; visible and invisible*. Paris: OECD,
    CERI. (Reprinted as Chapter 6 of Class, codes and control (Vol. 3).
    (1975) London: Routledge and Kegan Paul.
Bernstein, B. (1975). *Introduction*. In Class, codes and control (Vol. 3).
    London: Routledge and Kegan Paul.
Bernstein, B. (1977). Aspects of the relations between education and
    production. In *Class, codes and control* (Vol, 3, 2nd ed., pp. 174-200).
    London: Routledge and Kegan Paul.
Bernstein, B. (1990a). *The structuring of pedagogic discourse. Class, codes and
    control* (Vol. 4). London: Routledge.
Bernstein, B. (1990b). Elaborated and restricted codes: Overview and
    criticisms. In *The structuring of pedagogic discourse. Class, codes and con-
    trol* (Vol. 4, pp. 94-130). London: Routledge.
Corrigan, P. (1979). *Schooling the smash street kids*. Basingstoke, UK:
    Macmillan.
Fox, I. (1984). The demand for a public school education: A crisis of
    confidence in comprehensive schooling? In G. Walford (Ed.),
    British public schools: Policy and practice (pp. 45-63). Lewes, UK: Falmer
    Press.

Fox, I. (1985) *Private schools and public issues*. Basingstoke, UK: Macmillan.

Gibson, R. (1977). Bernstein's classification and framing: A critique. *Higher Education Review* 9, 23-45.

Gibson, R. (1984). *Structuralism and education*. London: Methuen.

Halsey, A.H., Heath, A.F., & Ridge, J.M. (1984). The political arithmetic of public schools. In G. Walford (Ed.), *British public schools: Policy and practice* (pp. 9-44). Lewes, UK: Falmer Press.

King, R. (1976). Bernstein's sociology of the school: Some propositions tested. *British Journal of Sociology*, 27, 430-443.

King, R. (1981). Bernstein's sociology of the school: A further testing. *British Journal of Sociology*, 32, 259-265.

Lambert, R. (1975). *The chance of a lifetime? A study of boarding education*. London: Weidenfeld & Nicolson.

Pring, R. (1975). Bernstein's classification and framing of knowledge. *Scottish Educational Studies*, 7, 67-74.

Rae, J. (1981). *The public school revolution*. London: Faber.

Rodger, J. (1985). Natural justice and the big public inquiry: A sociological perspective. *Sociological Review*, 33(3), 409-429.

Tapper, T., & Salter, B. (1984). Images of independent schooling: Exploring the perceptions of parents and politicians. In G. Walford (Ed.), *British public schools: Policy and practice* (pp. 179-207). Lewes, UK: Falmer Press.

Walford, G. (1981). Classification and framing in higher education. *Studies in Higher Education*, 6, 147-158.

Walford, G. (1983). Girls in boys' public school: A prelude to further research. *British Journal of Sociology of Education*, 4(1), 39-54.

Walford, G. (1984). The changing professionalism of public school teachers. In G. Walford (Ed.), *British public schools: Policy and practice* (pp. 111-135). Lewes, UK: Falmer.

Walford, G. (1986). *Life in public schools*. London: Methuen.

Walford, G. (1991). Private schooling into the 1990s. In G. Walford (Ed.), *Private schooling: Tradition, change and diversity* (pp. 1-13). London: Paul Chapman.

Walker, M. (1983). Control and consciousness in the colleges. *British Educational Research Journal*, 9(2), 129-140.

Willis, P. (1977). *Learning to labour*. Farnborough, UK: Saxon House.

11

Theorizing Social Relations Within Urban Schooling: A Sociohistorical Analysis

Gerald Grace
University of Durham

This chapter takes as its starting point Bernstein's (1977, p. 24) observation that "the structure of social relationships determines the principles of communication and so the shaping of forms of consciousness. It follows that changing the structure of social relationships can change the principles of communication and so change forms of consciousness." An attempt is made, at a theoretical and sociohistorical level, to make explicit the changing nature of social relations in urban working-class schooling in England and to reflect on their possible implications for changes in communication and consciousness. It is argued that the dominant and founding principle of social and pedagogic relations within English working-class schooling in the 19th century was that of hierarchical respect.

Analysis across a longer historical period shows changes in the structure of social relationships with new forms arising and consequent internal conflicts and contradictions appearing in the urban schooling system of the modern English state. Five modes of social relations are suggested as discernible in the last hundred years of English urban schooling, that is, those of hierarchical respect, liberal rapport, radical dialogue, class fraternity, and market exchange. The principles that regulate these modes express different conceptions of the roles of teachers and learners, of the nature of the educational process, and of the relations of the school to the wider society, economy, and polity. The ideological and political struggles that have focused on inner-city schooling are related to these conflicts of social relations, communication, and consciousness formation.

THE PRINCIPLE OF HIERARCHICAL RESPECT

Bernstein has argued that the heart of the schooling process does not reside primarily in the content of the educational encounter, but in its form, that is, within the social relations of the education encounter. It is here that principles of power and social control are realized and enter into and shape the consciousness of both teachers and pupils. The dominant principles of urban working-class schooling in the 19th and early 20th centuries celebrated the interrelated notions of hierarchy, boundary, discipline, loyalty, and civilization. The social relations of the educational encounter were one of the means for the cultural reproduction and extension of such notions within the social world and consciousness of the urban working class (see, for example, McCann 1977; Simon, 1974a).

Hierarchy of power and authority, with the legitimation of divine ordination, was realized within the school as well as within the wider social structure. In particular, the public school cult of the role of the headteacher as the epitome of secular and moral power had an important influence on the social relations of elementary, working-class schooling. For large urban schools especially, the power of the headteacher in terms of physical and moral sanctions was a visible and immediate expression of a wider structure of power and authority in the lives of the pupils. This hierarchy was repeated through clearly delineated levels of power and authority within the school, each level marked by a certain range of privilege and supported by a particular mode of public ritual (on the significance of ritual in schooling, see Bernstein, 1977, pp. 54-66). The principle governing relations within this hierarchical structure was that of *respect*. Respect was the visible manifestation in conduct and demeanor of an internal acceptance of the legitimacy of the social order. To be respectful was an acknowledgment of one's place within the structure, relative to the superior positions of others. To violate this principle was to be "insolent" and threatening to that established order.

The disruption of traditional patterns of social relations in large English cities consequent on rapid industrialization led to tendencies toward "insolence" among the urban working class. Thus it was that for 19th-century England respect became a celebrated virtue within the urban school and insolence an evil to be eradicated. A sense of boundary, of "everything in its proper place," characterized the whole social world of the school. This could be seen to apply to relations of role and position (the boundary between teachers and pupils), to relations of curriculum content (the boundary between subjects), and to relations of education and locality (the boundary between school and community). The constraints of space in crowded urban classrooms gave to the notion of boundary not only a symbolic but also a material and functional significance. A sense of boundary was locked into a particular sense of order.

In its symbolic aspects, the *discovery of boundary* informed much of the pedagogic activity of the school. The classificatory principle which was at the heart of the elementary school curriculum expressed itself not only through formal grammatical and arithmetical rules but also through the classificatory mode of much natural history and elementary natural science teaching. The act of classification was the act of establishing the importance of boundary.

Discipline also had its material and symbolic manifestations. Large classes, difficult working conditions in schools, and elements of working-class resistance to formal schooling generated situations in which the proofs of a "proper teacher" were to be found in a strongly imposed framework. This was a functional imperative of the urban classroom—yet it was always more than this. Discipline, in the form of explicit and imposed social control, was seen to be a necessary antidote to the tendencies toward anarchy embodied in the "urban mob." Working-class schools were a first line of defense and containment against this deeper threat, and therefore it is not surprising that "good discipline" featured highly in their evaluation by superiors (Grace, 1978). The principle of discipline had not only these wider sociopolitical correlates, but also obvious economic and military linkages. Growing European economic and military competition in the late 19th century gave to the notion of discipline in English urban working-class schooling a new significance. The foundations for the discipline of the factory and the discipline of the military were increasingly looked for in school regimes that emphasized exact obedience and close attention and that attempted the socialization and control of body posture and physical movement (for an interesting discussion of this, see Hurt, 1977).

In these ways the social relations of the urban school were some sort of microcosm of other structures of social relations for which its pupils were destined. Symbolically, the idea of discipline, in relation to the curriculum and pedagogy of the urban school, stood for the virtues of the protestant ethic—hard work, rigor, perseverance, and the experience of some pain or ordeal in the process of learning. In such contexts, learning was not intended to be intrinsically pleasurable or to exalt the position and the mind of the learner, but rather to involve the *submission* of the learner to the structures, authority, and sheer weight of established knowledge. The discipline of learning was concerned first to establish a consciousness of *ignorance* in the mind of the pupil (a state comparable to the recognition of original sin). In light of this recognition, the drudgery and rote of learning appeared as the legitimated and necessary means for attaining some enlightenment (a state comparable to salvation). Such a concept of the necessary discipline of study was at the heart of the pedagogy of the urban school and patterned its social relations in particular ways. The good teacher was demanding, the good pupil was diligent in application, and the regulative principle of their pedagogical relation was that of cultural discipleship.

If a sense of respect and of discipleship were important objectives of the social relations of urban schooling, the creation of a sense of loyalty was a crucial one. In the socialization of the urban working class, the establishment of a sense of respect might be seen to be the initial challenge, but unless some deeper sense of loyalty to existing institutions could be developed, the sociopolitical situation would remain problematic. Loyalty might be engendered by the reproduction in urban schools, albeit on a humbler scale, of some of the cultural forms and rituals that characterized the education of the upper classes. In particular, competitive games and the team spirit played an important part in the attempt to create a sense of corporate loyalty, which had wider sociopolitical implications. The headteachers of urban elementary schools sought to generate "loyalty to the school" as a countervailing ideological force to the deeper loyalties of class and neighborhood. In this they were only ever partially successful. Urban working-class schools were too embedded in the close networks of the locality to make this a real possibility, and they lacked the necessary control of spaces—physical, temporal, and symbolic, in which significant identity changes and changes of social allegiance might be accomplished.

Nevertheless, the social relations of such schools were marked by persistent efforts to obtain such allegiance from the urban working class. Loyalty to the school was but one manifestation of an ideological structure that found its apotheosis in the ideology of nationalism and of patriotism. Both forms sought to establish an allegiance to corporate entities transcending class and locality and to invest such allegiance with moral worth.[1] The good teacher and the good pupil were expected to demonstrate loyalty to the institution, even though such loyalty might frequently require the suspension of rationality and independent thought.

---

[1] At another level, that of imperialism, Simon (1974b, pp. 165-175) examines the educational implications of empire.

The last of the mediations of the dominant principle of respect that characterized urban working-class schooling in the 19th century and early 20th century was that of "civilization." The principle of civilization was the dynamic manifestation of a supreme cultural confidence. It was a conviction that "the best that has been thought and known" was the property of an elite whose duty it was to guard the cultural treasure and to make appropriate mediations of it in appropriate circumstances. For men such as Matthew Arnold, the philistinism and barbarity attendant on industrialization and urbanization required as an antidote the extension of "civilization." The act of civilizing the urban working class involved their exposure to the refining and elevating qualities of selected cultural elements in language, art, music, literature, and poetry. The products of superior minds might thus serve to extend sense and sensibility among the population at large and to provide some encounter with "sweetness and light." This encounter would be firmly contexted within an explicit framework of cultural hierarchy that celebrated the superiority of received cultural forms and left the recipient in no doubt as to the barbarity and poverty of his or her own cultural forms and practices.

The social relations of the 19th-century urban school were formed within an explicit cultural hierarchy involving an ethic of civilization transmission. The teachers themselves were frequently aware of, or made aware of, their own deficiencies of culture, and this caused them to seek to "improve" themselves with great attention to cultural detail and correctness. Their own function and role as cultural transmitters was marked with insecurities. Their own consciousness of "lack of culture" was realized again in the lack of culture of their pupils that repeated elements of their own social and class biographies. Such socialized insecurities engendered an attitude of deference and awe in their encounter with high culture. Such culture was perceived as the creation of superior minds in another time—a great cultural mystery that the elementary school teacher only partly comprehended but that he or she knew to be, or believed to be, profoundly enriching.

Thus the principle of civilization in the urban elementary school involved the transmission not only of selected elements of high culture, but more crucially of a sense of awe and deference in relation to them. The principle of civilization involved the recognition of cultural greatness in others and the generation of an appropriate sense of deference (if not of comprehension) in the presence of such greatness.

The question that must now be considered is the extent to which the principle of hierarchy, and its mediations in notions of boundary, discipline, loyalty, and civilization in urban working-class schooling, was challenged by new and emergent principles arising in the 20th century and especially in the 1960s and 1970s with important consequences for the social relations of urban schools. Studies in urban education have shown that by the 1960s and 1970s, the teachers within urban working-class schools in England had become more socially and culturally differentiated, and this contributed toward changes in the principles regulating pedagogic activity and patterning social relations within the schools (see Grace, 1978).

The principle of hierarchical respect that had persisted well into the 20th century was on the defensive in English urban schools by the 1960s. Wider social and cultural change that had involved a weakening in the authority of hierarchy, of boundary, of institution, and of role, had been compounded by the existence of crisis conditions in inner-city schools, especially in London in the 1960s and early 1970s. The crucial correlates of continuity and certainty in the maintenance of a stable social order were more dramatically fractured at that time in working-class inner-city schools than in any other type of educational institution.

The crisis of teacher supply for such schools in the late 1960s and early 1970s resulted in considerable institutional instability and the enforced recruitment of a highly differentiated and cosmopolitan teaching group. Not only did this admit to the schools teachers with a wide range of political and educational ideologies, many with egalitarian premises, but constantly changing patterns of social relations appeared to herald a state of anomie. Such conditions undermined the principle of hierarchical respect in schooling and any mode of social relations based on it. The pupils perceived the instability of the institutional structure and were quick to exploit the spaces that became available for the subversion of respect. In this, they were supported by some teachers who saw in the principle of respect an outmoded and unacceptable ideology of hierarchy and domination. Thus, an essential consciousness of order and timelessness that urban schools in an earlier period had sought to create became crucially weakened in the 1960s and 1970s.

Some teachers sought to maintain the principle of hierarchical respect in changed conditions. For such teachers, respect was the crucial regulative principle of institutional relationships. It continued to celebrate the appropriate and proper social distance between pupil and teacher, between young teacher and senior teacher, and between all teachers and the headteacher. In other words, respect was seen as the necessary regulator of appropriate distance, appropriate behavior, and acceptable presentation of self in schooling. It was seen as the enemy of casualness and familiarity in the classroom and the school. Traditional teachers attempted to defend such vestiges of ritual as remained in the urban school, and they retained expectations for strong leadership from the headteacher. Discipline in the form of explicit and imposed social control was seen to be essential to the generation of respect and to accord with what it was claimed many working-class parents wanted from the schools. These concerns accounted for the hostility shown toward young teachers of egalitarian persuasion at this time and especially toward "soft progressive" headteachers. Both were seen to be engaged in forms of institutional treason, but whereas the errors of the former could be seen to be naive, the errors of the latter were culpable.

In a cultural sense, the principle of respect was also on the defensive by the 1960s. For some urban teachers, particularly those with a conscious sense of "scholarship success" from humble origins, many of the developments in the curriculum and pedagogy of urban schools at this time were seen to represent an erosion of standards and a weakening of the central cultural mission of such schools. Having acquired, through their own educational socialization, a sense of respect for an established corpus of knowledge and for the discipline required to acquire it, they saw both of these features increasingly belittled. Cultural critiques of the 1960s and early 1970s, frequently mediated by their younger colleagues, attacked the whole cultural structure of which they were a part. The notion of cultural hierarchy was undermined; the established boundaries of knowledge were labeled "arbitrary" and counterproductive; the discipline of study was seen to be a feature of youth "alienation"; the transmission mode of pedagogy was called "imposition"; and yesterday's work of civilization was denounced as today's work of cultural domination. In countering these notions, traditionalists claimed that the principle of respect in cultural terms was an essential correlate of academic success, and that principles of cultural egalitarianism or relativism were a betrayal of the fundamental work of the urban school. In taking this stance, such teachers' concern that respect should be generated toward the corpus of knowledge and the indices of scholarship was not unrelated to considerations of respect for their own authority position. All such undermining activity had in their view the effect of devaluing the role of the cultural transmitter as such and of weakening respect for the teacher. In particular, the cultural transmitter was in danger of losing the priest-like associations of the role, associations that had to do with the mediation of excellence and the possession of special qualities. Such uncertainties produced for such teachers a crisis of legitimation in cultural forms and a loss of that sense of confidence and cultural superiority that had marked the earlier "civilizing" function of urban schools. For traditionalist teachers, a sense of cultural anomie could only be resisted by continuing to uphold a respect for "standards," for without a respect for standards not only would the cultural outcomes of the school become problematic, but also the whole structure of its social relations, and beyond that the social relations of the wider society.[2]

THE PRINCIPLE OF LIBERAL RAPPORT

If the principle of respect in urban education in the 1960s and 1970s was on the defensive, the principle of rapport appeared to be rising to dominance. Rapport was seen to be the principle for a liberal era of schooling. It celebrated the importance of friendliness and good interpersonal relations, of understanding the young adult and "youth culture", of sympathizing with social and economic disadvantages, and of demonstrating pastoral concern for the learner. The social relations of urban schooling in the 1960s and 1970s were marked by a strong and persistent effort to achieve rapport at personal, institutional, and cultural levels. At the personal level, the principle of rapport was most clearly realized in the dominant liberal and individualistic educational ethic that theoretically required the recognition of the uniqueness of each pupil and of his or her particular needs and personality dispositions.

Within the rapport relation some teachers claimed to relate to their pupils in terms of a vivid individualism that made them blind to considerations of social class, locality, or even ethnic identity. The good teacher in the urban school was seen to achieve rapport in the classroom by taking the time and trouble "to get to know" his or her pupils as whole human beings. The requirements of obtaining this intimate knowledge of the pupils might necessitate the teacher becoming involved in the wider life of the neighborhood and in engaging in home visits. The epitome of the principle of rapport at this time was to be found in the increasing appointments of full-time school counsellors in inner-city schools. At an institutional level, the principle of rapport was also manifested in the strong and increasingly powerful pastoral care systems that were established in urban working-class secondary schools. The formal designation of a group of teachers as primarily agents of good human relations within urban working-class schools was without historic precedent and was evidence of the importance that was attached to this function in urban education, especially in the large comprehensive schools.

The rise of rapport as a dominant principle in 1960s urban education was partly a response to the diffusion of more humane and psy-

---

[2]For an elaboration of these arguments, see the early literature of right-wing criticisms of inner-city schools (e.g., Boyson, 1975; Cox & Boyson, 1975).

chologistic theories of learning that were salient at this time. It was also partly a response to crisis conditions in inner-city schools. Not only could it be persuasively argued that pupils in modern urban schools would learn better if treated in a friendly and adult way, but it could also be powerfully argued that no other alternative was possible. The weakening of institutional functioning in many inner-city schools in the late 1960s and early 1970s and the accelerated weakening in principles of respect created the necessity for a new regulative principle in the social relations of schooling. Rapport offered the advantage of appearing as a new educational principle, a new ingredient in particular forms of professional expertise in teaching, and as an essential principle for institutional cohesion. Rapport also had the considerable advantage of muting features of hierarchy without radically changing them.

If rapport accomplished a reduction of the social distance between teacher and pupil and helped in the generation of a new and approachable image for headteachers, it also had important consequences for school-community relations. The strong boundary of the urban "citadel" school vis-a-vis its locality was weakened, and the ideology of school-community partnership encouraged. The intentions of greater community liaison were many and various, but one had to do with ending previous states of community warfare and resistance in relation to the urban school and of replacing them with cooperation. Rapport between school and community was looked to as a new principle in urban education.

In cultural and pedagogic terms, a greater relation of rapport was planned. With a weakening of principles of respect toward established cultural forms and a weakening in the legitimations for notions of the essential discipline of study, a search for new regulative principles took place. During the 1960s and 1970s, developments in the curriculum of urban schools that celebrated the importance of relevance, interest, enjoyment, self-direction, and community relatedness can be seen as parts of a schooling response to a changed cultural milieu. The "good" school and the "good" teacher sought to create an integrated environment for learning in which the pupil would experience a sense of rapport in the act of learning. Multicultural education became a legitimated response to the growing ethnic diversity of the schools. Multiculturalism as "rapport" was looked to for the amelioration of racism in schools.[3] By various forms of curriculum change, it was intended that a sense of boundary, of cultural alienation and distance, and of cultural exclusion should be eradicated from the consciousness of pupils.

---

[3]Multiculturalism as a means of obtaining greater cultural understanding and rapport in multiethnic urban schools was criticized by antiracist teachers for avoiding the power relations of racism and for an unwillingness to confront these directly in antiracist education.

Liberal rapport in its cultural and pedagogical manifestations is an attractive principle. It is related to sincere attempts to integrate education with the life experience of the urban pupil and to remove much that is distant and dull from the cultural message of the school. It is associated with enlightened and progressive responsiveness to changes in theories of learning, to changing pupil expectations, and to a changing social and cultural context. In inner-city schools in particular it appeared to be the obvious liberal principle for dealing with the cultural challenges and opportunities presented by a multiethnic population. It is apparently a principle for the promotion of harmony and for the de-fusing of conflict in schooling. At the same time there are problematic aspects related to its rise to dominance in modern urban schools. It could be claimed that the rise of rapport might signal the death of legitimate demand, that is, of a requirement that all pupils should encounter, in relative terms, the difficult, the precise, and the exacting. In this sense, the principle of rapport may become a hindrance to the full intellectual development of urban working-class pupils. Second, and more generally, the principle of rapport has the effect of *muting* features of power, control, and hierarchy without radically changing them. It is thus a superficial "solution" to various structural and cultural problems in education and in society, problems that some teachers want to claim should be made increasingly visible for more fundamental change.

Insofar as social relations within urban schooling in the 1960s and 1970s were premised on principles of rapport, they appeared to offer the possibility of reduction of conflicts of various kinds and of the emergence of a situation of harmony. But from both traditionalist teacher and radical teacher perspectives, such harmony could only be achieved at the price of avoiding fundamental questions that the existence of hierarchy generates. In other words, rapport alone can be seen to be the principle of a superficial liberalism that seeks to avoid, rather than confront directly, the apparently immutable features of hierarchy and of its manifestations in classism, racism, and sexism.[4]

---

[4]The Inner London Education Authority (ILEA) was prepared to confront these issues directly in its 1983 series of publications, *Race, Sex and Class*, that were sent to all ILEA schools (see Morrell, 1984). Its willingness to do so is not unconnected with its later political abolition.

THE PRINCIPLE OF RADICAL DIALOGUE AND EMANCIPATION

It is precisely the claim to have engaged in more fundamental analysis of these questions that characterized those urban teachers who sought to advance principles of pedagogic dialogue and of antiracist and antisexist education as the basis of the social relations of the urban school. Such teachers were the mediators of radical forms of pedagogic communications and consciousness that drew their inspiration from libertarian writings, feminist and antiracist literature, and from the writings of Paulo Freire.[5] For such teachers there was an urgent need for the social relations of urban schooling to be transformed by a coming to dominance of the principles of dialogue and emancipation. Whereas principles of respect were regarded as Victorian anachronisms and principles of rapport seen as the manipulative strategies of a new teacher professionalism, principles of dialogue and emancipation held out the possibilities for radical transformation of educational experience and human and cultural relations. Principles of dialogue, especially in a Freirian mode, celebrate egalitarianism and were intended to undermine hierarchy in all its forms. The student and the realizations of his or her culture were not merely to be "related to" as in the liberal pedagogic mode, but to become an important and central constituent of the educational process.

The principle of dialogue dignifies the "student" and the status of his or her language, theorizing, and culture. More than this, it signals an attempt in the pedagogic relationship to obliterate the very categories of "student" and of "teacher" and of the hierarchic order that they represent and to replace them with the egalitarian concept of "cultural participant." It seeks to transform the urban school from its historic function of *imposed cultural transmission* to one of *comprehensive cultural creation*, that is, the school would become an arena for the representation of a rich variety of cultural patterns, forms of communication, and levels of consciousness. Principles of dialogue in this sense sought radical transformations in concepts of knowledge as the cultural capital of an elite, in established modes for the production of knowledge, and in the social relations of the educational process. From this radical perspective knowledge possession and creation was to be the property of all, the mode of its production was to be dialogic and communal, and the social relations of the educational encounter were to be egalitarian. The urban school within this framework was to become not an agency for the civilization (or cultural domination) of the working class and of ethnic minorities, but an agency for the realization of the cultural potentialities of that class and of those communities.

---

[5]For texts influential at the time, see Freire (1972, 1974). For a later text, see Freire (1985). For other literature in this genre, see Giroux (1983) and Livingstone (1987).

At an institutional level, the principle of dialogue has consequences for power and authority. Radical teachers in urban schools in the 1960s and 1970s opposed traditional authoritarian structures and were sceptical that liberal innovations in "participation" represented any real transfer of power. In the context of institutional management, the exponents of principles of dialogue sought a real redistribution of power, a diminution (and ultimate abolition) of hierarchical distinctions, and the emergence of egalitarian school councils as decision-making agencies. At its most ambitious this involved an extension to urban working-class youth of elements of power and decision making within their own educational institutions.

Such intentions represented the most dramatic antithesis to the founding preoccupations of popular urban education in England and potentially the most radical transformation of its social relations. In confronting directly the features of hierarchy whether at a cultural, racial, gender, or institutional level, the mediators of principles of dialogue in urban schools could claim to hold a fundamentally radical stance within education. Such radicalism, however, had many vulnerabilities. Although able to obtain some influence in inner-city schools during their crisis period, a changed social, political, economic, and educational environment in the 1980s was inimical to radical intentions.

Principles of dialogue and emancipation were criticized from traditionalist positions as being anarchic and relativist, and they were attacked by some Left teachers as being diversionary. Although the principles of dialogue and emancipation acknowledged a form of fraternity in urban schooling, it was seen by a sector of teachers on the Left as a fraternity lacking its proper historical location in class analysis and in class struggle.

THE PRINCIPLE OF CLASS FRATERNITY

It was to remedy this situation that a sector of urban teachers in various locations worked in the 1970s to establish the principle of *fraternity* in its proper political context, as the basis for the social relations of the urban working-class school. Such teachers, generally Marxist or Broad Left in political commitment, applied the language of class analysis to the work of schools. From this perspective the school was seen to be a factory for the reproduction of a labor force with those qualities required by a capitalist economy.[6] Teachers were represented as work-

---

[6]The work of Bowles and Gintis (1976) was particularly influential at this time.

ers (at the level of mental production) engaged in the processing of the next generation of (largely) manual or service workers. The contradictions and crises experienced within urban schools were seen to be manifestations of wider contradictions and crises endemic in a capitalist social formation, and their eradication was looked for as a result of wider structural and political transformations. To expect any significant transformations to be mediated through the schools was regarded as part of a liberal mythology of social change. At the same time, however, urban schools were recognized as an important potential site of the class struggle. The alienation and resistance of a growing section of urban youth, black and white, was seen to be an as-yet incoherent expression of class resistance that required support. Such support could be realized in the principle of class fraternity that is the dynamic constituent of class solidarity.

The principle of class fraternity claimed to make possible a radical transformation of the social relations of the urban school. It celebrated the potential unity of urban teachers and of their working-class pupils, black and white, in a common struggle against structural inequalities of wealth and power, racism and sexism. In this sense, politically conscious urban teachers would become not the agents of a controlling enterprise, but allies of the pupils in a common sociopolitical struggle for a better society.[7] They would provide the knowledge that would realize power for working-class communities, the "really useful knowledge" of political, social, and economic relations in a capitalist world. The principle of class fraternity far more than the principle of radical dialogue would, it was claimed, transcend the encapsulated world of education and the school and extend the consciousness and "structural vision" of those who worked within it.

However, attempts to restructure the social relations of the urban school on the basis of a principle of class fraternity faced considerable problems. The most obvious was that of achieving a sense of fraternity, first at the level of the teachers. The highly differentiated nature of the teacher population in urban schools in the 1970s and a long history of intraoccupational fragmentation and conflict presented a formidable challenge. Fraternity presupposes (in the manner in which it was formulated by some urban teachers) a world view in which the class struggle is the real and central feature of social relations. It presupposes that teachers will be prepared to renounce their long and historic struggle for legitimated professionalism to embrace willingly the status

---

[7]As Bowles and Gintis (1976, p 287) put it, "we must fight for curriculum which is personally liberating and politically enlightening; we must reject our pretensions as professionals—pretensions which lead only to a defeatist quietism and isolation—and ally with other members of the working class."

of worker. It is clear that the realization of such fraternity could only come about as the result of a significant consciousness change within the teacher occupational group, and this was not forthcoming.

A further problem concerned the realization of class fraternity at the level of teacher-pupil relations. At this level fraternity presupposes a unity of the teachers with that section of the school population (the "lads" or the resisters) that has always constituted the traditional enemy of the pedagogue. The means to fraternity here were not obvious or straightforward. Although a considerable amount of unity might be achieved with (previously alienated) black pupils in a common struggle against the class relations underpinning racism and fascism, there remained the challenge of those "lads" who were associated with such racism and fascism (see Willis, 1977, for an elaboration on the culture of "the lads"). How could class fraternity be established in these conditions?

In a wider context, any attempt to establish the principle of class fraternity as an important principle in urban schooling had to face widespread inhibitions in English culture concerning the unity of the political and the educational. The problem for the mediators of class fraternity was that they brought to the level of the explicit that which remains at the level of the implicit in the other and competing principles of urban schooling. In other words, class fraternity (as formulated by its supporters in urban schools) was explicitly political (and therefore seen as corrupting the educational), whereas principles of respect, rapport, and even of dialogue appeared to retain an educational and cultural legitimacy, albeit in the case of the latter a deeply suspect one. Fraternity, in short, made visible the political relations of urban education in an uncompromising and challenging way.

The fraternity principle in urban education was too threatening to the established order of the school and of wider social relations to gain significant support from urban teachers in the 1970s. It remained as the ideological commitment of a relatively small group of "teacher heroes" (the expression is that of Althusser, 1972) in the inner-city schools. Nevertheless, the presence of such teachers provided part of the target for right-wing criticisms of subversion in inner-city schooling and of the misuse of educational autonomy in the schooling system. The moral panic generated by these means contributed to a political strategy of reassertion of control and discipline in urban working-class schooling in the 1980s.

THE PRINCIPLE OF MARKET EXCHANGE

The reassertion of control and discipline in urban working-class schooling in England in the 1980s and 1990s has been attempted by using the
discipline of market relations. The 1980s has been a decade of claimed
radical, cultural transformation of schooling. The schooling system, as
late as the 1970s, was characterized by a culture of relative autonomy
and of strong insulation from external agencies. Within these strong
insulations, which included insulations from parents and employers, a
variety of pedagogic forms and of relations with pupils could and did
exist. By the late 1970s, growing criticism of a lack of accountability in
urban schools and of the existence of forms of subversion and anarchy
within them prepared the ground for a major attempt by radical-conser-
vative state agencies to bring education to account by the application of
market principles (for an account of this, see Education Group II, 1991).

The attempted commodification and marketization of education
in the 1980s and 1990s can be seen as the last stage in an historical
process of the secularization of the school in England. Bernstein (1990, p.
86) observed that the era of hierarchical respect and of autonomous visible pedagogy in English education "had the cover of the sacred." The
social and cultural distance of the school, its strong insulations, and its
moral climate helped to preserve a residual sense of its sacred origins, of
the "otherness" of its mission. However, Bernstein noted that one of the
profound transformations arising from the dominant market ideology of
the 1980s is a market-oriented visible pedagogy, "a truly secular form
born out of the context of cost efficient education" (p. 86).

The principles of market accountability, market exchange, and
enterprise are now firmly enshrined in the charters of most urban
schools, albeit in documents that ironically are called *mission statements*.
The culture of enterprise is in the process of displacing earlier cultures
and subcultures of schooling based on mediations of the sacred, the liberal professional, or the emancipatory. Within the culture of education
as enterprise, radical transformations are being attempted. Knowledge
is claimed to be a commodity in the marketplace (see Grace, 1989). The
school is perceived as a production-function center whose effectiveness
is to be judged in terms of a measurable value-added product.
Headteachers and teachers are counseled to become market entrepre-
neurs in their particular division of the education business. Parents are
empowered in their relation with schools as they are ideologically
reconstructed as consumers and shareholders in the cultural enterprise.

In contemporary urban schools the principle of market
exchange is becoming increasingly influential as the regulator of head-
teacher-teacher-pupil relations. As a result of strong market account-

ability in schooling, the headteacher as senior entrepreneur and the teacher as assistent entrepreneur are expected to be resourceful in the realization of measurable success. The pupil, within the culture of enterprise, is at one and the same time both an object for investment and entrepreneur in the making. In these circumstances teachers are expected to "deliver" appropriate curriculum packages and skill resources to urban working-class pupils who in turn are expected to deliver marketable success for the school.[8]

Historically, urban schools have been located in the centers of entrepreneurial activity but largely insulated from such activity. One of the consequences of breaking the boundary between the school and the world of enterprise could be that urban working-class pupils, black and white, will have opportunities to demonstrate entrepreneurial intelligence and achievement that has found no legitimate place in the schooling of the past. Thus the principle of market exchange and of enterprise does have a potential for breaking the culture of academic failure long associated with urban working-class schools.

The market principle in schooling has, however, internal contradictions that threaten that outcome through the reconstitution of hierarchy in various forms. Bernstein (1990, pp. 86-87) argued that "specialisation of curricula within a dominant market-oriented visible pedagogy allows for an almost perfect reproduction of the hierarchy of the economy within the school or between schools (as in the case of 'magnet' schools) through the grading of curricula" and he suggested that "the explicit commitment to greater choice by parents and pupils is not a celebration of a participatory democracy but a thin cover for the old stratification of schools and curricula" (p. 87). This argument is supported by Ball (1993, p. 16) who concluded that available data "clearly show the exclusionary effects of systems of selection and choice in terms of racial segregation and discrimination. . . . The market provides a mechanism for the reinvention and legitimation of hierarchy and differentiation via the ideology of diversity, competition and choice."

It is here that the internal contradictions and oppositions of urban schooling reform under current ideological and political conditions in England become fully apparent. Although the ideology of market accountability in schooling claims to be the agency for greater openness, opportunity, and efficiency, the ideology of greater parental choice allows for the reconstitution of the impediments of hierarchy. Although the representatives of "moral values" within New Right formu-

---

[8]In the market exchange relation, those pupils who cannot deliver marketable success for a school are likely to be seen as a source of deficit in a real sense. The possible implications for policies of selection, recruitment, and retention of pupils arising from this are profound.

lations call on schools, especially inner-city schools, to find a new sense of moral and spiritual purpose, the commodification and commercialization of schooling is profoundly inimical to these ends. Although teachers and pupils are expected to relate together in a culture of education as enterprise, central state regulation of schooling has reached an historically unprecedented level in this century (see Simon, 1991). Thus the latest phase in the development of urban education reform in England is marked by deep contradictions (see Coulby & Bash, 1991; Whitty, 1992). Although radical transformation is claimed, it is possible to discern in contemporary conditions the reconstitution of hierarchy and of other cultural and pedagogical features redolent of 19th-century urban schooling in the Victorian era.

OVERVIEW

Across a long historical period, transitions have occurred in the social relations of the educational encounter in English urban schooling. These transitions have been related to wider structural, political, cultural, and economic change in English society. Five modes of social relations have been suggested as discernible in English urban schooling in the last hundred years, and these are now summarized in programmatic form (following Bernstein) as shown in Table 11.1.

Table 11.1. Social Relations in Urban Schooling: A Theoretical Matrix

Teacher Construct	Principle of Relation	Pupil Construct	Knowledge Construct	Hierarchy
Master	Hierarchical respect	Scholar	Sacred	Celebrated
Professional	Liberal rapport	Client	Integrated	Muted
Participant	Radical dialogue	Participant	Discovery	Challenged
Worker	Class fraternity	Worker	Power	Challenged
Entrepreneur	Market exchange	Entrepreneur	Commodity	Reconstituted

The theoretical matrix represents ideal-type forms, and it is not argued here that a distinct historical and linear sequence can be inferred or that the constructs suggested are exclusive. These are matters for further study and research. The intention has been to think through the social relations within urban schooling as they relate to wider networks of power relations. As Bernstein (1990, p. 168) remarked:

> Education is a relay for power relations external to it. The degree of success of the relay is not here the point. The education system's pedagogic communication is simply a relay for something other than itself. Pedagogic communication in the school . . . is the relay for class relations; the relay for gender relations; the relay for religious relations; for regional relations. Pedagogic communication is a relay for patterns of dominance external to itself.

REFERENCES

Althusser, L. (1972). Ideology and ideological state apparatuses. In B.R. Cosin (Ed.), *Education, structure and society*. Harmondsworth: Penguin.

Ball, S.J. (1993). Education markets, choice and social class: The market as a class strategy in the UK and USA. *British Journal of Sociology of Education*, 14(1), 3-19

Bernstein, B. (1977). *Class, codes and control: Vol.3: Towards a theory of educational transmissions* (2nd ed.). London: Routledge & Kegan Paul.

Bernstein, B. (1990). *The structuring of pedagogic discourse: Class, codes and control: Vol. 4*. London: Routledge & Kegan Paul.

Bowles, S., & Gintis, H. (1976). *Schooling in capitalist America: Educational reform and the contradictions of economic life*. London: Routledge & Kegan Paul.

Boyson, R. (1975). *The crisis in education*. London: Woburn Press.

Coulby, D., & Bash, L. (Eds.). (1991). *Contradiction and conflict: The 1988 Education Act in action*. London: Cassell.

Cox, C.B., & Boyson, R. (Eds.). (1975). *Black Paper, 1975*. London: Dent.

Education Group II. (1991). *Education limited: Schooling and training and the New Right since 1979*. London: Unwin Hyman.

Freire, P. (1972). *Cultural action for freedom*. Harmondsworth: Penguin,

Freire, P. (1974). *Education for critical consciousness*. London: Sheed & Ward.

Freire, P. (1985). *The politics of education: Culture, power and liberation*. London: Macmillan.

Giroux, H. (1983). *Theory and resistance in education: A pedagogy for the opposition*. London: Heinemann.

Grace, G.R. (1978). *Teachers, ideology and control: A study in urban education.* London; Routledge & Kegan Paul.

Grace, G.R. (Ed.). (1984). *Education and the city: Theory, history, and contemporary practice.* London: Routledge & Kegan Paul.

Grace, G.R. (1989). Education: Commodity or public good? *British Journal of Educational Studies,* XXXVII(3), 207-221.

Hurt, J.S. (1977). Drill, discipline and the elementary school ethos. In P. McCann (Ed.), *Popular education and socialisation in the nineteenth century* (pp. 167-191). London: Methuen.

Livingstone, D.W. (Ed.). (1987). *Critical pedagogy and cultural power.* Boston: Bergin & Garvey.

McCann, P. (Ed.). (1977). *Popular education and socialisation in the nineteenth century.* London: Methuen.

Morrell, F. (1984). Policy for schools in inner London. In G. Grace (Ed.), *Education and the city: Theory, history, and contemporary practice* (pp. 195-209). London: Routledge & Kegan Paul.

Simon, B. (1974a). *The two nations and the educational structure 1780-1870.* London: Lawrence & Wishart.

Simon, B. (1974b). *Education and the labour movement 1870-1920.* London: Lawrence & Wishart.

Simon, B. (1991). *Education and the social order 1940-1990.* London: Lawrence & Wishart

Whitty, G. (1992). Urban education in England and Wales. In D. Coulby, C. Jones, & D. Harris (Eds.), *Urban education: World yearbook of education 1992* (pp, 39-53). London: Kogan Page.

Willis, P. (1977). *Learning to labour: How working class kids get working class jobs.* Farnborough: Saxon.

12

Delicate Boundaries: Bernstein, Sacks and the Machinery of Interaction

David Silverman
London University

At first sight, there would seem to be very few intellectual links between an ethnographer like myself and the work of Basil Bernstein. Although, as Atkinson (1984) noted, structuralism and interactionism have a common interest in the social construction of reality, they differ widely over what is involved in that construction. As he put it:"The structuralist will tend to see significance in the systems of classification and ordering; the interactionist will see meaning as the emergent outcome of transactions between actors or groups of actors" (p. 145).

A further difference is that, like interactionists, my work tends to derive from empirical research and to be inductive. Conversely, Bernstein's structuralist analyses derive from the establishment of principles and are, therefore, deductive. Even sympathetic critics like Atkinson (1984) have remarked on the "relative lack of clear empirical demonstration" (p. 32) in Bernstein's work.

However, one can make too much of such apparent differences. The research I report in this chapter is hardly interactionist. Rather it derives from the work of Harvey Sacks which, as we shall see, has surprising links with Bernstein's structuralism.

Like Bernstein, I have an abiding interest in how language operates. Sometimes this has taken me in quite an abstract, theoretical direction, as in the book with Torode (Silverman & Torode, 1980). In that book, we analyzed several theories of language as practices that sought to construct a particular relationship between "appearance" and "reality." One chapter even dealt with Labov's (1972) debate with Bernstein about the operation of linguistic "codes."

Our position was more sympathetic to Bernstein than Labov's. It was based on a redefinition of *restricted* and *elaborated* codes: "In the sense of *elaborating* the difference between 'appearance' and 'reality' on the one hand, and of *restricting* 'reality' to an identity with 'appearance' on the other" (Silverman & Torode,1980, p 181).

Shortly after, Atkinson (1984) acknowledged that our reading, although unconventional, "preserves and develops the underlying spirit of . . . (Bernstein's) work" (1984, p. 108). Indeed, Bernstein repaid the compliment, taking up our concept of "voice" (a form of speaking used by speakers but not equivalent to any one speaker) in a subsequent publication (Bernstein, 1981).

Since then, I have intermittently used theories of the "speaking subject" that fit far more closely to Bernstein's structuralism than to what is seen as the more humanistic, interactionist tradition. For instance, in a semiotic analysis of Roeg's film *Bad Timing*, I focused on the construction of subjects within a verbal and visual narrative (Silverman, 1993a).

It would be relatively easy to demonstrate the links between this semiotic work and Bernstein's structuralism—indeed, this is what I planned in an early outline of this chapter. Instead, I want to attempt to demonstrate another, more unexpected, link—between Bernstein's structuralism and a piece of research inspired by Harvey Sacks.

At least if I can demonstrate that, in some respects, Sacks and Bernstein are working in the same territory, I can start to break down some of the boundaries policed by social theory.

In two books on methodology (Silverman, 1985, 1993a), I have argued against the mind-numbing effect of polarities in theory and research. Elsewhere, I have used Douglas's (1975) account of the role of anomaly in boundary maintenance to speculate on why British sociologists tend to group together into "schools."

This is, predictably, close to Bernstein's notion of boundary: "the social arrangements and practices whereby domains of . . . knowledge and experience are kept separate" (Atkinson, 1984, p. 27). As Atkinson emphasized, the concept of "boundary" is "fundamental to much of the Bernstein corpus" (p. 27).

By the end of this chapter, I hope that the reader will come to suspect the auspices of that boundary in social thought that seems to separate Bernstein's Durkheimian neo- Structuralism from Sacks' version of ethnomethodology. First, however, it is necessary to set out

Sacks's approach. Sacks's own work has recently appeared in two volumes (Sacks, 1992a, 1992b). For a much more detailed review of Sacks's work, see Silverman (1993c).

SACKS ON DESCRIPTION

As Schegloff's extensive introductions to each volume make clear, Sacks's early work can be seen as a dialogue with two programs of the 1960s, offered by Homans and Chomsky.

Homans's (1961) aimed to replace common sense with a scientific sociology. Using proverbs as a case in point, Sacks showed, contrary to Homans, that the point is not proverbs' "defects" or "inconsistencies" but "what's done with them" (1992a, p. 422). Sacks had no time for attempts to begin with "operational definitions" of phenomena, and he made much play with such definitions as used in Introductory Sociology textbooks (p. 30). Instead, he says, we need to see how participants themselves employ definitions, without assuming that it is immediately obvious what is important or most basic. For instance, in an answer to a question that asks how you can use conversational data to address a traditional sociological problem, Sacks said: "The first rule is to learn to be interested in what it is you've got. I take it that what you want to do is pose those problems that the data bears" (p. 471).

Chomsky's (1965) concern with generative rules ties in with Sacks's concern to construct an apparatus that would generate observed outcomes. However, unlike both Chomsky and Saussure, who are principally concerned with deciphering the rules of language beneath imagined cases, Sacks seeks to understand the rules that participants attend to in sequences of conversation. So, for instance, whereas Saussure was interested in the organization of a menu (and Bernstein was interested in the organization of a curriculum), Sacks is concerned with the sequential implications of a particular order from the menu (e.g., how "I think I'll have roast beef" is treated as a "proposal" for others, e.g., "Oh I just had roast beef last night"; 1992b, p. 76).

In contemporary philosophy, Sacks was attracted to speech-act theory. However, Austin (1962) and Searle (1965) did not study actual talk but worked with invented examples and their own intuitions about what it makes sense to say. For Sacks, on the contrary:

> What we need to do . . . is to watch conversations. . . . I don't say that we should rely on our recollection for conversation, because it's very bad. . . . One can invent new sentences and feel comfortable with them (as happens in philosophy and linguistics). One cannot invent new sequences of

conversation and feel happy with them. You may be able to take "a question and answer", but if we have to extend it very far, then the issue of
whether somebody would really say that, after, say, the fifth utterance, is
one which we could not confidently argue. One doesn't have a strong
intuition for sequencing in conversation. (1992b, p. 5)

Sacks undoubtedly owed a great debt to Garfinkel's focus on the
indexicality of utterances and how indexicality is resolved "for all practical purposes." Unlike Garfinkel (1967), but like Durkheim and Bernstein,
Sacks aimed for a cumulative science that offered "stable accounts of
human behaviour (through) producing accounts of the methods and
procedures for producing it" (Schegloff in Sacks, 1992a, p. xxxi).

As already noted, unlike Bernstein, Sacks's work is distinctly
inductive. As Schegloff put it, the work is driven by the observation of
actual talk with actual outcomes. The question one poses is simply:
How was this outcome accomplished? The method is straightforward:
"begin with some observations, then find the problem for which these
observations could serve as . . . the solution" (p. xlviii).

Among contemporary sociologists not doing ethnomethodology, Sacks was also influenced by Goffman, who had been involved with
his dissertation at Berkeley (not always constructively). Particularly in
the earliest lectures, we see Sacks's interest in Goffman's (1963) work
on ceremonial orders. However, Sacks wants to understand "ceremony"
by reference to the sequential analysis of conversations. For instance,
we know that the proper return to "how are you feeling?" is "fine." This
means that if you want to treat it as a question about your feelings you
have to request permission (e.g.. "It's a long story" to which the next
party may say, "That's alright, I have time"). This means that "everyone
has to lie" because people attend to "the procedural location of their
answers" and, in part, produce answers by reference to "the various
uses that the answer may have for next actions that may be done" (p.
565). Thus Goffman's (1981) attempt to separate "ritual" and "system"
requirements would have been a nonstarter for Sacks.

However, Sacks's reading in the social sciences extended far
beyond Goffman and Homans. Schegloff noted the wide range of
Sacks's reading, citing C.Wright Mills, Parsons, and the Chicago School
as important influences. Like Goffman, it seems that Sacks was also
influenced by Simmel to whom he referred as "one of the greatest of all
sociologists" (1992b, p. 132).

Of course, Sacks also covers more familiar territory but shifts
our focus in a most original way. He cites Gluckman on "the reasonable
wrongdoer in Barotse law" in order to raise the issue of "how a human
gets built who will produce his activities such that they're graspable in
this way" (p. 119).

Like Bernstein, but unlike most interactionist sociologists, Sacks is thus explicitly concerned with the construction of human subjects. Again, like Bernstein, Sacks operates with a highly structural version of "culture" but one deployed in local contexts.

Thus Sacks approaches "culture" as an "inference-making machine" (p. 119): a descriptive apparatus, administered and used in specific contexts. For instance, Sacks looked at the first two sentences of a children's story: "The baby cried. The mommy picked it up." Why do we hear the "mommy" as the mother of this "baby"? Sacks asked: "Is it some kind of magic? One of my tasks is going to be to construct an apparatus for that fact to occur. That is, how we come to hear it in that fashion" (1992a, p. 236).

Based on this treatment of culture, using his interest in the work of the Opies, Sacks treats "socialization" as embedded in the sets of skills learned and deployed when children play games and address adults. In particular, Sacks reveals the role of "You know what Mummy?" as a way of getting into conversation, thereby preserving the adult's control of its direction.

Such observations allow Sacks to get a hold on conventional categories, such as "memory," "experience," and "culture" that are very different from what we take to be the "humanist" position of nonstructuralists. For instance, "memory" is treated as something interactional. So "memory" resides in organizational features of conversation: "What one remembers stands in some close relationship to what it is that's just been done, and if you don't get a chance to say it, when you then get a chance to say it, you've forgotten it" (1992a, p. 27).

Like "memory," Sacks also shows that "experience" exists through a powerful descriptive apparatus. So having "no one to turn to" is the outcome of an organized search procedure through a hierarchy of persons and a set of assumptions about when it might be appropriate to turn to each person (for instance, not turning to a spouse with a problem engendered by one's adulterous relationship).

This means that "culture," in Sacks's hands, becomes a set of devices. As Schegloff put it, in a way that might be written by Bernstein himself, for Sacks, "persons, their experiences, and the stored versions of experiences in stories are the device by which culture reproduces itself and adapts to changing social circumstances" (1992b, p. xl).

Like the Durkheimians, Sacks rejected the antiscientific position of some interactionists (e.g., Blumer). Sacks wanted to do a *better* science. For instance, he criticized laboratory studies only for their lack of success, not for their aim of producing a "science of society." So laboratory studies of, say, "short-term memory" fail because they ask the wrong question, namely, "do people understand what somebody else says?" Instead, researchers should be asking: "is there some *procedure* people use which has, as its product, a showing that they heard and understood?" (1992, p. 30, emphasis added).

Having set the intellectual agenda, we are now in a better position to follow Sacks's account of description. As we shall see, this seems to follow an agenda that is quite different from that of Bernstein.

Sacks begins with this problem: Sociology seeks to describe and classify without attending to how members describe and classify. As Sacks put it:

> All the sociology we read is unanalytic, in the sense that they simply put some category in. They make sense to us in doing that, but they're doing that simply as another Member. They haven't described the phenomena they're seeking to describe—or that they ought to be seeking to describe. What they need to do is to give us some procedure for choosing that category which is used to present some piece of information. And that brings us back to the question, are there procedures that Members have for selecting categories? One of my aims is to show that there are. (1992a, pp. 41-42)

For instance, certain things are known about any category, for example, people of a certain age or gender. If you want to escape such category-bound implications, you can counter by accounting for why the category should not be read in this way here (e.g., "I'm 48 but . . ."). However, people use sayings such as "boys will be boys" that serve as "anti-modifier modifiers," asserting that, in the last instance, the category is omni-relevant (p. 45). The precise relevance of a category is also established by categorizing the categorizer, for example, if B categorizes C as "old," you might categorize B in order to decide how *you* would categorize C (p. 45).

Similarly, categories can usually be read off the activities in which people engage. Thus, to hear a report of someone crying *may* be heard as the activity of a baby. Similarly, a person who properly picks a baby up *may* be heard of as a "mother." Moreover, if both baby and mother are mentioned, we will try to hear them as a "team"—so that if the mother picks up the baby, we will hear the mother as not any mother but as the mother of this baby.

However, people may try to avoid the normally category-bound implications of certain activity descriptions. For instance, Sacks discussed the American South where, according to some whites, even when blacks engage in activities appropriate to anybody, they are not to be seen as "anybody," but as "blacks-*imitating*-whites."

Sacks also noted the commonplace assumption that members of subcultures resist being categorized by other groups. For instance, he showed how "hotrodder" may be preferred to "teenager" by a young person. The logic of this is fully understood by reference to Sacks's account of the apparatus of descriptive categories (membership categorization devices) and activies (category-bound activities). For when adults refer to "teenagers," they give themselves access to the known category-bound activities in which teenagers may engage. By preferring an alternative term ("hotrodders") with category- bound activities known only to the "in-group," young people assert ownership of the descriptive apparatus (1992a, pp. 169-175).

Moreover, Sacks noted, this attention to descriptive categories occurs even in those many situations in which we are talking to strangers and there is no apparent battle over which category to use. He mentioned the case of people telling interviewers doing surveys that they watch less television than they actually do: "It's interesting in that they're controlling an impression of themselves for somebody who couldn't matter less" (p. 580).

Sacks argued that this happens because we can be held responsible not only for our descriptions but for the *inferences* that can be drawn from them, that is, the sort of person who would say such a thing about themselves or others.

However, descriptions are not just assembled for ourselves but are recipient designed for others. We help others infer certain things from our descriptions by indicating if the hearer should seek to use them to find some person already known to them. So using descriptions such as "Joe," "Tom," or "Harry" allow hearers to search for someone already known.

Having paved the way, I now analyze some data extracts using Sacks's account of description. By focusing on the issue of "delicate" topics, however, the analysis indirectly takes us back to one of Bernstein's central concerns. I consider how the "boundary" between "delicate" and "non- delicate" matters works in practice.

ASSEMBLING "DELICATE" DESCRIPTIONS

Following Sacks, Jefferson (1985) noted our preference for descriptions that start off by exploring routine, normal, or nonproblematic explanations of events. Counseling for HIV and AIDS, with the presumably nonroutine, abnormal issues of sexuality and death that it topicalizes, presents a nice test for members' attempts to maintain a life-as-usual explanatory framework. Using data from such a setting, I now explore how counselors and their clients cooperatively mark and manage the nonroutine or "delicate" implications of their communication.

However, straight off, there would appear to be something counterintuitive in our observations. Does not "professionality" consist, in part, as Parsons (1951) told us, of maintaining a position of affective neutrality? May not professionals achieve that neutrality by bypassing or refusing to countenance the delicate or embarrassing aspects of their work? Again, may not clients exclude such aspects from their encounters with professionals simply by ignoring them? In short, why should these people mark items as delicate because this creates the very problem that needs to be managed?

In these materials, as it turns out, the parties do not passively ignore potentially delicate matters. Instead, in a massively recurrent manner, they mark such matters by what may be called "expressive caution" (Greatbatch; personal communication, 1992), represented by speech perturbations and delays.

Using Sacks's (1972, 1992a) account of how descriptions are organized, I show how a failure by either professional or client to mark a potentially delicate item would carry strong implications about the moral status of clients. Following Heath's (1989) work on "embarrassment" in the context of doctors' conduct of physical examinations of their patients, I then go on to examine how, having marked an item as delicate, both parties cooperatively restore a life-as-normal framework.

Throughout, I assemble a case for viewing delicate matters as a locally produced and managed phenomenon. This follows Bergmann's (1989) discussion of how, in psychiatric interviews, certain matters are treated with "caution," in an indirect and euphemistic manner. However, as he noted, we do not need to ask what motivates this caution:

> By describing something with caution and discretion, this "something" is turned into a matter, which is in need of being formulated cautiously and discreetly. Sociologically viewed, there is not first an embarrassing, delicate, morally dubious event or improper behaviour about which people then speak with caution and discretion, instead the delicate and notorious character of an event is constituted by the very act of talking about it cautiously and discreetly. (Bergmann, 1989, pp. 38-39)

In Maynard's (1991) data, delicate issues were marked by doctors in their delivery of diagnostic news to the parents of mentally handicapped children. In Bergmann's (1989) work, psychiatrists doing intake interviews cautiously introduced certain topics. In our data on counseling interviews, professionals used expressive caution before touching on potentially delicate topics, that is, they delayed their delivery and/or use of perspective display sequences and downgrades. Our data, however, allow us to show that the marking and management of delicacy is not a one-sided professional matter. In this chapter, I show

how expressive caution is cooperatively accomplished between professional and client.

Most of my analysis is concerned with a long extract taken from a pretest counseling interview in a British testing center (for detailed work on many such extracts, see Silverman & Peräkylä, 1990).

The extract begins about three minutes after the start of the consultation. Transcription conventions are contained in an appendix at the end of this chapter.

```
   1 8B-5
 1    C:     Let's finish this HIV thing. .hhhhh So (.) do you
 2           understand about the anti-bodies.=
 3    P:     =Yes I |do:.
 4    C:           |Ri:ght. .hh So: .h how lo:ng is it since you
 5           think (.) you might have been at ri:sk (.) of being
 6           infected with HIV.
 7    P:     Well uh- (0.4) uhuh to tell you the truth it's only
 8           I- like er Friday I had a phone call from a .h ex-
 9           girlfriend- my boyfriend's ex-girlfriend .hh to say
10           that uh:m (0.5) she'd been to the VD clinic (0.2)
11           and uhm she thought that I should go:, (0.2) bu:t
12           (.) (since) then I've never worried. It was only (.)
13           after the phone-ca:ll.
14    C:     Oh ri:ght.=
15    P:     =That I thought that well I'd better go check it
16           o(h)u(h)t. .hhhh You kno:|w.
17    C:                              |So: the thing is you see
18           w- wh- what abou:t contacts before your present
19           boyfriend if I might ask about (tha:|:t).
20    P:                                         |Well I had (.)
21           since my: divorce in eighty-two (.) I've only had
22           two relationships.
23    C:     Right.
24    P:     And uh:m (0.2) one lasted for eight years and one
25           lasted for three year:s.
26    C:     Uh huh
27    P:     So I don't- I haven't worried
28    C:     No sure.
29    P:     you know because uh- those are the only two me:n.
30           Bu:t (.) on saying tha::t (0.2) my latest boyfriend
31           (.) is the only one that I've well had to worry
32           about because of the phone-ca:ll.
33           I'v|e never worried before.
34    C:        |(Yea:h).
35    C:     How long have you been with your latest boyfriend.
36    P:     Three months.
37    C:     Three months.
38    P:     Yea:h.
39    C:     Right. .hhhhh So: (.) we are only just really on the
40           time limit for this HIV for your present boyfriend
41           |then aren't u- aren't we.
```

```
42    P:    |Yea:h.
43    P:    |Mm hm
44    C:    |.hhh Uhm .hhh d'you know if any of your: your er
45           partners have been drug users.=Intra|venous drug=
46    P:                                          |No:.
47    C:    =|users is our main |uhm you- you've never used=
48    P:     |They haven't.     |Mm
49    C:    =needles for yourself |(either.=No). .hh ⌋ ask=
50    P:                          |No:
51    C:    =everybody those questions.=I haven't saved them
52           |up for you. .hhhh Obviously when we're talking=
53    P:     |(That's okay yeah).
54    C:    =about HIV .hhhh uhm (.) the intravenous drug using
55           population are a population that are at ɾi:sk.
56    P:    Yea|:h.
57    C:        |Because (.) if they share needles (.) then
58           they're sharing (.) infection with the blood on the
59           needles obvious|ly.
60    P:                    |Mm h|m
61    C:                         |.hhhhhh Uhm (0.5) d'you know if
62           any of your partners have been bisexual.
63    P:    No they haven't.=
64    C:    =No?
65    P:    No:.
66           (1.5)
67    C:    Ri:ght. .hhh Uh:m (0.5) ꜱo (0.6) er I'll just finish
68           telling you about it and then when I get to the end
69           you can decide whether you actually want the test or
70           not.=|Because it ʰas to be your=
71    P:          |Mm
72    C:    =decision anyway.=|Okay.
73    P:                      |Mm hm
```

The transcript begins just as C has completed a long sequence of information about the nature of an HIV test (data not shown). By line 7 of this extract, however, P is into a much longer turn at talk. This is tied into a question asked by C which sets off the long question-answer chain shown in this extract.

I look first at how P sets up her reply to C's question beginning at line 7 as compared to her answer at line 3. P was quickly into her earlier answer—indeed the transcript indicates the absence of even the slightest pause between the answer and the preceding question. Here, by contrast, there is considerable hesitation before P gets into her answer.

At line 3, P can latch her "yes" immediately to the completion of C's turn because this is the candidate answer hearable from the question's juxtapositioning with the agenda statement. This is not to say that P could not have said that she did not understand about anti-bodies, merely that what is, in this context, a problematic answer would normally be marked. However, in lines 7-8, P precisely does mark her answer as problematic through considerable expressive caution which includes two hesitations (uh, uhuh), a pause, two downgrades (well, only), a repair (I like er), and a preface (to tell you the truth). P's use of "only" to describe how long she has been worried suggests that she is setting up her answer as delicate because she hears C's question as implying that most people will spend a lot of time deliberating before coming for an HIV test.

However, I am more concerned here with such expressive caution in the description of sexual activities. Note that I do not begin with the assumption that sexual matters and the like are intrinsically "delicate" because of cultural taboos, and so on. Any such assumption is defeasible because we can visualize sequential features and other local circumstances when such taboos do not operate (see Extract 2 later). Instead, I am concerned with how expressive caution works in the local production of delicacy.

I begin by looking further at P's utterance in line 7 "to tell you the truth." As will be shown, the story that P tells between lines 7 and 13 involves a highly organized set of disclosures that delay certain items. Before making a set of observations, I reproduce this passage next:

```
7      P:      Well uh- (0.4) uhuh to tell you the truth it's only
8              I- like er Friday I had a phone call from a .h ex-
9              girlfriend- my boyfriend's ex-girlfriend .hh to say
10             that uh:m (0.5) she'd been to the VD clinic (0.2)
11             and uhm she thought that I should go:, (0.2) bu:t
12             (.) (since) then I've never worried. It was only (.)
13             the phone-ca:ll.
14     C:      Oh ri:ght.=
15     P:      =That I thought that well I'd better go check it
16             o(h)u(h)t. .hhhh You kno:|w.
```

1. The story begins with the report of a phone call. Straight off we can remark that phone calls are a routine part of ordinary modern existence. This sets up a nice contrast with C's question about the relatively extraordinary topic of thinking about one's risk of being infected with HIV. How do we account for this contrast? We can find a parallel in the reports of witnesses to the assassination of President Kennedy who typically prefaced their accounts by referring to their original thoughts that perhaps what they had heard were the sounds of an ordinary event, such as a car backfiring. As Sacks observed: "there is a preference for descriptions which start off by exploring routine, normal or non-problematic explanations of unex-

pected events: members are engaged in finding out only how it is that what is going on is usual" (Sacks, 1984, p. 419)

2. After the phone call is reported in speech that exhibits none of the perturbations present in the beginning of the turn, P moves once again into a very turbulent delivery pattern from the end of line 8 to the end of line 10. Before she says "ex-girlfriend," P takes an inbreath and then after a short pause she repairs her description into "my boyfriend's ex-girlfriend." Clearly, expressive caution is being displayed here. What work is being done in the production of such perturbations? First, in naming an associate (here boyfriend's ex-girlfriend), one implies a description of oneself—in this case the standardized relational pair (Sacks, 1972) of boyfriend-girlfriend. Because of this self-involvement, descriptions of certain types of associates may be foreshadowed as delicate matters. By referring to the ex-girlfriend of your boyfriend, you describe yourself as having a boyfriend who has had at least one earlier partner. Now the fact of having a relationship with someone who has had at least another partner may not be extraordinary. However, reporting such a fact may be heard as a category-bound activity with potentially delicate implications (e.g., casting doubt on whether this present relationship may be temporary, etc.). Indeed, P's use of "ex" in the description "ex-girlfriend" suggests that we are to hear her boyfriend as engaged in serial monogamy (i.e., as not promiscuous) which creates, by implication, the SRP of "faithful partners." This may have something to do with her repair from her original formulation of "a .h ex-girlfriend."

3. The hesitation and repair prior to this report thus constitutes a nice solution to the problems of delicacy that may arise in describing one's sexual partners—proceed with expressive caution by delaying such descriptions. Moreover, such caution is not just self-interested. It shows a fine attention to what a recipient may want to hear. By producing a minimal amount of potentially delicate items at a first turn after a question, one leaves it up to the recipient to decide whether to treat it as a gloss that needs unpacking, for example, via a probe or a demand for specification. Such requests provide a favorable environment for disclosing items marked as delicate because such items can now be produced as demanded by C rather than as volunteered by P.

4. Further turbulences (a hesitation and a half-second pause) occur in P's delivery of the item "she'd been to the VD clinic"

(line 10). Here we are concerned with a description of an activity rather than an associate. As Sacks (1972) also noted, activities are category bound because they imply the kind of persons who might engage in them, for example, "crying" may be heard as being done by a baby. However, although a baby crying may be heard as "normal," this is unlikely to be the case with going "to the VD clinic." P's expressive caution in the delivery of this item nicely marks the delicate implications of having a boyfriend who has had an affair with someone who has gone to a VD clinic. The delay also marks the speaker as someone-who-does-not-normally-talk-about- people-going-to-VD-clinics. Throughout, P's own visit for an HIV test (in what may be described as "a VD clinic" is produced as something that arises from someone else's suggestion (her boyfriend's ex-girlfriend) and from someone else's actions (her boyfriend who presumably had infected the ex-girlfriend).

5. Now P produces her reasons for seeking a test in terms of her caller's wishes ("she thought that I should go") (line 11) and her own sense of the situation ("I thought that well I'd better go check it o(h)u(h)t") (lines 15-16). Note the appeal to doing what someone else thinks best and to the responsibility of "checking out" things. Both delay the description of one's own sexual activities while trading off life-as-usual situations that serve to downgrade the unusual and delicate business of seeking an HIV test. Now P's rapid visit for an HIV test is reconstituted as depicting a responsible person (who realizes she must rapidly "check it out") rather than someone who has not reflected sufficiently (recognized in her earlier "it's only I-like er Friday").

In the discussed passage, we have seen how both parties steer away from problematic explanations of such an unexpected event as seeking an HIV test. As Sacks (1984) put it, members are "engaged in finding out only how it is that what is going on is usual" (p. 419). But the cooperative accomplishment of expressive caution sits uneasily with the prescribed tasks of HIV counseling that require that clients address their risks in specific terms (see Peräkylä & Bor, 1990).

I have already noted how C's requests for specification may provide a more favorable environment than open-ended questions for P to present delicate material. Although P's initial descriptions can appear perfectly adequate at the time, such requests redefine them as indefinite references that constitute an invitation to their recipient to request more information.

Bearing in mind the expressive caution about delicate items, two questions remain: (a) how do Cs set up their requests for specification; and (b) how do Ps expand (what are now received as) insufficiently precise references?

The next nine lines of the extract bear on these questions:

```
17    C:                                  |So: the thing is you see
18          w- wh- what abou:t contacts before your present
19          boyfriend if I might ask about (tha:|:t).
20    P:                                  |Well I had (.)
21          since my: divorce in eighty-two (.) I've only had
22          two relationships.
23    C:    Right.
24    P:    And uh:m (0.2) one lasted for eight years and one
25          lasted for three year:s.
```

The following observations can be made regarding C's request for specification (lines 17-19):

1. P's expressive caution serves to mark a delicate matter but does not directly answer C's question (at lines 4-6). C has, therefore, still to establish just how long P may have been at risk. C's "so" (line 17) locates her upcoming question as the natural upshot of P's account, whereas her reference to P's boyfriend (line 19) nicely ties her question to P's own description. Moreover, C's initial question:

    how lo:ng is it since you think (.) you might have been at ri:sk

    has already provided for the possibility that P may have been at risk longer than she suspects and thus warrants the line of questioning beginning here.

2. Before introducing her own term "contacts," C marks its potentially delicate character by a set of perturbations ("w- wh- what abou:t contacts"). Having "contacts," although the standard term used by professionals in STD clinics, can be heard by clients as an activity bound to the category of "promiscuous person." Indeed, we see that this is a deviant case because elsewhere both parties recurrently strive to locate patients' sexual activities in the context of long-term relationships.

3. As Schegloff (1980) pointed out, various types of action projection can serve to mark and request formal permission for potentially delicate or risqué actions. So here C adds a little rider to her question ("if I might ask about (tha:|:t)."). Although, unlike question projections, this request comes after, rather than before, the question, it serves the same

function of marking that C understands that this may be heard as a delicate topic.

Here, then, C has skilfully prepared the ground for exploring a potentially delicate topic. In doing so, she has provided some kind of a favorable environment in which P can specify her indefinite reference.

Faced with C's request for specification, P does tell more in relatively undisturbed speech. But note two things. First, she converts the C's professional item "contacts" into "relationships." This transforms the SRPs involved: compare the description of sexual partners as contacts (for STDs) to ones involved in relationships (implying that the sexual activity is necessarily contexted in "commitments" and other nonsexual matters).

Second, note that the P prefaces her response by "since my divorce." This does a lot of interesting work:

- it gives a favorable context to read her upcoming MCD "relationships" (by implying that prior to her divorce she was only involved in one relationship).
- it makes several relationships permissible to a "single" woman (but only one after the other as she later makes clear).Even though the years do not add up (8 plus 3 years from 1982 take us to 1991 and the interview takes place in 1989), we hear her as engaged in consecutive monogamy—just as in her earlier description of her boyfriend's "ex-girlfriend."

As C's disturbed delivery of the term *contacts* showed, professionals display caution in organizing questions about potentially delicate matters. In turn, one of the strategies available to clients is to portray themselves in a favorable light—as in P's appeal to a pattern of serial monogamy.

However, we should not emphasize the separate strategies of each party. As was already noted, the identification and management of delicacy tends to be a cooperative matter. This is nicely shown in this later passage:

```
45    C:    |.hhh Uhm .hhh d'you know if any of your: your er
46          partners have been drug users.=Intra|venous drug=
47    P:                                         |No:.
48    C:    =|users is our main |uhm you- you've never used=
49    P:     |They haven't.      |Mm
50    C:    =needles for yourself |(either.=No). .hh I ask=
51    P:                          |No:
52    C:    =everybody those questions.=I haven't saved them
53          |up for you. .hhhh Obviously when we're talking=
54    P:    |(That's okay yeah).
```

```
55      C:      =about HIV .hhhh uhm (.) the intravenous drug using
56              population are a population that are at ri:sk.
57      P:      Yea|:h.
58      C:           |Because (.) if they share needles (.) then
59              they're sharing (.) infection with the blood on the
60              needles obvious|ly.
61      P:                     |Mm h|m
62      C:                          |.hhhhhh Uhm (0.5) d'you know if
63              any of your partners have been bisexual.
64      P:      No they haven't.=
```

The task of pretest counseling involves asking clients to assess the nature of their risk of having been exposed to HIV. In this passage, both parties have to cope with the implications of discussing potentially delicate aspects of the status of P's sexual contacts.

The extract is closely analyzed next to show how delicacy is nicely marked and managed. Namely:

1. C prefaces her question at line 44 by "d'you know." We can see the power of this preface by imagining an alternative way of posing the question:

    *C: Have any of your partners been drug users?

    Putting the question this way would imply that P is the kind of person who *knowingly* might associate with drug users. So this form of the question can be a category-bound activity, in which its recipient is to be heard in the category of a-person-who-might-consort-with-drug-users. The C's preface is a neat device to overcome this hearing. It allows P, if necessary, to reveal that she had subsequently discovered that a partner was a drug user, without any kind of implication that she would not knowingly associate with that category of person.

2. In line 46, C uses the category "partner." Note the expressive caution ("er") that precedes it. Massively recurrent in these materials are such delays in the first delivery (by both professionals and clients) of descriptive categories relating to sexual associates and activities. However, note that the category "partner" may be less damaging to the propriety of P's behavior than "contact"—C's earlier term. Although both relate to sexual activity, the SRP "partner-partner" is less implicative of promiscuity than the pair "contact-contact." Again, is shown, both professionals and clients in these sessions strive to present client behavior in the best possible light.

3. Note how, on line 50, P overlaps with C's talk in order to produce a reply at the first available turn-transition point. In this way, nondelicate matters are marked by unqualified delivery at the first opportunity. Equally, at lines 47-49, P marks her answer ("no . . . they haven't") as preferred by producing it early and without qualification, overlapping with C's elaboration of her question. Moreover, at line 47, P does not embed her "no" in C's "d'you know" format. Thereby, she elides the possibility that she could be the sort of person who did not fully "know" all her partners.

4. Again, see how, on lines 48-50, C redesigns her next question. This may be in order to reorient toward P's presentation of herself, dropping the "d'you know" format and offering a negative answer as the preferred one. More plausibly, C is now asking about P herself, not some other about whom her knowledge might be incomplete. (For a treatment of how we talk about our own and other's experiences, see Peräkylä & Silverman, 1991b).

5. C's justification of her line of questioning (Intra|venous drug users is our main; I ask everybody those questions.=I haven't saved them up for you) works as a retrospective justification for asking such a question. It serves neatly to counter the category-bound implications of the activity of asking someone if they have had sex with drug users. Without the elaboration, the implication might be that C had reason to suspect that P might be the sort of person who would engage in such an activity. The elaboration, however, seems to be about to make clear that the question has not been generated by anything that P has said or done—other than presenting herself at a clinic in which "intravenous drug users is our main" (client population?). This is underlined by C's observation "I haven't saved them up for you."

6. P's agreement tokens on line 54 ("that's okay yeah") show her acceptance of C's elaboration and thus marks her continued recipiency for this line of questioning. This allows C to tag on a further question (about "bisexual partners") whose delicacy is nicely marked and managed by the same "d'you know" format as used on line 45.

SUMMARY

The analysis of this extract has allowed me to distinguish a number of practices involved in the local production and management of "delicate" items. These include:

1. C's and P's use of "expressive caution" to mark potentially delicate objects, that is, they delay their delivery, engage in various speech perturbations, and use elaborations and story prefaces to mark and manage delicate items.
2. C's and P's showing a preference for descriptions that start off by exploring routine, normal, or nonproblematic explanations of unexpected events
3. C's and P's endeavoring to put P in a "positive" light, for example, by countering implications of P's promiscuity
4. P's producing a minimal amount of potentially delicate items at a first turn after a question, leaving it up to the recipient to decide whether to treat it as a gloss that needs unpacking
5. C's providing a favorable environment for disclosing delicate information by using perspective-display sequences, downgrades, prospective and retrospective justifications for questions, and requests for specification.

Our full corpus of materials involves some 200 consultations from 10 testing centers in Britain, the United States, and Trinidad. In the context of this chapter, however, there is only space to review one further extract. This is chosen to substantiate the point that what is a "delicate" topic is entirely a "local" matter.

Because neither party is a "cultural dope" (Garfinkel, 1967), what is proper behavior is always a local matter—locally produced and sustained. This means that sometimes nonpromiscuity can be heard as being made accountable.

Extract 2 begins with C asking about P's present partner:

```
                  2 8A-3
1    C:                      How long have you been with him?

2    P:        Six months.

3    C:        Six months. (0.3) When were you last with anyone
4              before that?

5    P:        About thr(h)ee years. .hhh=

6    C:        About three yea|rs.

7    P:—>                     |hhh I'm a Catholic.=heh
8              he|h .hhhhh

9    C:             |Ri:ght.
```

In Extract 2, C's repetition of P's utterance ("about three years" (lines 5-6) can be heard to make it accountable. Not having a sexual partner for three years at a stretch now may look to be inappropriate to the category-bound activity of seeking an HIV test. Note how P does indeed now offer an account, appealing to a religious MCD (arrowed).

Here P marks a joke, but C does not join in. For C to join in P's laughter at this point might imply that C was laughing at P's religion. In these consultations, P's preferences, whether sexual or religious, are not routinely heard by C as a laughing matter.

Although it is always tempting to appeal to apparently self- evident norms of interaction, close investigation of such local practices reveals that people are far from being "cultural dopes." Consequently, the appealing prospect of a sociology of embarrassment must begin by clearly delineating the local production of the phenomenon itself.

THE MACHINERY OF INTERACTION

Although it might be assumed that analysis of "descriptions" is concerned with "content," whereas the sequencing of talk addresses "forms," this assumption is mistaken. As his address of his data shows, Sacks's contribution to our understanding of description is not intended to stand apart from his account of the sequential organization of talk. For instance "recipient design" is, for members, both a descriptive and sequential consideration.

Underlying both sets of concerns is a Chomskyian-like desire to unearth the apparatus or machinery that would reproduce whatever members do. As Sacks himself put it:

> The kind of phenomena we are dealing with are always transcriptions of actual occurrences, in their actual sequence. And I take it our business is to try to construct the *machinery* that would produce those occurrences. That is, we find and name some objects, and find and name some rules for using those objects, where the rules for using those objects will produce those objects. (1992, p. 113; emphasis added)

A significant corpus of work has emerged over the years, stemming from Sacks's pioneering observations (e.g., Baker, 1984; Drew, 1978; Jayyusi, 1984; McHoul, 1982; Silverman & Peräkylä, 1990; Watson, 1978).

This work has raised some vital methodological questions for ethnographers and anyone else attempting to construct sociology as an "observational" discipline. Sacks put the issue succinctly:

> Suppose you're an anthropologist or sociologist standing somewhere.
> You see somebody do some action, and you see it to be some activity.
> How can you go about formulating who is it that did it, for the purpos-
> es of your report? Can you use at least what you might take to be the
> most conservative formulation—his name? Knowing, of course, that
> any category you choose would have the(se) kinds of systematic prob-
> lems: how would you go about selecting a given category from the set
> that would equally well characterise or identify that person at hand?
> (1992a, pp. 467-468).

Sacks shows how you cannot resolve such problems simply "by
taking the best possible notes at the time and making your decisions
afterwards" (p. 468). Instead, our aim should be to try to understand
when and how members do descriptions, seeking thereby to describe the
apparatus through which members' descriptions are properly produced.

CONCLUSION

Like the ethnographers of the Chicago School, Sacks was all for the
careful observation of detail. Nonetheless, like Bernstein, he rejected
the romantic baggage now attached to "subjectivist" sociologies concerned with "authentic" presentations of "experience" (cf. Silverman,
1989).

As we have already seen, for Sacks, "experience" exists through
a powerful descriptive apparatus. For instance, he warned his students
against worrying about the speed with which people do things:

> Don't worry about how fast they're thinking. First of all, don't worry
> about whether they're "thinking". Just try to come to terms with how it
> is that the thing comes off. Because you'll find that they can do these
> things. Just take any other area of natural science and see, for example,
> how fast molecules do things. And they don't have very good brains.
> So just let the materials fall as they may. (1992a, p. 11)

This way of treating social order helps to reopen a debate
between ethnography and Durkheim (see Gubrium, 1988). To be sure,
Garfinkel (1967) had already acknowledged a debt to Durkheim's conception of the "moral order." But Garfinkel also makes clear that, unlike
Durkheim, his aim was to discover the moral order "within" whatever
members were doing.

Durkheim is much more relevant to Sacks than to Garfinkel.
Like Bernstein, Sacks espouses many of the features of Durkheimian
sociology. Not only does he share Durkheim's antipsychologistic thrust,

but, unlike Garfinkel, Sacks makes no bones about doing a "science" aimed at understanding "culture." It's just that you no longer need to use such a gloss as "culture" when you can closely observe the "machinery" that collectivity members use to produce particular outcomes. When studying a conversation, as Sacks (1992a) clearly put it:

> Our aim is . . . to transform . . . our view of what happened here as some interaction as the thing that we're studying, to interactions being spewed out by machinery, the machinery being what we're trying to find; where, in order to find it, we've got to get a whole bunch of its products. (p. 169)

Like Sacks, Bernstein's work transgresses the simplistic boundaries between "macro" and "micro" sociology. As Atkinson (1984) put it: "While radically different from the humanist, individualistic bent of much so-called micro-sociology. . . . Bernstein's . . . meta-theory cuts across simplistic distinctions between small-scale and societal scope of analysis" (p. 32)

Both Bernstein and Sacks's work has been arbitrarily positioned on one side or the other of the macro/micro divide. They have also tended to be safely tucked away in specialist areas of the discipline: the sociology of language for Sacks, and the sociology of education for Bernstein.

I share Atkinson's regret about the way Bernstein's work is limited in this way. Like him, I believe Bernstein is better seen "as one of the most original and creative British sociologists" (1984, p. 7). As I have tried to demonstrate, Sacks's work is ostensibly at the other end of the sociological spectrum from Bernstein. Ironically, by repositioning Sacks, we see how both writers share certain similar research imperatives unconnected with the current fashion for "authentic" accounts of "experience."

THE TRANSCRIPTION SYMBOLS

*	* What?	Invented example
	C2: quite a | while Mo: | yea	Left brackets indicate the point at which a current speakers talk is overlapped by another's talk.
=	W: that I'm aware of = C: =Yes. Would you confirm that?	Equal signs, one at the end of a line and one at the beginning,

		indicate no gap between the two lines.
(.4)	Yes (.2) yeah	Numbers in parentheses indicates elapsed time in silence in tenths of a second.
(.)	to get (.) treatment	A dot in parentheses indicates a time gap, probabaly no more than one-tenth of a second.
_____	What's up?	Underscoring indicates some form of stress, via pitch and/or amplitude.
::	O:kay?	Colons indicate prolongation of the immediately prior sound. The length of the row of colons indicates the length of the prolongation.
WORD	Ive got ENOUGH TO WORRY ABOUT	Capitals, except at the beginnings of lines, indicate especially loud sounds relative to the surrounding talk.
.hhhh	I feel that (.2) .hhh	A row of hs prefixed by a dot indicates an inbreath; without a dot, an outbreath. The length of the row of h's indicates the length of the in- or outbreath.
( )	future risks and ( ) and life ( )	Empty parentheses indicates the transcribers inability to hear what was said.
(word)	Would you see (there) anthing positive	Parenthesized words are possible hearings.
(( ))	Confirm that ((continues))	Double parentheses contains author's descriptions rather than transcriptions.

REFERENCES

Atkinson, P. (1984). *Language, structure and reproduction: An introduction to the sociology of Basil Bernstein*. London: Methuen.

Austin, J.L. (1962). *How to do things with words*. Oxford: Clarendon Press.

Baker, C.D. (1984). The "search for adultness": Membership work in adolescent-adult talk. *Human Studies*, 7(3/4), 301-324.

Bergmann, J. (1989). Veiled morality: Notes on discretion in psychiatry. In P.-A. Forstrop (Ed.), *Discourse in professional and everyday culture*. Linkoping: University of Linkoping, Studies in Communication: SIC 28.

Bernstein, B. (1981). Codes, modalities and the process of cultural reproduction—a model. *Language in Society*, 10(3), 327-363.

Chomsky, N. (1965). *Aspects of the theory of syntax*. Cambridge: MIT Press.

Douglas, M. (1975). *Implicit meanings*. London: Routledge.

Drew, P. (1978). Accusations: The occasioned use of members' knowledge of "religious geography" in describing events. *Sociology*, 12, 1-22.

Garfinkel, E. (1967). *Studies in ethnomethodology*. Englewood Cliffs, NJ: Prentice-Hall.

Goffman, E. (1963). *Behavior in public places*. New York: Free Press.

Goffman, E. (1981). *Forms of talk*. Oxford: Basil Blackwell.

Gubrium, J. (1988). *Analyzing field reality* (Qualitative Research Methods Series 8). Newbury Park, CA: Sage.

Heath, C. (1989). Embarrassment and interactional organization. In P. Drew & A. Wootton (Eds.), *Erving Goffman: Exploring the interaction order* (pp. 136-160). Cambridge, UK: Polity.

Homans, G.C. (1961). *Social behaviour: Its elementary forms*. New York: Harcourt Brace.

Jayyusi, L. (1984). *Categorization and the moral order*. London: Routledge.

Jefferson, G. (1985). On the interactional unpackaging of a "gloss." *Language in Society*, 14, 435-466.

Labov, W. (1972). The logic of nonstandard English. In P.P. Giglioli (Ed.), *Language and social context* (pp. 179-216). Harmondsworth: Penguin.

Maynard, D.W. (1991). Interaction and asymmetry in clinical discourse. *American Journal of Sociology*, 97(2), 448-495.

McHoul, A.W. (1982). *Telling how texts talk: Essays on reading and ethnomethodology*. London: Routledge.

Parsons, T. (1951). *The social system*. Glencoe, IL: Free Press.

Peräkylä, A., & Bor, R. (1990). Interactional problems of addressing "dreaded issues" in HIV-counselling. *AIDS Care*, 2(4), 325-338.

Peräkylä, A., & Silverman, D. (1991a). Owning experience: Describing the experience of other persons. *Text*, 11(3), 441-480.

Peräkylä, A., & Silverman, D. (1991b). Reinterpreting speech-exchange systems: Communication formats in AIDS counselling. *Sociology*, 25(4), 627-651.

Sacks, H. (1972). An initial investigation of the usability of conversational data for doing sociology. In D. Sudnow (Ed.), *Studies in social interaction* (pp. 31-74). New York: Free Press.

Sacks, H. (1984). On doing "being ordinary." In J.M. Atkinson & J.C. Heritage (Eds.), *Structures of social action* (pp. 413-429). Cambridge: Cambridge University Press.

Sacks, H. (1992a). *Lectures on conversation* (Vol. 1, G. Jefferson, ed., with an Introduction by Emmanuel Schegloff). Oxford: Blackwell.

Sacks, H. (1992b). *Lectures on conversation* (Vol. 2). Oxford: Blackwell.

Schegloff, E.A. (1980). Preliminaries to preliminaries: "Can I ask you a question?" *Sociological Inquiry*, 50(3/4), 104-152.

Searle, J. (1965). *Speech acts*. Cambridge: Cambridge University Press.

Silverman, D. (1985). *Qualitative methodology and sociology: Describing the social world*. Aldershot, UK: Gower Publications.

Silverman, D. (1989). Six rules of qualitative research: A post-romantic argument. *Symbolic Interaction*, 12(2), 215-230.

Silverman, D. (1993a). Unfixing the subject: Viewing "Bad Timing." In C. Jenks (Ed.), *Cultural reproduction* (pp. 163-187). London: Routledge.

Silverman, D. (1993b). *Interpreting qualitative data: Methods for analyzing talk, text and interaction*. London: Sage.

Silverman, D. (1993c). The machinery of interaction: Remaking social science. *Sociological Review*, 41(4), 731-752.

Silverman, D., & Peräkylä, A. (1990). AIDS counselling: The interactional organization of talk about "delicate" issues. *Sociology of Health and Illness*, 12(3), 293-318.

Silverman, D., & Torode, B. (1980). *The material word: Some theories of language and its limits*. London: Routledge & Kegan Paul.

Watson, D.R. (1978) Categorization, authorization and blame-negotiation in conversation. *Sociology*, 12, 105-113.

13

Bernstein and Ricoeur: Contours for the Social Understanding of Narratives and Selves

Hilary Dickinson
University of Greenwich
Michael Erben
University of Southhampton

> Once we have understood its importance, the claim that the concept of an action is secondary to that of an intelligible (ie narrative) action will perhaps appear less bizarre, and, so too will the claim that the notion of "an" action, while of the highest practical importance, is always a potentially misleading abstraction. An action is a moment in a possible or actual history or in a number of such histories. (MacIntyre, 1985, p. 214)

The importance of understanding individuals as narrative beings within the context of society is only just becoming an area of general concern in sociology (Erben, 1993). However, for some time now we have found in our own teaching and research into life-course patterns that description and explanation of biographical narrative has developed an increasingly strong resonance in attempting to understand how the constraining and liberating features of social life unfold. What we propose is that by highlighting a crucial element of Bernstein's and Ricoeur's work—namely, the treatment of narrative—it is possible to establish a number of coordinates that represent a considerable development in the protocols for researching the nature of selves and narratives.

By narratives we mean the types, varieties, and patterns of the stories (or biographical features) that compose parts of the life-course experiences that characterize the way individuals carry themselves through and contribute toward the constitution of social contexts. It is the manner in which such narratives occur and are recognized by the participants themselves and by others that forms the establishment of an important mode of social explanation. Such an area of social study has, as we have suggested, only barely been formalized. Nonetheless, it can claim some sophisticated if disparate practitioners. Bernstein and Ricoeur have not, as far as we know, been previously linked. However, we feel that although they have very different intellectual antecedents—Bernstein as a sociologist of pedagogics and Ricoeur as an hermeneutical phenomenologist—they are both concerned with developing a way of understanding personal identity among social forces or, put another way, of developing a social theory of personal identity.

They approach these substantive issues in different ways and with different accents, inflections, and examples. For Bernstein, the dominant theme is a sociology of regulation, whereas for Ricoeur it is the social meaning of time. Nevertheless, it is our view that together they offer the possibility for a fuller conception of narrativity than is singly available to either. Both are linked by the agreement that to be denied the experience of social life through narratives is to be rendered powerless not only at a formal level but in the act of interpretation itself. This chapter is not concerned with the formal explication of Bernstein's ideas. This has already been excellently done by Atkinson (1985). Knowledge of the variety of Bernstein's codes through the four volumes of *Class, Codes and Control* (1971, 1973, 1977, 1990) are taken for granted. Similarly, although we are mainly concerned with the three volumes of Ricoeur's *Time and Narrative* (1984, 1985, 1988), we are not offering a general systematic discussion of his hermeneutics. This is readily available in Clarke (1992). What the chapter seeks to be is a disquisition on the nature of narrative and narration as exemplified in the works of two highly important social theorists.

However, before addressing specifically the ideas of Bernstein and Ricoeur in this regard, the next section examines more generally the concept of narrativity and the ways that social scientists and historians have begun to use it to illuminate the life-course experiences of individuals. It is against this background that one can see more clearly the way in which many aspects of Bernstein's and Ricoeur's work prefigure and resonate with work more explicitly on narrativity.

NARRATIVITY IN SOCIAL LIFE

Four fundamental points may be made about any narrative. First, a narrative organizes the actions and events it tells of into a meaningful whole. Whether implicitly or explicitly, it explicates the meaning of the events and sets them into a social framework of regular expectations and obligations, into a moral framework (and we would include here devices that indicate the narrator's rejection of a moral framework), and (frequently) into a cosmic framework. On a grand scale the cosmic framework of the story of Oedipus involves ideas about destiny and the Fates as, on a more modest scale, does the self-story of an examinee who takes a lucky mascot into an examination.

The second point is that what the narrative is organizing, at a deeper level than that of a social, moral or cosmic framework, is the human experience of temporality. Narrativity, for Ricoeur, is a solution to what he terms the *aporias*—the doubts, uncertainty, and flux—of time. Narrative—public and private, real and fictional—continuously links the past with the present and the future thus rendering the present meaningful in terms of what went before and what will (probably) come after:

> Historical stories and fictional stories resemble one another because whatever the difference between their immediate contents (real events and imaginary events respectively), their ultimate content is the same— the structures of human time. There is nothing more real for human beings than the experience of temporality. (White, 1991, p. 151)

The meaningful framework of a narrative and its organization of temporality are points so fundamental that they may best be regarded as two aspects of the defining characteristic of a narrative. Ricoeur makes a distinction between a mere listing of events—a chronicle—and a narrative, which is characterized by the possession of a plot. The plot provides the structures of meaning that unite the events into a meaningful entity in time, relating the temporal disjunctures and transitions of the narrative to one another and rendering them comprehensible and meaningful (White, 1991, pp. 148-151).

These two central issues—structures of meaning and the organization of temporality—provide a fruitful *point d'appui* for an issue crucial to sociology—the notion of personal identity, the "self," and the transformation of the self over time. In a narrative of the self—an autobiographical account—the narrator is both the "self" and also provides an account of the "self"—or indeed of "selves" as there is the possibility of the story that runs: "That's what I was like then—but now I'm a completely different person." It is evident that such a way of conceptualizing personal identity has much in common with the familiar Meadian notion of the central self—the "I"—and the various aspects of that self—the "mes"—which are the many social roles that are evoked by, or deliberately acted out in, different social settings. However, there are at least two respects in which a narrative model of the self offers possibilities for richer analysis than does the Meadian model. In the Meadian model it is clear how different social situations evoke different roles, or "mes" from an individual, but the means by which an individual can choose to be certain kinds of "me" rather than others is not explicated. Second, the means by which personal identity may be transformed, or more crucially, transform itself over time is not made clear. In a narrative model the narrating self can explain how the social self, or selves, seeks to play roles or act autonomously; and in regard to changes in personal identity too, the narrating self can explain and account for these changes. However, the narrating self may merely describe such changes rather than explain and account for them. Returning to the points made earlier about the framing of the narrative (social, moral, and cosmic) one may note that different narrative conventions demand different degrees of explicitness in reflection on the interior life. A high degree of explicitness and reflectiveness is found in the account of someone in analysis, whereas very little is found in ritualized forms of greeting.

Another respect in which a narrative model of personal identity is more powerful than a Meadian model is found in the way it can connect the individual with the social context. Any story of the self is embedded in a narrative that uses the frameworks and conventions of a particular social and historical milieu. This observation connects with the third fundamental point to be made about narrativity—that the principle of narrativity in human life blurs the boundaries between "real" events and "fictional" events. This is not to deny that there are many contexts in which the distinction between real and imaginary is of great importance—for historians, sociologists, lawyers, and journalists to name only a few. But the recognition that the narrative *principle* is the same for real events as for imaginary events is important in specific contexts for sociology. It can enable the sociologist to focus attention on the structures of meaning that narrative gives to temporality and social relations and to the presentation of the self within temporality. As the novelist invents the motivations of his or her characters and their personal change and development, the "real" process of experiencing, describing, and accounting for personal change in oneself takes the form of a fictional account. It would be equally appropriate to say that fictional narratives use the same kind of structuring as do those of real-life stories. In fact, the two kinds of narratives mutually influence one another as life and art imitate one another. Just as the boundary between real and imaginary events is blurred, so is the boundary between the "great" narrative and the small personal narrative. The principle is the same whether we have an individual composing his or her life story in internal reflection, a diary, or to a confidant or, on the other hand, a novelist or historian at work for publication.

The fourth point to be made about narrative is that narrative is expressed through language—indeed that narrative is impossible except through language. This interconnectedness of language and narrative perhaps seems obvious, but it is worth stressing in the context of Bernstein's work in view of his focus on language. It may be observed that narrative can be expressed pictorially as, for example, in Hogarth's series of engravings of Modern Moral Subjects, church paintings of stories from the Old and New Testaments, or strip cartoons; but in all these cases the story of the pictures needs to be supported in words—captions, titles, sermons, and so on—because the pictures alone are not enough (Erben, 1994).

In the last few years theories about narrativity have produced a range of empirical research in the social sciences, and to perhaps a greater extent, in oral history. For example, Murray (1989), Passerini (1989), and Chanfrault-Duchet (1991) examined the way in which life stories told to the researcher may be structured using recognizable genres of narrative, such as comedy, tragedy, or the picaresque. Murray (1989) examined how the narrative models of "romance" and "comedy" were used to express aspects of personal identity by people giving accounts of how they had trained for and run in a marathon. The romantic model involves elements of explaining how one had tested oneself in relation to morally desirable and undesirable courses of action, and/or of personal achievement in a test of physical and moral endurance. In the comic model there is an "amused distance from the possible competitive role, and this lightness distinguished them from those pursuing a social identity project [i.e., the romantic]" (p. 186).

Thomson's (1990) "Anzac Memories: Putting Popular Memory Theory into Practice in Australia," uses the personal narratives of veterans from World War I to examine the interplay between public and personal memory and the process by which people seek to compose and structure personal memories with which they are comfortable. Thus for one of his respondents, the fact that an enduring public construction of the war was of glory and bravery, whereas his personal memory was of discomfort, pain, and terror, produced an uncomfortable situation about which the respondent was hesitant to talk. But public memory has shifted; the influence of perceptions of the Vietnam war, of films such as *Apocalypse Now*, has tarnished the image of militarism and has made terror and avoidance of war seem to be not cowardice, but a sensible reaction. This shift in public memory has enabled this respondent to compose a different kind of sense from his wartime memories, a private memory in which the horror of war no longer needs to be denied expression, and his own reactions no longer need to be defined as cowardly. In showing how the interplay between public and private memory and between fictional and real events can re-structure both public and private memories, Thomson's research exemplifies the explanatory power of narrativity theory.

BERNSTEIN

Bernstein from his earliest to his most recent work has had a concern with narrative and narrativity. The way in which beings translate themselves into their surroundings—join in the stories of those that form their social arena—has been a permanent and abiding theme in his work. In 1958, he noticed how when a group of post office messenger boys were required to produce formal spoken narratives they evidenced a marked degree of harmonization with the narrative rules, not of formal discourse, but, of a set of shared implicit meanings found among their families and friends. Narratives are again the subject of analysis in the much discussed piece of research (Bernstein, 1971, p. 178), in which middle-class and working-class children were asked to tell the story that was presented to them pictorially. The middle-class children tended to make meaning explicit—and as a result, the reader or hearer of their account does not need the pictures to make sense of the story. The working-class children tended to leave meaning implicit—to make sense of their accounts the reader needs the pictures. Though subsequent commentators have frequently misinterpreted this to indicate that the working-class children were deficient linguistically, what in fact is at issue is different narrative conventions. This is made clear later in the same chapter when Bernstein discussed situations in which different contexts evoked restricted accounts from middle-class children.

Of Bernstein's early work, the piece that most explicitly addressed questions of different narrative conventions is his review of *The Lore and Language of Schoolchildren* by Iona and Peter Opie (Bernstein, 1971). He discussed the way that the peer group language of children "reinforces solidarity with the group" rather than expressing individuality; and that it is the "very impersonality [of the group discourse] which enables the child or young adolescent to operate with savage or unfeeling terms quite freely, without a sense of guilt or shame" (p. 72). Bernstein refers here to the traditional stories and rhymes of playground oral culture. These narratives of playground culture are traditional in two senses;

some of them are passed on from one generation of children to another but, more importantly, the form of the narratives is traditional, a form that demands a show of solidarity with the group and prohibits expression of personal feeling (especially tender feeling) and reflection. The form and verbal expression of playground stories and rhymes follows strict rules for narrative structuring. In commenting on this, Bernstein concentrated on the linguistic features of the stories and fitted them into his emerging theories of codes; but it can be seen how close this is to theories about the structuring of narrative.

In 1977, Bernstein observed in describing how families managed matters ranging from the placing of a postcard to the setting of an aspidistra that ways of integrating the narrative possibilities of expression varied historically among similar social groups. This was more than a matter of social class (although it certainly was, in part, that)—it was more a matter of how different groups experienced and expressed their socialization within the power relations of the wider society. For Bernstein it is interesting to note the similarity in terms of power relations between highly formal upper middle-class Edwardians and contemporary free-and-easy middle-class academic intellectuals while at the same time observing their quite opposite rules of daily conduct. These changes in the narratives, in the daily stories of such groups, provide the exposure, reveal the orchestration, that demonstrates how the narratives themselves work. The narrative versions such groups have of themselves, partly forged by structural socioeconomic change and partly formed by their own educational experiences, are what interests Bernstein. Perhaps what we can say is that although each group might (if we can suppose a time shift to enable the groups to observe one another) find much to reproach in the other, both groups share narratives in which the world looks permeable to their influence. Their narrative conceptualizations include an assemblage of possibilities that make alteration of the governance of the social a possibility. Of course, there are many seeming exceptions to these rules—but these instances are for Bernstein not exceptions but the prefiguring moments of stasis or change. It is possible to see the narrative of innovative Edwardian ruling turn into ritualization and degeneration—at that moment it is possible for a member of the haute bourgeoisie and an exploited worker to become identical, not in material conditions, but in the character of their narrative selves (Galsworthy, 1922; Mann, 1924; Seabrook, 1967).

Bernstein's sociology, we may say, is centrally concerned with the fluidity of the biographical as it intersects with the fluidity of the social. Nothing could be further from the truth that Bernstein leaves the individual out of his constructions and formulations. The individual to be an individual must be part of a social relation. This social relation is characterized by regulation. This regulation is for Bernstein achieved through pedagogic communication—by which he means the varieties of communication performed in the transmission and acquisition of language. Such pedagogic communication can take place in the home, in the nursery, between friends, at the school, or in the locality. However, it is more than a route for the transport of received outlooks on gender, chemistry, class, literature, religion, mathematics, and so on. For although the individual stands in relation to those texts in terms of already acquired texts relating to them, what is also being transmitted are the internal constituents of the text itself; these constituents are the means of *ordering* the information to be imparted. These pedagogic discourses, these communicative settings, are essentially the imagining moments during which that which is to be learned (instrumentally and/or expressively) is experienced through a continual process of interpersonal recontextualizing. The individual's life, the trajectory of living, is a process of endlessly celebrating and challenging this fact, of confirming acceptance and requiring change. For Bernstein, the recognition of this state is also the recognition of the individual in her or his tensions between the pulls of anxiety and harmony that form the mix of sociality and ego (Lacan, 1968).

How a person sees the world, interprets the world, and brings that world back inside them is done in terms of some sort of coding. Bernstein employs the term code, which he has used from his earliest to his most recent works, to mean the acts (normally hidden) that valorize regulation; acts which he has analyzed to reveal the regulatory processes contained therein. Codes are then the acts of cultural transmission by which society is sustained. Bernstein's approach to those aspects of social life that could be analyzed using terminology and concepts from theories of narrativity employs a different terminology—that of code. But, as was indicated, there is a great deal of overlap and resonance between the fundamental ideas at issue. For the social, moral, and cosmic framework that situates the events of a narrative into a culturally meaningful entity, Bernstein uses the overarching concept of code. Codes, whether linguistic, whether regulating the performance of social roles or regulating conduct, or whether mediating learning, are culturally accepted frameworks of meaning that govern the responses of individuals in the gamut of social situations of daily life.

A person's narrative journey through a day will encounter, create, and utilize many forms of coding activities—restricted/elaborated, positional/personal, strong/weak framings, visible/invisible pedagogies, and so on. The possibilities of the permeability, or not, of boundaries will be contemplated. The thoughts that play through our minds ("Does Mary love me?", "I am cooking," "I am anxious," "Where is the taxi?") are all experienced and elicit actions in terms of where we place, and are placed within, the coding features that join our cognitive and moral acts.

Further, given that no two individuals (no matter how close) live the same lives, their codings in their external actions and in their internal lives will always be different; in fact, this is how difference and complementarity are established. Of course, this does not mean to say that there are not marked degrees of similarity within groups. That the well-off, well-educated upper middle classes are likely to have dispositions more reminiscent of some codes than others, whereas those kept poor and constantly denied access to education will not share this repertoire of codes, is a point constantly made by Bernstein. Codes for Bernstein will axiomatically become complicit in whichever forms of narrative are associated with power.

However, codings are not always satisfying even unto themselves; they do not always produce the full narrative; they can never in a complex society entirely close the curtain; chinks of light from other codes, relaying other narratives, are always peeking in to make our current narratives stop and ponder difference. Additionally, we can be prevented by the burden of articulation to so explain and make clear to ourselves the sources of our high moments that they may dissolve; in the moment we see the sun setting through an olive grove, we may regret that our simple, unembellished response is being transmuted through the other more formalized parts of our lives. We have a desire to translate our positional reactions into our personal expressions. This difficulty, this inability to express one code and then one narrative in the form of another, is something that we learn to live with and also, most interestingly, to adumbrate and speculate on and therefore to understand better.

The way regulatory activities are internalized is through the rehearsals of their narratives—by example, by practice, and, highly importantly, by recounting. It is via these methods, by an appreciation of the sequencing of life through time in a deliberate way, that the individual may utilize the narratives of self and others to contextualize her- or himself and innovate within the social arena. Any fracturing, denying, or stultifying of these processes will make innovation less likely and more precarious. Complex societies are arranged so that frustrated narratives will be commonplace. However, it is the degree of frustration that is important and, almost always, needless to say, it is those with the least power and cultural capital that are most negatively affected. As Hardy (1968) has said of narrative, "We dream in narrative, day-dream in narrative, remember, anticipate, hope, despair, believe, doubt, plan, revise, criticise, construct, gossip, learn, hate, and love by narrative" (p. 5).

If Bernstein supplied a manner of describing the regulatory

modes of cultural transmission, it is Ricoeur who explicitly addressed the moral imperatives behind, and hermeneutical considerations on, the human act of narration. Bernstein's formulations, although highly descriptive, do not allow, or are too methodologically circumscribed, to reach more fully than they do into the heart of the cultural. It is here that Ricoeur can supply the other part of a shared narrational project and go a long way to providing the hermeneutical depth of the socio-logical outline.

RICOEUR

For Ricoeur, the *social imaginary*, by which he means the collection of stories, histories, and narrative that compose the coordinating princi-ple of our purchase on existence make up *social reality* itself (Ricoeur, 1984, p. 77). Ricoeur observes these narratives working at a variety of levels, from the national to the everyday. That is, although all societies invoke themselves in sociopolitical *imaginaries* that represent mythic or symbolic discourses of narrative, narratives are also the medium of exchange at the everyday level. It is at this quotidian level that we engage with most acts of narrative and by which our narrative compe-tence is established. As such it is through this generation of narrative competence that we fully understand our own actions and sufferings (Kemp, 1989).

This process of self-understanding can only exist for Ricoeur in the practice of the mediation of cultural signs, a mediation that is achieved through the recognition of a universal feature of existence—namely, time and its passage. Time is experienced by persons at both the naturalistic and reflective level, and life is composed of the narra-tives by which time is experienced. These narratives place on exis-tence—past, present and future—a cohering feature constituting the reasons for thoughts and actions. For Ricoeur, then, narrativity offers a philosophical solution to the problem of how to describe and discuss identity. He argues that we equate life with the stories it represents. We do not see our jobs, our feelings concerning a dropped plate, or the contemplation of our deaths or those of others in any terms other than as events within a narrative—be they trivial or momentous. The acts of recounting these narratives to ourselves or to others are the way, to use Dilthey's term, we establish the "coherence of life" (Dilthey, 1961, p. 17).

What we have established is not the ease of life but the recog-nition that life and the identities that compose it are of a narrative kind. This is why for Ricoeur our forms of telling stories are so impor-tant, because their contemplation will inform us how we construct, at a more prosaic level, ourselves. Ricoeur quoted from Proust's great novel to give an example of his point:

> But to return to myself, I thought more modestly of my book, and one could not exactly say that I thought of those who would read it, of my readers. Because they would not according to me be my readers, but the real readers of themselves, my book being only like one of those magnifying glasses offered to a customer by the optician at Combray. It was my book, and thanks to it I enabled them to read what lay within themselves. (Proust, cited in Ricoeur, 1991b, p. 198)

It does not matter for Ricoeur that this quotation should arise from a semi- autobiographical novel because in this case it provides a discussion of what yourself is and how others are in relation to it.

We understand what action is; we interpret action by perceiving it through a network we can describe as a semantics of action (Ricoeur, 1991a, p. 28). That is, those performances we are witness to gain their familiarity because we apprehend them as moments in "plots" (*les intrigues*) of stories known to us, or, as ones we have sufficient syntactical fragments of that we may devise them. We may say then that human life in its purely biological state is in its prenarrational moment and that its actualization is as an "activity and a passion in search of a narrative" (Ricoeur, 1991a, p. 29). The narrative is constituted by the plots of stories that transform the paradigmatic order of narrative into ever revised and revitalized paradigmatic orders. To understand a narrative by "emplotment" (*mise en intrigue*) is to devise a system that provides the researcher with a point of mediation to interpret the sense of time's passage, to obtain a narrative purchase.

Ricoeur argues that these processes of emplotment are forms of engagement greater than having a perspective. It is more a process of interpretation in terms of revision and accretion—that is, engagement does not pretend to the majesty of total explanation. We are not able totally to replicate a narrative; we cannot re-give it in language, there is no such thing as a full-scale map; and, further, we can never overcome "the ineluctably aporetic nature of the human experience of time" (White, 1991, p. 144). The meaning of human lives for Ricoeur is apprehended by an engagement with the plots through which they are lived. The benefit of this lack of total completeness, this approximation, is that narrative is interpreted by the mechanism of its own epistemological foundations—and as such prevents the fetishing of both the social context and the individual.

It is then not surprising that Ricoeur has said (1986) that "telling a story is the most permanent act of societies . . . in telling stories, cultures create themselves" (p. 7). These stories, as we mentioned earlier,

can refer to competing accounts of national destiny or be the establishment of reciprocity in small groups. It is less useful to Ricoeur to deny
certain narratives and to proclaim others than advance the view that it is
in the readiness to refigure narratives that ethical procedures are pursued. It is for this reason that he argues that the connection between
the recognition of narrative and moral understanding is simultaneously
"a relation of presupposition and relation of transformation" (Ricoeur
1984, p. 55). Each narrative that is engaged with must make certain pre-
suppositions, "a familiarity with terms such as agent, goal, means, circumstance, etc." (Ricoeur, 1984, pp. 56-57). However, the constituents of
narrative are not of themselves constrained by a particular narrative. In
Ricoeur's terms, narratives are not a matter of a simple succession of
stories, but of a development of "discursive features . . . syntactic features, whose function is to engender the composing of modes of discourse worthy of being called narratives." (p. 21). These activities are
operationalized through the grammar of narratives, that is, through the
available compositional elements of narratives immanent to a culture
and that represent the building blocks of conceptual reciprocity.

The high regard in which Ricoeur's work is held by both continental and Anglo-American philosophers centers, above all, on the
notion of narrative (Wood, 1991). This is not only because he develops
a shared social meaning for philosophical analysis by his recognition
that both for philosophy and human life in general there is nothing
more real for individuals than the "experience of temporality" (Rée,
1991), but also, that part of that reality is occupied with loss, personal
confusion, and the "mystery . . . of being-in-time" (White, 1991, p. 142).
The fact that narrativity is the language that has temporality as its ultimate referent must mean that it is through this medium that the aporias of existence, as well as its harmonies, are recognized.

Each social event needs to be recognized to be available for
conceptual understanding; and it is recognized by locating it within a
temporal schema. As such the experience of time can never be merely
serial, rather, it engages the already existing narrative texts as the constituting features of consciousness in the world—the manner in which
events occur for the receiving narrative is not like a radar beam steadily
counting approaching aircraft, but, by "inaugurations, transitions, termi-
nations" (White, 1991, p. 148). Events are then analyzed by the process
of making them narrative, not by passively registering the world, but by
working up the material given in perception and fashioning it so "that it
creates something new, in precisely the same way that human agents by
their actions fashion distinctive forms of historical life out of the world
they inherit as their past" (White, 1992, p. 150). Narratives have meaning
because human actions produce meaning, and this meaning is under-

stood in a form of continuity that although it formally separates past and future is experienced as reflection and prefiguration.

BERNSTEIN AND RICOEUR

The similarities of subject matter, if not interpretive method, which link Bernstein and Ricoeur, are, given their very disparate backgrounds, quite remarkable. The reflections and intentions of individuals are seen as produced by and producing the narratives that also constitute the basic characterization of their actions; in other words, not only do human beings recount stories, but they are also constituted as story-telling creatures. For both Bernstein and Ricoeur it is not only a general point concerning communication that narratives be mutually comprehensible, but of special interest is the *degree* to which they are mutually comprehensible. Both are concerned with the social circumstances that constrain individuals in the production of narratives.

One of the features of reduced narrative possibilities, argue Bernstein and Ricoeur, is the inability (usually consequent on powerlessness or oppression) of individuals and groups to promote innovation. Unless the horizon of expectation can be approached from a repertoire of narratives containing figurations of the possibility of change, then those narratives will be either foreshortened or unrealistically speculative. This is so because possibilities of change need to be contextualized by universalistic rather than particularistic, self-confirming codes (Bernstein) or, obversely, because change when divorced from realistic narratives of innovation becomes merely fanciful and devoid of meaning (Ricoeur). In Kearney's (1989) terms: "The universal loses contact with the actual. Expectancy becomes disassociated from experience. The *ought* floats free from the *is*" (p. 23; emphasis in original). The conditions under which this most readily occurs, when, for example, pedagogic transmission is most reduced, is at the point where individuals have the least opportunity or desire to become engaged with narrative. This may be in modern societies a result of poverty, mass unemployment, and a close proximity with a crude and simplistic mass media. As such we are reminded that narratives are not simply routes of cognitive sophistication but also the pathways of ethics.

The narratives of experience wait to have their transformative features exploited by the narratives of expectancy. Unless this exploitation can occur—unless the narrative of experience can be intelligible to the narrative of expectancy—then narratives will remain in positional, strongly classified forms. These narratives, although universally understood and perfectly meaningful, will be predictable because they rehearse the past without building on tradition in order to transform it. Of course, these distinctions made by Bernstein and Ricoeur are abstract and analytical. In reality they are to be encountered in a thousand partial ways, and no consciousness is entirely one or the other. If humans are peculiar by conceptualizing action in terms of narrative, they can never be entirely free from its insistent conservative structures, nor can they ever entirely resist its refiguring possibilities.

Although the networks that form the contours of narratives may be highly limiting, nonetheless, the narrative impulse can be realized in markedly unpromising circumstances. The place that both Bernstein and Ricoeur give to the need for and importance of teaching is recognition of this. It is in the sustaining and promoting of those relationships that can enlarge the temporal and causal components in the narratives of others that virtuous acts find their own narrative expression. At its most basic level this starts with children in which what is at stake is far more than do-goodery or a reified concern with "proper" English. It is rather a way of recognizing that a neglect of narrative accounts will restrict the ability of children to produce for themselves a sense of narrative being a route to *both* reassurance and innovation, a way of providing a sense of the temporal and causal; as MacIntyre has said: "deprive children of stories and you leave them unscripted, anxious stutterers." (p. 216). Bernstein's sociology of regulation and Ricoeur's philosophy of interpretation act as complex and extensive explications of this ethical point.

At the heart of both Bernstein and Ricoeur is an attempt to descibe the arc that links the possibilities of moral reasoning with existential embodiment. For both thinkers group norms are the rationalized forms of phenemenological motivation; and it is the process by which this is achieved that permits existence to be explained to itself. The moral injunction of Bernstein's and Ricoeur's thought is that this process be adumbrated and refined because it is in the process that the ethics of communication become uncovered. The fact that the process of achieving group norms is always, ultimately, incomplete is a feature of human society itself. The process, although rich in the possibilities of improved communication, nonetheless describes a lack at its very center. It is paradoxical that the mechanism by which humans gain the most understanding of themselves also indicates their incompleteness. It is, then, by uncovering the strength and lacunae of the narratological structure of reason itself that Ricoeur has developed hermeneutics, and it is in the performances of narrating activities that Bernstein has provided a glimpse of its systematization.

REFERENCES

Atkinson, P. (1985). *Language, structure and reproduction—an introduction to the sociology of Basil Bernstein*. London: Methuen.

Bernstein, B. (1958). Some sociological determinants of perception. *British Journal of Sociology*, 9(2), 159-174.

Bernstein, B. (1971). *Class, codes and control* (Vol.1). London: Routledge and Kegan Paul.

Bernstein, B. (1973). *Class, codes and control* (Vol.2). London: Routledge and Kegan Paul.

Bernstein, B. (1977). *Class, codes and control* (Vol.3). London: Routledge and Kegan Paul.

Bernstein, B. (1990). *Class, codes and control* (Vol.4). London: Routledge and Kegan Paul.

Chanfrault-Duchet, M.-F. (1991). Narrative structures, social models and symbolic representation in the life story. In S.B. Gluck & D. Patai (Eds.), *Women's words: The feminist practice of oral history* (pp. 77-92). London: Routledge.

Clarke, S.H. (1992). *Paul Ricoeur*. London: Routledge.

Dilthey, W. (1961). *Meaning in history*. London: Allen and Unwin.

Erben, M. (1993). The problem of other lives. *Sociology*, 27(1), 15-25.

Erben, M. (1994). Pictorial biography: Hogarth's *Marriage A-la-Mode*. *Auto/Biography*, 2(2), 44-58.

Galsworthy, J. (1922). *The man of property*. London: Heinemann.

Hardy, B. (1968). Towards a poetics of fiction: An approach through narrative. *Novel*, 2(1), 5-14.

Kearney, R. (1989). Paul Ricoeur and the hermeneutic imagination. In T.P. Kemp & D. Rasmussen (Eds.), *The narrative path* (pp. 1-32). Cambridge, MA: MIT Press.

Kemp, T.P. (1989). Toward a narrative ethics. In T.P. Kemp & D. Rasmussen (Eds.), *The narrative path* (pp. 65-88). Cambridge, MA: MIT Press.

Lacan, J. (1968). The mirror-phase as formation of the function of I. *New Left Review*, 51, 71-77.

MacIntyre, A. (1985). *After virtue* (2nd ed.). London: Duckworth.

Mann, T. (1924). *Buddenbrooks* (2 Vols., trans. H.T. Lowe-Porter). London: Martin Secker.

Murray, K. (1989). The construction of identity in the narratives of romance and comedy. In J. Shotter & K. Gergen (Eds.), *Texts of identity* (pp. 175-205). London: Sage.

Passerini, L. (1989). Women's personal narratives: Myths, experiences and emotions. In Personal Narratives Group (Ed.), *Interpreting Women's Lives: Feminist Theory and Personal Narratives* (pp. 189-197).

Bloomington and Indianapolis: Indiana University Press.

Rée, J. (1991). Narrative and philosophical experience. In D. Wood (Ed.), *On Paul Ricoeur: Narrative and Interpretation* (pp. 74-83). London: Routledge.

Ricoeur, P. (1984). *Time and narrative* (Vol. 1). Chicago: Chicago University Press.

Ricoeur, P. (1985). *Time and narrative* (Vol. 2). Chicago: Chicago University Press.

Ricoeur, P. (1986, February 7). Interview. *Le Monde*, p.8.

Ricoeur, P. (1988). *Time and narrative* (Vol. 3). Chicago: Chicago University Press.

Ricoeur, P. (1991a). Life in quest of narrative. In D. Wood (Ed.), *On Paul Ricoeur: Narrative and interpretation* (pp. 20-33). London: Routledge.

Ricoeur, P. (1991b). Narrative identity. In D. Wood (Ed.), *On Paul Ricoeur: Narrative and interpretation* (pp. 188-200). London: Routledge.

Seabrook, J. (1967). *The unpriveleged*. London: Longmans.

Thomson, A. (1990). Anzac memories: Putting popular memory theory into practice. *Oral History, 18*(1), 25-31.

White, H. (1991). The Metaphysics of narrativity. In D. Wood (Ed.), *On Paul Ricoeur: Narrative and interpretation*. London: Routledge.

Wood, D. (Ed.). (1991). *On Paul Ricoeur: Narrative and interpretation*. London: Routledge.

14

Postmetaphysical Discourse and Pedagogy

Robert Young
University of Sydney

Enthusiasm for poststructuralist thought has had a considerable impact on social philosophy and theory. Now we are seeing the emergence of a more cautious appraisal and increasingly incisive criticism (e.g., Callinicos, 1989; Gallagher, 1992; Toulmin, 1990;). But the most interesting aspect of the phenomenon has been the way in which poststructuralism seemed to meet a deep need. How else to explain the incautious extravagances of "cultural studies," literary theory, certain feminisms, and much recent social theorizing.

Where earlier manifestations of "the linguistic turn" had made only limited reconnaissances, poststructuralism has marched an army. Phenomenology, ethnomethodology, various strands of hermeneutics, and the Frankfurt School were, it seems, but scouts for this army. Every metaphor has its day, and the notion of language, then sign system, code, and finally discourse, "dispositif," and so on, as metaphors for society, culture, and social reality is having its day today. Once I numbered myself among the advocates of this development, but the turn has turned too far. However, I recognize that critics of this way of seeing do not always take sufficient note of the nature of the needs that poststructuralism appears to meet. The exaggerations of some of its proponents do not detract from the insights of its more luminous practitioners. A retreat to neo-Marxism, one of the earliest alternatives to the apparent infelicities and inconsistencies of Foucault and Derrida (particularly in the hands of their North American fans; e.g., Nicholson,

1992), is looking less and less plausible. Perhaps it would be vain to expect that there could be a decisive outcome when the heirs of Nietzsche and Heidegger contest with the heirs of Marx on terrain thoroughly familiar to all the warring parties (Hoy, 1991).

It is not possible here to provide a balanced appraisal of poststructuralism and an outline of those insights it has provided that can be valued even when other, more sweeping claims are rejected. Nor will space allow me to justify the claim that poststructuralism has met particular needs with any extended analysis of those needs. Readers will have to read between the lines to glean an idea of these things from the following discussion. What I show in this chapter, very briefly to be sure, is that there is an alternative to poststructuralism, which preserves what is valuable in its central metaphors, but which avoids its more absolutist and antinomian uses. And I do this through a discussion of ideology, discourse, and pedagogy under the rubric of a "postmetaphysical pragmatism" that is guided by a textual rather than physicalist transactional realism. In rejecting modernity, there is an alternative to a mirror image of it. Foucault (198j276

1·), and "Derrida Anglicized," came close to a simple inversion of modernity. (Foucault himself tends to demonize modernity into Adorno's "totally administered society." His hierophants only simplify. But Derrida, at least, has actively protested against the misuse of his ideas |Derrida, 1984|). The great weakness of poststructuralism is what Rorty (1991(has called *textualism*—the extension of the notion of text to all "readable" reality, to all *social* reality. This amounts to a reduction of society to culture. Poststructuralism's insights derive from the fruitfulness of this extension and from the methodological value of going one step further than Husserl (1962) and "bracketing" relations between signifier and signified (as well as between the sign taken as a whole and the world). But the value of these metamethodological ploys is greatly reduced if everything is treated as text and the brackets are never removed.

It is also possible to recognize that a humane, critical, and nuanced postmodernity can be constructed out of cultural resources that have been available since long before Foucault's "archaeology." It should not surprise one to learn that Adorno (1967) was talking of contextuality of thought, including science, of sensuality, art, and the body, and of Nietzschean failure of the concept, before Foucault took up his chair in Paris. Adorno and others have been called "critical modernists," but a label of that kind would not meet with approval in the present apocalyptic mood. Perhaps in a special high sense of the term *metaphysics*, it might be safer to keep faith with the *fin de siécle* atmosphere and call the approach adopted here *postmetaphysical*. That has been

Habermas's (1987b) choice.

There are a number of contenders for hegemony among post-metaphysical theories, some of which are still incomplete. Nor can any more than the slightest sketch of theories of this kind be given here. Again, brevity compels one to focus on the meeting points of various strands of thought, on common ground and complementarity, and for the moment at least, to gloss over many difficulties, incoherencies, and pleonastic resemblances. I begin with a discussion of the ontology of the later Dewey, particularly with regard to ethical inquiry, to connect this with the Habermas-inspired discussion of discourse ethics and to note resemblances with neo-Aristotelian thought. The contextual, nonuniversalist, and textual nature of this thought is brought out. Discussions of notions of education, ideology, discourse, pedagogy, and of the role of the intellectual point to some of the implications of non-Parisian alternatives to poststructuralism. Although the discussion is confined largely to the ethical-political "domain," it could well be argued that, in the theory of knowledge, an even stronger case could be made, but again, space precludes a treatment of the reasons why a textually turned transactional realism is superior to nonrealist alternatives.

DEWEY'S POSTMETAPHYSICAL "METAPHYSICS"

There is no clearer exposition of the necessity of metaphysics and the possibility of a kind of metaphysics that escapes the thrust of recent postmodern criticism of essentialism and universalism than Boisvert's discussion of "Rorty, Dewey and Post-Modern Metaphysics" (1989). I do not intend to go beyond this in the present discussion. Before beginning, though, it should be said that rather than continue as Boisvert does, to use the word *metaphysics*, I chose to take up another of Boisvert's suggestions and call this necessary kind of reasoning *ecological ontology* (Boisvert, 1988, p. 183).

In *Experience and Nature* (1925/1982) and *Logic: The Theory of Inquiry* (1938), Dewey outlined what can be called his mature or "late" position. Dewey's view is distinctly postmodern, in the sense that it strongly rejects the kind of views those who use the terms *postmodern* or *poststructuralist* have also resolutely opposed.

It might surprise some who think of Dewey as an ethical universalist to realize that in his discussion of Plato, Dewey espouses a particularistic notion of social ethics. For Plato (and as MacIntyre, 1988, showed, Aristotle too), action has its own logic. Of course, action is to be distinguished from mere behavior. But Dewey's position is balanced between two extremes. Culturally meaningful doing—action—may bear many relations to any particular end, but the logic of its meaning is the realization of ends. As Gallagher (1992) made clear, in his timely analysis of hermeneutic theory, such a perspective picks up a postmodern strand in hermeneutic thought. Heidegger was among those who held that human action was a process in a dialectic between actuality and possibility and, with postmodernity generally, held that human identity was not a fixed essential identity and that "the unity of subjectivity is not a substantial unity but a unity of process constantly recovering itself" (Gallagher, 1992, p. 53). Cultures may hypostatize and naturalize particular ideals, but the business of practice is in a dialectical relation with these, as speech is with language (Taylor, 1984). This view of action overcomes the weakness in theories of language as action as identified by Derrida, but it meets criticisms of Derrida's weaknesses when it comes to politics by developing an account of both the production of language and the productivity of language (Benhabib, 1986; Fraser, 1981; Levin, 1981).

In contrast with Dewey, Rorty (1982) dichotomized philosophers into "metaphysicians" and "intellectuals," producing a new dualism. Rorty's metaphysicians are absolutists whose goal is to establish some sort of foundation on which knowledge may be built, whereas intellectuals, like Rorty himself, are those who enjoy conversations for their own sake, without yearning after the quest for certainty and knowledge of "reality." Here, Rorty aligns himself more closely with Derrida's critique of the metaphysics of presence and with poststructuralist ideas generally than with Dewey.

Dewey's position is more dialectical. Form, including textual form, emerges historically, as systems change. We can attempt to understand the configurations of circumstances (situations) in which we find ourselves and act to change the more problematic aspects of them, giving rise to new, quite real, but historically temporary, forms or situations. Problems are not solved in the imagination, but require real action, including the construction, production, interpretation, and deconstruction of texts. And imagined solutions are not always real solutions. That depends not only on invention, but on their adequacy with respect to the concrete particularities of place or situation. The dialogue between imagination and experience is called *inquiry*, but there is a dimension of inquiry in art and literature, just as there is a dimension of art and literature in inquiry. Nevertheless, as Derrida (1984) himself has argued, the genre distinction between inquiry and more expressive forms must be maintained. Inquiry requires both a kind of metaphysician and a conversationalist, as well as the forms of methodological suspicion that Derrida privileges.

As Boisvert made quite clear, the rejection of an absolute, ahistorical metaphysics is only the rejection of one kind of metaphysics—the notion that there is a deeper reality of which the historical flux of events is only a manifestation. But it is not necessary to abandon any and every notion of reality when abandoning this metaphysics. What is necessary is a shift in the conception of the nature of reality, from absolute, but veiled form, to a view in which the flux is the reality and reality is flux—whereas at any given time, it is real, circumstantial, and systematically interrelated. Similarly, the rejection of a metaphysics of the text, which is a metaphysics of the presence of signified (and object), does not imply the rejection of a metaphysics of the transactional reality and presence of texts themselves. Thus, we might not wish to agree with the sweeping and absolutist character of Derrida's rejection of the ontogenetic dimension of Heidegger's inquiries. However much we may problematize the world relations of textual meanings, we may still wish to speak of nontextual features of context. Of course, we must linguistify this to make it talk-about-able, but its prior existence, resistance, and independence of particular ways of talking is what is at stake. The error lies in all those hermeneutic theories that, like Gadamer's (1975), reduce social reality and its explanations to the explanation of meanings or that, like Derrida's (1978), reduce it to the suspicious transformation of them.

In such an ecological ontology, we live in a world of what Boisvert called "sursistences":

> events with significations established as a result of varied sorts of interactions with humans. The realm of existence carries within it the possibilities for various types of meaning. The lived world into which humans are born is composed of sursistences, culturally conditioned meanings which have emerged via the various sorts of participation of humans within their |situations|. (Boisvert, 1989, pp. 185-186)

We seek "goods" in this process in the same way we walk—by lurching from one unbalanced moment to another. We solve problems only to create new situations from which new problems emerge. As Dewey (1925/1982, pp. 67-68) explained, we move forward by experimenting with our situation to secure and extend goods we have already defined, and we sift our experience in such a way that we learn to define or redefine our goods.

Dewey always sought to go beyond both cultural relativism and cultural absolutism (or ethnocentrism). Unlike Rorty, who believes that philosophy should limit itself to comparing, contrasting, and thereby understanding cultural traditions, Dewey sought a nonethnocentric basis for cultural criticism.

DISCOURSE ETHICS

With Rorty (1982, pp. 3-18) we can agree that philosophy (and indeed sociology) is a conversation, but with Habermas (1982) we can take the view that the rules of conversation have constitutive power. That is, it is in meaningful interaction, particularly communicative interaction, that we constitute (i.e., make real) the learning process whereby we come to understand the goods we seek, our own lives, and the movement of our conduct. Although our reality may involve more than texts, our inquiries about it begin and end with texts, and changing those texts changes our reality, *but only to the extent that it is textual.*

Of course, the theses of Habermas-inspired discourse ethics are controversial, and there is no possibility of defending any particular version of them here. The point that I make is simply that the way in which discourse theories of ethics are developing brings them on the one hand into closer and closer complementarity to Dewey's ecological ontology, providing an ethical-political methodology for Dewey's onto-genetic process, and on the other hand, into a realist view of the productivity of texts. The parallel here is with the relationship the old metaphysics had with its epistemology. Just as Habermas, with the postmoderns, has rejected the old metaphysics of essence, so he has rejected the epistemological method of solving the cognitive problems it raises—in favor of, arguably, an implicit, new metaphysics of a genetic ontological kind and a communicative-interactive philosophy rather than one of consciousness-based method (Habermas, 1977) of dealing with the cognitive problem. However, Habermas also rejected textualism. Social analysis must deal with that which is beyond text, even beyond meaning: "the objective framework of social action is not exhausted by the dimension of . . . meaning" (Habermas, 1977, p. 361).

Habermas reformulated Kant's categorical imperative in a concrete ethical-political form. From an ethics based on a principle that individual thinkers take into account monologically (that ethically acceptable rules must be such that everyone could accept them), Habermas moved to actual discourses. This move entailed the idea of a cooperative process of argumentation in which parties to a discourse are able to form a common will, which is also by that fact, to the extent that it is textual, a common world. A practical safeguard in such discourses is the fact that each individual is best able to determine his or her own interests (needs and wants). "Best able" does not mean "perfectly able" because the terms in which needs and wants are identified are themselves capable of discursive scrutiny, in critique of the culture in which they are embedded. This critique becomes the critique of cultural traditions and, as shown later, MacIntyre has something *methodologically* useful to say about this, too.

Ethical claims are analogous to truth claims—they admit of validity and invalidity. They produce new meanings in new texts (or reproduce old meanings). That is, they are also ethical acts. They are claims that emerge in contexts of action. Their meanings and the productive process itself are conditioned by nontextual realities. That is, resolution of ethical problems is not simply cognitive or passive, nor is it simply directed by desire. Habermas's conception of the political is the "concrete universalisation" of ethical agreement and associated practices. Habermas argues that there is no need for a separate line of argument to make the connection between the norms discovered/agreed in argumentation and the regulation of action because practical (i.e., normative) discourses, as defined by Habermas (1990), "are always related to the concrete point of departure of a disturbed normative agreement" (p. 100).

In this sense discourses emerge from what Dewey calls problems, specifically, ethical/political or "practical" problems. The nature of the possible complementarity between Habermas's procedural account of ethical problem solving and Dewey's account of problem situations begins to emerge. By embedding Kant's transcendental principle of ethics (categorical imperative) in concrete, problem-generated, historically, and culturally located argumentation, which in the ethical/cultural domain is also constitutive action, Habermas provides a procedural/logical account of Dewey's ontogenetic view of social reality. He argues, in addition, that this view, although emerging from European philosophy, is not ethnocentric because the idea of discursive resolution of validity claims in a way that is binding on participants is found in all cultures. However, he accepts that the political conditions of a problem situation limit the possibility of entering into such discourses *and* the viability of any outcomes.

Discursive problem solving is differentially institutionalized in different cultures, and even in cultures in which it is honored in universalistic terms (e.g., European cultures), it is "repeatedly thrust aside by the instruments of force" (Habermas, 1990, p. 103). Force here is a nontextual real. Note, however, that the universalization spoken of here is not inconsistent with local substantive diversity. The concrete practices spoken of are consistent with this because they are problem-solving practices, not substantive norms. Poststructuralist analyses of colonial discourse have drawn attention to the need to go beyond mere oppositionary discourses or "nativist" discourses. But this can only occur when there is a dialogical process. In this politically constitutive dialogue a development from a hybrid colonial-nativist discourse leads to a discourse that transcends both. (Niranjana, 1992)

Where Habermas and the poststructuralists part company is

where the positive possibilities of discourse start to emerge. Deconstruction can reveal only metaphysical commitments; it cannot lead to a better metaphysics. For his part, Foucault takes the view that power/knowledge is an inseparable combination. Habermas's view is that these are only contingently and relatively true statements. They are sweeping and exaggerated. He argues that the writings of the poststructuralists and the claims expressed in them make up a performatory contradiction. This contradiction is constituted by claims that no discourse can claim greater truth relative to others, or that all truth claims are inextricably enmeshed in a regime of power and the writings themselves, which make the implicit claim that clever Derrida and wily Foucault have seen through all this. It is much the same sort of performatory contradiction that we are faced with when a Cretan tells us that all Cretans are liars. Habermas (1987b) recognizes the implication of power in what passes for knowledge in society, but holds that the idea of truth (which is always conditionally but never absolutely counterfactual) helps to understand conditions under which dialogue can be freer than the existing influence of power.

Accordingly, Habermas defines the political problem as the problem of emancipation from nondiscursive methods of problem solving, and the character of politics is defined as the concrete universalization of these methods (Howard, 1988). Ideology is first procedurally defined. Its existential correlate is the exclusion of individuals and particularly classes (categories) of individuals from the ontogenetic poetic of their polity, culture, and identity. It is this exclusion that marks colonial discourses. However, deconstruction is only one of the necessary tools for critique of colonial discourse because deconstruction is a form of "immanent critique" and, like all immanent critique, is tied to the resources of the critical domain to which it is immanent. Some form of historicism and some form of realism are necessary to the movement beyond the critical domain to which deconstruction is tied, namely, actually or presently existing texts. Thus, the politics of identity and culture are opened up, not simply as the result of the criticism of the core ideas of a single culture complex—such as power/knowledge in modernity—but as the result of a methodology that is based on a general understanding of both the emergent, nonessential character of human ontologies in all cultures and the contingent actuality of the same. The political importance of this level of analytical capability is further explored next.

MACINTYRE'S AND DEWEY'S COUNTER-FACTUALISM

As Sleeper (1985) pointed out, the logic of the adaptive/learning process described by Dewey has "ontological implications." And as

Garrison (1990; see also Boisvert, 1988; Sleeper, 1985) recently reminded us, the metaphysics or ontogenetics of this has an Aristotelian
dynamic. The contingently ontic character of the actualized emerges
from the range of the ontologically possible. This was also Heidegger's
position. There is always a tension between the actual and the potential, and each person is aware of this in his or her own experience.
Things could be otherwise better. In the concrete present this is also
worked out in a dialectic between the desiring imagination and the
experienced situation—a dialectic the energy or tension of which we
call *problem*. The desiring imagination presents us with some understanding of the end, of a possible resolution of all tensions, and of rest
and peace. This is always counterfactual, yet real in its effects, because
we act in the present in terms of it, and in our experience of our actions
and the outcomes of them we revise, renew, or replace our desires and
imaginings. The "ideal speech situation" was an attempt by Habermas
to characterize the desiring imagination of a state of full mutual understanding between persons. Although Habermas no longer uses this
counterfactual tool, he continues to endorse the necessity of a counterfactual account of the conditions of understanding as an assumption of
all speakers who set out to understand each other (Habermas, 1990).

    And it is, perhaps surprisingly to some, MacIntyre's (1988)
Christian neo-Aristotelianism that provides us with some clues as to
why it may be necessary to retain what Benhabib (1989-90) in her discussion of Habermas and neo-Aristotelianism called the sense of a
"larger ethical context in which morality is always but an aspect" (p. 27).
It is from our hopes and our desiring imagination at this logical level
that we find the resources to transcend the particularity of cultural traditions of morality. Essentially, MacIntyre gives a Lakatosian account of
the (theory) rivalry of moral traditions. Only when a tradition fails to
enable its members to deal effectively with experience and an alternative tradition appears to offer some resources to do this and some persons find themselves able to live biculturally and bilingually, and so
develop a new set of solutions to problems, are we enabled to pass
beyond a particular, failing ethical discourse to a more effective one.
This process is obviously compromised by culturally correlated asym-
metries of power of the kind that characterize colonial situations. It is
clear enough, I think, that something like this process is what is happening today in the world of social thought generally and specifically in
ethical theory. At least, that is my interpretation. One may agree with
Williams (1985) that recognition of the embeddedness of ethical theories in their culturally specific backgrounds may be a precondition of
any postmodern ethical discourse, throwing all ethical theories into
doubt, but also agree with MacIntyre (and Habermas) that this is but a

necessary step in the development of valid moral reasoning. Not valid once and for all, but valid in Dewey's (1925/1982) sense of substantiating "frail goods" and extending secure ones and searching for those goods of which all we sense is a "precarious promise"(pp. 67-68).

THE POLITICAL FORM OF THE EMANCIPATION
OF DESIRING IMAGINATION

Discussions of the emancipation of desire often focus on sexuality. Perhaps it is heretical to say that the importance of sexuality and differences of sexual preference has been much overrated. It may be even more heretical to argue that in addition to freedom *to* desire we need to embrace the possibility of freedom *from* desire or, at least, freedom from the particularity of desire and the tyranny of the imagined objects of desire of any particular tradition, culture, or "orientation." When marginalized and oppressed groups are identified, we ought first to recognize that it is their exclusion from the ontogenetic poetic that is the first problem of their situation, not the specific content of their desire that is thereby unrealized, because the latter may change but the dynamics of exclusion/participation are a permanent feature of the exercise of power in the human condition.

Although all interpretive activity occurs *out of* the unexamined preinterpretations of the life world—biases, *vorhabe*, tradition, a language—all traditions have an image or dream of a state of being beyond any and all specific components of the tradition and thus beyond the tradition itself. This is a dream of a standing outside or ekstasis a.k.a. ecstasy, in which particularity and contingency is transcended. It is this normally counterfactual image that plays the key methodological role in our ability to go beyond the way traditions give us ourselves. Normally, language speaks for us, but we sometimes speak language. That is one way languages change. If we must guard against the modernist illusion that we always speak language, that we can overcome tradition and readily master our fate, equally, then we must guard against the postmodernist absolute—that we never do (see Gallagher, 1992, chap. 4)

But oppressed groups often demand participation in the transformative historical, culture, and identity-creating process at the expense of the desire of others. The political problem of participation, whether viewed intranationally or internationally, is that of a plurality of desiring imaginations and the incoherence created by their particularity. From a strictly logical point of view, it would appear that two solutions are possible: either a pluralism of the multicultural variety—a kind of museum of many rooms/exhibits—or an intercultural dialogue in which the first topic of conversation is the identification of a conceptually counterfactual conception of the good, thick enough to go behind the particularity of the presently diverse desires of a plurality of oppressed groups, to constitute new, shared understandings (possibly procedural) grounded in diversity. In a world in which all cultures are developing a recognition of the plurality of our common humanity, we see for the first time the possibility of an ekstasis that we can share.

In earlier critical theory, the organizational form of the desiring imagination of this capitalist age was the Party. Critical theory is sometimes defined as "the self clarification of the struggles and wishes [desires] of the age." But such a definition of critical theory is grossly historicist. The spirit of the age was the counterfactual self-recognition of the proletariat. The Party was not only the organizational form of the politics of those desires, but also the educative agent of their recognition (Fraser, 1989, p. 113). But at a time when we recognize the plurality of particular struggles—of women, African Americans, indigenous peoples in colonized situations, religious minorities, "lifestyle" minorities (such as gay people)—and we add an interethnic and international, even global dimension to the analysis—the particularity of the cause of the working classes in capitalist societies becomes evident. We must also recognize the corollary of this: the particularity of all causes.

In pluralist polities, an emancipatory politics pragmatically requires a coalition of minorities and subaltern groups. That coalition may be built on a temporary foundation of political expediency, but eventually it must be founded on a noncoercive, nonvanguardist identification of common ethical ground. An analysis that goes behind the assemblage of dispositifs in an order of power/knowledge to a recognition of the power of counterfactual desiring imagination and to a recognition of its common possession by such groups is a necessary antidote to the more Parisian versions of poststructuralism and an essential ingredient of a politics that goes beyond the "dictatorship of the proletariat" or any other group or contingent coalition of groups.

Ideology is both situation and process, in which the desiring imagination of categories of people are excluded from the ontogenesis of the future context of their own biography. Particular metaphors, concepts, and narratives are manifestations of this situation of exclusion and the one-sided processes of transformation that occur in it.

If so, ideology-critique must exist in a struggle for an effective voice for excluded groups. When the political order of a given polity has reached the level of generally discursive processes, as it has in the "liberal democracies," this struggle is primarily a problem of political organization or media access and education, and a problem of the role of critical intellectuals in the politics of culture and identity, *and* the struggle among intellectuals for the conceptual basis of a possible common politics for all groups and classes, including those already "included." It is a politics of education. In this politics, intellectuals must be organic, but not simply organic to particular oppressed groups. They must be prophetically organic to the future unity of interest of presently diverse oppressed groups. In societies in which force is the immediate medium of control of the voices, the struggle may take on a more direct and classical organizational character.

A PEDAGOGY FOR EDUCATING THE DESIRING IMAGINATION

One of the dangers of a too ready instrumentalization of the curriculum, film making, painting, or writing in the service of a political program is the reduction of the learning process to the transmission of what Dewey called "inert" or dead knowledge. Such an instrumentalization, often recommended today in the cause of one or another oppressed group, runs the risk of putting the dialectic of possibility and actuality to death in the name of freedom.

As Garrison has shown in his perspicuous discussion of the metaphysics of Greene's Deweyian conception of freedom (Garrison, 1990; Greene, 1988), any adequate conception of the various dimensions and uses of the dialectic of the good, including the particular form it takes in schooling, must avoid the dogmatism of a monological imagination. He pointed out that true freedom consists in an open process of learning in which the desiring imagination's confrontation with the present form of things is constantly tempered by reasoned reflection:

> Reason above cannot secure freedom. Reason cannot release the imagination, neither can it inflame our passions. It is, rather, the role of reason to constrain the *excesses* of unfettered imagination and desire, the result of which is not freedom at all but capriciousness. To be free it is necessary to educate not only reason, but the imagination and the passions as well. (Garrison, 1990, p. 201)

Here reason is to be understood holistically, rather than cognitively, if Garrison is not to be misread. Reason is the tempering of desire and imagination by realism. Desire and imagination are what keeps reason living. The educative process occurs in the dialectic between reason and the desiring imagination. This educative process involves the reality test of relationships with members of other groups, other cultures, and understanding of *their* desires and imagination, and the process of discursive inquiry through which shared or *public* goods may be identified. The problem with instrumental rather than inquiry-oriented understanding of the formative processes (schooling, mass media, science, public discussion, etc) is the reification of a one-sided moment in human developmental history, even if that one side is the side of some particular oppressed group or de facto coalition of groups. The result will be unsatisfactory and may well have the unintended consequence of legitimating the existing systems in ways that have much the same essentializing effect as the discourse of the dominant groups in society (as critics of "nativism" argue; Niranjana, 1992). Perversely, a blind antiuniversalism is likely to support a politically real hegemony.

Western schooling systems presently rest on a modernist understanding of the enlightening role of education, the truth of the content to be taught, and the inquiry orientation of pedagogy. One may well agree with postmodern critics that this educational culture constitutes a "device," as Bernstein (1985) calls it, for freezing the social order in its present form, by socializing populations in a form of consciousness (subjectivity) appropriate for the prevailing order of power. Bernstein's structuralism was perfectly adequate to an anticipation of the main outlines of Foucault's analysis of the modern regime of power/knowledge, pastoral (new middle class) power, and governmentalization. But this does not mean that there is no conception of enlightenment, truth, or truthfulness that can escape these criticisms. If we abandon any notion of a dialectical-critical movement, whether of the kind outlined here or not, we are left in a kind of postmodern pessimism and privatism that is similar in its effects, if not its causes, to that produced by excessively functionalist Marxist theory.

The educative process, shared in a special way by schooling (as the institutional structure for the education of the young), is the process of inquiry by means of which we address our situation. It is first a holistic and spiritual process, in which we assess the present condition of our dividedness and the adequacy or inadequacy of our self-understanding. Within these metaphysical and metamethodological considerations, other more specific ethical (and cognitive) questions take their place. The discipline of education is a historically progressive diagnostic study of the conditions of life and of the immanent, constitutive theorizing of this life, and the relation between the two. Pedagogy is our local and particular role in this wider process. Accordingly, its logic is similar to that of the practical syllogism—it involves local and particular premises, values, and more general principles.

In Habermas's terms, it is a study of life worlds and the public world, the breakdown of the former, and the contradictory and constrained character of the latter, and the processes and strategies through which life worlds are increasingly colonized by forms of nonrational force such as administrative power and economic need (money).

It is also a study of the ways these processes of colonization may be effectively resisted through the healing of the wounds in the public domain brought about by counterinstitutional means of bringing all voices into a public process of reconstruction and recontextualization of life-world-level meanings, identities, and values (Habermas, 1987a).

Meaning is constituted not only by the relation of *language-signs* to languages (différance), but also by the relationship of *utterances* to concrete life contexts, mediated by the validity judgments of speakers and hearers, who listen, speak, and make claims on each other out of their desiring imagination. Niranjana (1992), following Benjamin, argued that postcolonial retranslations of indigenous texts are *claims*, just as colonial translations are claims. The presences claimed may be absent in the sense of the old metaphysics, but they are present in their apprehension by those who accept the claims they make on us. All texts make claims. So, too, ideology *and* critique are constituted in utterances of surrender or intimate betrayal, or small accesses of courage to assert oneself by making claims in the ontogenetic plane of transformation of the real. Arguments are political, cultural, and auto-genetic deeds. The overall or general direction of our argumentative self-constitution defines what we might properly call *spiritual* in a post-metaphysical sense of the term. And this much can be common ground between religious and non-religious people becuase there is no necessary contradiction between the human capacity to make holistic meaning in living and the additional assumptions yielded by religious faith.

For the most part, this discussion has been confined to the ethical/political domain. But perhaps the most pressing questions educators face today are questions concerning the spiritual status of the educative process. Ethics only begins when some general value slope or metaethical bias is already embraced. The term *spiritual* indicates, at the least, the possibility of some such general tilt, shape, or wholeness in the metaphysical (ontogenetic) dimension. Perhaps we could call it *hope*, or *telos*, if we recognized the dialectical character of our engagement with any postulated telos. The conditions of our age, its struggles, and its desires demand a new, postmetaphysical approach to pedagogy, but this does not mean an approach without a spiritual dimension. The problems of intercultural politics, cultural critique, and learning demand we go beyond a merely poststructuralist understanding of them. There must be a balance between cultural pluralism and shared ground if we are to live peaceably on one planet. There must be a recognition of the productivity of texts as well as the existing awareness of the textuality of production if we are to harmonize our desiring imaginations within the limits of our common biosphere. For some of us the need for a spiritual oneness in a vast universe is also of surpassing importance. A balance is

not possible unless we theorize some escape from poststructuralism's
hall of mirrors. A critical, textually turned transactional realism—a kind
of pragmatism both metaphysically and metatheoretically—is better
than an infinite regress of reflections in which the only presences are yet
more reflections. The resources for this are available.

REFERENCES

Adorno, T. (1967). *Negative dialectics.* New York: The Seabury Press.
Benhabib, S. (1986). *Critique, norm and utopia.* New York: Columbia
    University Press.
Benhabib, S. (1989-90). In the shadow of Aristotle and Hegel:
    Communicative ethics and current controversies in practical phi-
    losophy. *The Philosophical Forum,* XXI(1-2), 1-31.
Bernstein, B. (1985). On pedagogic discourse. In J. Richardson (Ed.),
    Handbook of theory and research in the sociology of education. Westport, CT:
    Greenwood Press.
Boisvert, R. (1988). *Dewey's metaphysics.* New York: Fordham University
    Press.
Boisvert, R. (1989). Rorty, Dewey and post-modern metaphysics. *The*
    Southern Journal of Philosophy, 27(2), 173-193.
Callinicos, A. (1989). *Against postmodernism: A Marxist critique.* Cambridge,
    UK: Polity Press.
Derrida, J. (1978). *Writing and difference.* London: Routledge and Kegan
    Paul.
Derrida, J. (1984). On an apocalyptic tone recently adopted in philoso-
    phy. *The Oxford Literary Review,* VI(2), 3-37.
Dewey, J. (1938). *Logic: The theory of inquiry.* New York: Irvington
    Publishers.
Dewey, J. (1982). *Experience and nature, the later works* (Vol.1). Carbondale:
    Southern Illinois University Press. (Original work published in
    1982)
Foucault, M. (1981). Is it useless to revolt? *Philosophy and Social Criticism,*
    8(3), 1-9.
Fraser, N. (1981). Foucault on modern power: Empirical insights and
    normative confusions. *Praxis International,* 1(3), 272-287.
Fraser, N. (1989). *Unruly practices: Power, discourse and gender in contemporary*
    social theory. Minneapolis: University of Minnesota Press.
Gadamer, H.-G. (1975). *Truth and method.* New York: Seabury Press.
Gallagher, S. (1992). *Hermeneutics and education.* Albany: State University
    of New York Press.
Garrison, J. (1990). Greene's dialectics of freedom and Dewey's natural-

istic existential metaphysics. *Educational Theory*, 40(2), 193-209.

Greene, M. (1988). The dialectic of freedom. New York: Teachers College Press.

Habermas, J. (1977). A review of Gadamer's Truth and Method. In F. Dallmayr & T. McCarthy (Eds.), *Understanding and social inquiry* (pp. 357-373). Great Bend, IN: University of Notre Dame Press.

Habermas, J. (1982). *The theory of communicative action* (Vol. I). London: Heinemann Educational Books.

Habermas, J. (1987a). *The philosophical discourse of modernity*. Cambridge, UK: Polity Press.

Habermas, J. (1987b). *Nachmetaphysiches Denken*. Frankfurt: Suhrkamp.

Habermas, J. (1990). Discourse ethics: Notes on a program of philosophical justification. In S. Benhabib & F. Dallmayr (Eds.), *The communicative ethics controversy* (pp. 60-110). Cambridge, MA: MIT Press.

Howard, D. (1988). *The Marxist legacy*. London: Macmillan.

Hoy, D. (1991). Splitting the difference: Habermas' critique of Derrida. *Praxis International*, 8(4), 47-464.

Husserl, E. (1962). *Phenomenology and the crisis of philosophy*. New York: Harper.

Levin, D. (1981). The body politic: The embodiment of praxis in Foucault and Habermas. *Praxis International*, 1(3), 301-315.

MacIntyre, A. (1988). *Whose justice? Which rationality?* Great Bend, IN: University of Notre Dame Press.

Nicholson, L. (1992). On the postmodern barricades: Feminism, politics and theory. In S. Seidmann & D. Wagner (Eds.), *Postmodernism and social theory* (pp. 82-90). Cambridge, UK: Blackwell.

Niranjana, T. (1992) *Siting translation*. Berkeley: University of California Press.

Rorty, R. (1982). *The consequences of pragmatism*. Minneapolis: University of Minnesota Press.

Rorty, R. (1991). *Objectivity, relativism and truth. Philosophical Papers* (Vol. I). New York: Cambridge University Press.

Sleeper, R. (1985). Rorty's pragmatism: Afloat in Neurath's boat, but why adrift? *Transactions of the Charles Peirce Society*, 21, 9-20.

Taylor, C. (1984). Foucault on freedom and truth. *Political Theory*, 12(2), 152-183.

Toulmin, S. (1990). *Cosmopolis: The hidden agenda of modernity*. New York: The Free Press.

Williams, B. (1985). *Ethics and the limits of philosophy*. Cambridge, MA: Harvard University Press.

Author Index

Subject Index